"Of Them Which Say They Are Jews"

"Of Them Which Say They Are Jews"

AND OTHER ESSAYS ON THE JEWISH STRUGGLE FOR SURVIVAL

By

HORACE M. KALLEN

Edited by

JUDAH PILCH

•

NEW YORK
BLOCH PUBLISHING COMPANY
5715–1954
A Centennial Publication

Library of Congress Catalog Card Number: 54-10964

PRINTED IN THE UNITED STATES OF AMERICA
PRESS OF Maurice Jacobs INC.
224 N. 15TH ST., PHILADELPHIA 2, PENNA.

Acknowledgments

Our grateful appreciation is expressed to the following organizations for the generous permission granted to reproduce some of Dr. Kallen's essays from their respective publications: American Jewish Congress (*Judaism*); American Jewish Committee (*Contemporary Jewish Record* and *American Jewish Year Book*); American Academy of Political and Social Science (*Annals*); Hadassah (Brochure on Louis D. Brandeis); Hadassah and Harper & Bros. (*The American Jew: A Composite Portrait*); National Council for Jewish Education (*Jewish Education*); and the Zionist Organization of America (*New Palestine*).

The publication of this book was made possible through the generosity of Dr. Phil W. Lown, a vice-president of the American Association for Jewish Education

CONTENTS

Editor's Introduction

DR. KALLEN is first and last a philosopher whose philosophy keeps him in active and responsible participation in the issues of the daily life. His interests have ranged over the social sciences, psychology, social research and education during nearly half a century. Unlike other American intellectuals of Jewish connection (to use a Kallenian expression) who have kept aloof from the Jewish community and have not concerned themselves with its problems, Dr. Kallen has studied and labored to find solutions of all the major problems of Jewish survival both here and abroad.

Horace M. Kallen appears on the Jewish scene at a turbulent time in our history, in a period of crisis, when Jewish sufferings in the post-World War I era followed one another with little respite, reaching their climax in the Hitlerian holocaust, and when the great already receding centers of Jewish life in Europe were being liquidated and others in America and in Israel were coming to the fore. As a Jew acceptive of his personal responsibility for the Jewish being, Dr. Kallen took up the challenge of the Jewish struggle for survival amid the realities of the present-day world, and the exercise of the human right to shape his destiny and to develop his creative powers as Jew in accord with his own Jewish integrity. By tongue and pen Dr. Kallen undertook to deal with the critical issues of his day, and has done so with courage, vigor and profound conviction.

In planning this volume of Dr. Kallen's essays we have selected the writings which best convey his basic ideas and reflect his varied interests. His essays span the entire gamut of Jewish life in our time. In them he attempts to analyze and illumine the age-old problem of anti-Semitism, to discover what makes a Jew a Jew, to explore Jewish relationships to the world at large and to the United States in particular, and to examine the specific trends and ramifications of contemporary Jewish life.

The essays assembled in this book are arranged under three heads: *Modernity and Survival*, *Appraisals and Memories*, and *The Jewish Education of The American Jew*. They are, as it were, introduced by a significant essay, heretofore unpublished, on the American Jewish community, on the eve of its Tercentenary in this land, entitled "Anarchy and Order in American Jewry."

While at first glance the reader may recognize statements which keep recurring in the essays, he will find upon careful reading that the repetitions present, strictly speaking, different aspects of the identical theme, i. e. Jewish struggle for survival. Although written for different occasions and at longer or shorter intervals, the essays have a lasting quality about them and constitute an important new "guide to the perplexed of our time."

The selections reveal Kallen as most of all the American Jew. To him there is obviously no conflict between his loyalty to the American ideal and his acquiescence in his Jewish heritage. He is heir to both. The Bill of Rights, the Constitution, and the Declaration of Independence, which promulgated the principles of "live and let live, live and help live," as Kallen sums it up, have inspired men to live and fight for one abiding faith — democracy — affirming their right to be different, to live and act differently, and to interpret this faith as they conceive it. Pronouncements of the Jewish genius, which found expression in life and in letters, elaborated the conception of "Proclaim liberty throughout the land to all the inhabitants thereof" and also inspired thought and action in generations of men to struggle for the realization of the vision of Aharit Hayamim and to fight for the attainment of freedom. This idea "penetrated like wild fire into the quite compact and durable configuration of Jewish ways and their institutions."

Dr. Kallen finds in both Americanism and what he calls Hebraism, of which Judaism is a phase, a singleness of purpose embodied in a multiplicity of expressions and manifestations. "Judaism," Kallen points out, "like Hebraism is an indefinite manifold." "Jewish living," he maintains, is "a manifestation of multiplicity and variety" and not of "sameness." It is the all-including total of ideas and values of Jewish individuals and of groups, in one country or another, at this time or that. All of these values "together, and then some" characterize Jewish living. The oneness of Judaism is the singular idea of its plurality. Or as he puts it, "There is not *a* Jewish view of life. There are Jewish *views* of life. The views are *many*. Life with all its conflicts and antagonisms and hates, indeed through them, makes itself somewhat one."

The American ideal, too, is of a oneness that functions through and in multiplicity. It rests on faith in human freedom, on a common aspiration for all men, which affirms "each man's unalienable right to to be different," to live, to feel and to think differently, and yet to be "united with one another through their differences" and through their shared purpose to be of "service to the whole."

Kallen's synthesis of these two complementary traditions expresses an attitude toward life and men based on integrity, truth, and right. Thus his loyalty to one enriches and fructifies the other. His Jewishness makes him a more enlightened American and a more conscientious citizen of the world, and his Americanism makes him a nobler Jew. It is no wonder then that he attacks the notion that flight from Judaism will free the Jew from disaster and will insure for him a safer or richer life in the world of today. He would rather have us "replace the feeling that Judaism is disaster by a more positive emotion, a mood of courageous self-respect which will put *fight for* Judaism in place of *flight from* Judaism."

To Kallen, knowledge of Judaism is indispensable to a wholesome Jewish life. "Knowledge of its inner quality and outer values, of its nature and its significance to the Jew and of its role in the orchestration of the cultures of mankind," is not a liability but a great asset for every Jew. Hence his contention that American Jewish communities, like communities of different origins and cultures, can maintain their communal identity and give it free expression in their thoughts and modes of living, thus making their own specific contributions to the "free patterns of American national life" and orchestrating "into an integral solidarity with the spirit of American democracy."

Hence the Americanization of Jews does not mean their becoming indistinguishable from Christians; it means their developing the Jewish individuality in such a way that they live and work not merely as citizens of the nation, but as *Jewish* citizens of the nation.

To Kallen, the ideal of assimilation is therefore totally unworthy. As an American, he recognizes that assimilation would be detrimental not only to American Jews but to our country. For it would deprive the country of the potent, energizing influence of a vital and spirited "minority" which, like every one of the "minorities" that make up the majority, seems to be at its best when it is most deeply mindful of its venerable heritage. Jews again, who endeavor to make themselves "100% Americans," whatever that may mean, cut themselves off from their roots, and negate much of the faith that inspired and continues to inspire our country's thinkers and reformers. Dr. Kallen quotes the 19th Century historian and essayist, Lecky, who wrote, "Hebraic mortar cemented the foundation of American democracy." Thus no Hebraist, nor anybody otherwise imbued with Jewish culture and ideals, need feel that he is thereby in any way isolated from the main streams of American life. If anything, habituation in Jewish culture tends to bring one closer to the American Idea and its inspiration.

Holding these views, Dr. Kallen can not condone the practices of social and cultural segregation. As he sees it, the right to be different does not imply segregation from other communities. On the contrary, free social and cultural intercourse with all communal neighbors is the nourishing medium of growth for all communities which together make up the American people.

Dr. Kallen's phrase for this insight is *Cultural Pluralism*. It points to an all-pervasive process wherein "Each (group)," he writes, "is a spring of individuality from which flows a little stream of cultural difference that crosses the others, combines with them, and finally makes the great river of the nation's cultural life, as all the tributaries make the Missouri or the Columbia or the Mississippi. They effect a cultural union in which each different region and community has its own different part to play."

Kallen is quietly, not blatantly, proud of his Jewishness, a pride which derives from the knowledge that the values inherent in the Jewish cultural tradition are basically democratic.

He, too, like the rabbis of old, sees in Judaism the preponderant element of *Herut* (freedom) as against *Harut* (dogma). The Almighty, according to Jewish tradition, presented the Torah, not as dogma and creed, carved in stone, thus connoting authoritarianism and final pronouncement, but as teaching illuminated by the spirit of freedom, which calls upon man to be alert, wise, and decent, and to choose a life of dignity, worth, and self-respect.

From this deep conviction that communities of different cultures can live together and strengthen one another through a free trade in cultural values, follows the recognition that such an intercultural exchange underlies the healthy growth of the changing Jewish community, "as freely interacting member of the culture of America." From this conviction follows also Dr. Kallen's recognition that "Jewish education is the first and the last condition of Jewish living in America." Education is the only reliable guarantee, "for the survival of Jews as Jews." When Kallen thinks about Jewish education in America, it is not primarily the past which concerns him, but the present and the future. The Jewish school he envisions does not merely foster a study of past glories, but relates the entire Jewish past intimately to the pressures and tensions of the ever-changing present and the unknown future.

Exactly what happens when a child with no real awareness of his

Jewish background hears "*Jew*" hurled at him as an epithet? There is puzzlement, shock, which, if not accompanied by understanding of the place of the Jew in the general scheme of things, leads to a fierce longing to cast off the burden, to flee from Judaism, to reject it entirely, even to berate those who continue to embrace it, as "making it tough for the rest of us."

How much better off is the youngster (and by the same token the adult as well) who learns wisely to accept his Jewishness as a responsibility which challenges the best of his heart and mind, the responsibility of a man to be himself and not the shadow of another!

Kallen, like other Jewish intellectuals, indeed like all other Jews, has had to confront the Jew-hatred which still infests so much of our planet. But what he experienced did not cause him to flee from Jewish life; but to realize its inner worth, its inalienable right to live on and grow equally with other forms of human life, and its positive role in the give-and-take with the cultures of which civilization consists. Courageous loyalty to a cultural heritage, achieved by learning its nature and history and cultivating its services in intercultural relations, is a far healthier, more satisfying attitude than fear and flight. The task of education is to communicate this loyalty in this way, by the best means the science of education makes available.

This virtue of courageous loyalty, which one finds in Kallen, he extolls in Albert Einstein. Part of what he has written about Einstein can be equally said about Kallen himself: "By affirming his integrity as a Jew he has vindicated the integrity of the Jew as a man and a scientist, and has made his life a light and a leading for all Jews to inner freedom and outer respect. Of the great Jews of his generation, none has lifted the torch of self-respect so high for the Jew; in none has the courage born of inner freedom burnt so brightly. And in this and through this, none has been a more potent vindication of self-respect and freedom for all mankind."

How, then, face the anti-Semite if one is not to cease being a Jew? By identifying oneself, Kallen says, with democratic ideals. To be anti-Semitic in America — or anywhere else in this world, for that matter — is to be anti-democratic, just as it is anti-democratic to be anti-Negro, anti-Catholic, anti-minority. One of the most prized and protected virtues of a democracy is that it enables minorities to be heard, for the truth has very often been known to lie with the few rather than with the many.

There are those who feel that for an American Jew to concern himself more than a little with Israel is to display divided allegiance.

Kallen, who sees in American democracy the safeguarding, the right and opportunity to be different, and in the union of differences the enrichment and strength of America, cherishes a passionate interest in the present and future of Israel. As an American, he wants to live in a just world, in a happy and progressive country; as a Jew, he wants to know how his fellow Jews fare in other lands — whether they are persecuted or free, whether they live safely at home or are perforce obliged to wander from land to land. If his brothers in far countries are in trouble, if they have difficulty in entering the refuge of Israel, if those already in Israel find it necessary to meet first a British crisis, then an Arab crisis, and finally a UN crisis — Kallen, armed with tongue and pen, recognizes his duty to help.

Divided allegiance? Nonsense! To quote from the oath of allegiance to the flag of the United States, it is rather allegiance to the principle of "justice for all" — justice even for people who live outside the United States. For in the end, if those outside America suffer injustice, it is America too which suffers, and indeed all the world, which has suddenly and unalterably become a small place in which all members of the human race now live in close proximity. For freedom is possible only in a world society where each group and every individual is liberated from want and fear and is free, as Dr. Kallen puts it, "to think, to believe, to assemble, to speak and hear, to write and read, to produce or create or discover and to exchange the fruits of their thoughts and labors, without let or hindrance, on equal terms." Hence, a free society of Jews in Israel, of men and women who fled from every form of oppression, are entitled to look to their fellow Jews for those instruments and tools which would render their group life in Israel free and secure.

If one general expression can be used to describe the spirit of Dr. Kallen's essays, it is — *Ahavat Habriyot* (love of one's fellow man). *Ahavat Yisrael* (love of Israel) is naturally an integral part of this great devotion to mankind. Hence all Dr. Kallen's critical attitude toward our society springs from this one source. His reflections on life, consequently, are not dominated by a single principle or a set of principles which appear to govern the lives and works of many a liberal. For Kallen is guided not by formulas (from which he has endeavored to emancipate himself) but by man's day-by-day needs and by his lifelong aspirations for a better and kindlier world. Kallen is thus a true disciple of our prophets and sages.

JUDAH PILCH

Horace M. Kallen, Hebraist

By MILTON R. KONVITZ

FOR over forty years Professor Horace M. Kallen has been writing, speaking, organizing, and struggling for different strands of a single philosophical position: for pragmatism, cultural pluralism, humanism, the scientific method, civil liberties, the cooperative movement, and the democratic way of life. His single philosophical position always has been Hebraism.

In Hebraism he has found the law of his life, and this law he has loved with all his heart, with all his soul, and with all his might. This philosophy he has taught to thousands upon thousands of students at leading American universities, but mainly at the New School for Social Research (which he helped establish in 1919, when he was thirty-three years of age), and through his many significant books, articles, and public lectures. Using one metaphor or another, one subject or another, it is of Hebraism that he talks when he sits in his house, when he walks by the way, when he lies down and when he rises up.

What is Hebraism?

In the first place it is a category of thought which sees nature and life in perpetual flux; which sees all things under the aspect of time. It is a philosophy of existence in which time and change are real, in which history is significant, and in which biography is meaningful and precious. The Hebraist is on no "quest for certainty" — except the certainty of human experience itself — birth, love, pain, joy, death. The Hebraist rejects any form of predestination, foreknowledge, or any sense of immutable destiny; on the contrary, he believes in the reality and freedom of the will, and in individual responsibility for actions which follow from the will's reality and freedom.

Moral freedom and moral responsibility thus go hand in hand. The Hebraist believes in the possibility of a self-reformation, of *teshubah* — a turning of man from the ways of evil and death to the ways of righteousness and life. The Hebraist believes that even the citadel of God can be stormed by the human spirit and that God Himself can be made to recall — to use the language of our liturgy — His harsh decrees. Thus, even God is not immutable, and to Him, too, *our* times, *our* histories and *our* biographies are real and significant, even as He is to us active, functional, dynamic, and approachable.

Hebraism means, too, that the objects which time casts up on the shores of existence are real, and that their reality is their justification for existence. The real things are not the generalized forms of existence (not the essences of Santayana, or the Ideas of Plato, or the attributes and modes of Spinoza) but the things which come into being and pass away — the things which are apprehended under the aspect of *becoming* more than under the aspect of *being*. These things — a specific, particular Adam or Eve, David or Bathsheba, Moses or Deborah, a creature different from all other creatures that ever were or ever will be — have a right to be, a right to live, and a right to be different. It is *difference* that defines character; it is difference which *identifies* a person — it is the only thing that gives meaning to his identity. In so far as he has a right to live, a man has a right to be different.

Hebraism means, then, individualism; it means respect for the dignity of each man, woman, and child; it means the right to live, the right to be oneself, the right to be different. For it is to God, not to man, that each of us is beholden for the gift of his life and for the gift of a nature which makes each man an original Adam and each woman an original Eve.

Hebraism is thus committed to freedom, radical liberty; for radical (Biblical, Jeffersonian) individualism needs freedom no less than a fish needs water. Live and let live — this is a brief statement of its political commitment. But he who is different and who wants the right to be different, but who wants the right to be different only for himself, forfeits the right to be different. He is a totalitarian; he wants everyone to conform to his own notions and will; when he acts upon these notions, to coerce his fellows, to wipe out their differences, he forfeits his citizenship in democratic society.

Thus Hebraism is committed to a maximum of democratic freedom and to the preservation of inherent, inalienable individual ("minority") rights — rights in the spheres of human interest where differences matter most: religion, thought and speech, cooperation (the Constitution speaks of "assembly") among those of like religion or thought, and the freedom adequately (judicially, legally) to protect one's right to be oneself, to be different.

Hebraism means a commitment to righteousness, to strive to bring about what is *right*, to seek the ways of justice and mercy and peace. It means making an effort to find these ways and to construct the personal and social instruments which will tend to aid us in the achievement of the highest values. Hebraism thus places a high value upon the intelligence and the methods of science when used in the interests of a furtherance of life and righteousness. Values, actions, and tools justify themselves as and when they contribute to satisfying (in part) the heart's desire; and the heart learns what it desires and what it should desire as man works with and for ideals.

"To believe in life in the face of death, to believe in goodness in the face of evil, to hope for better times to come, to work at bringing them about," says Kallen, "— that is Hebraism."

Yes, that is Hebraism. At times, depending on the truth to be emphasized, Kallen has called this philosophy by other names — e. g., pragmatism or humanism. It is the philosophy to which Horace Kallen has been and is committed. It is not a philosophy which he merely avows intellectually; it is the philosophy to which he is committed existentially, with his whole person. It is the core and course of his inner life.

It is also the core and course of the lives of Jews throughout history. It is also the core and course of the lives of Americans and of all free peoples.

Proem: Anarchy and Order in American Jewry

Anarchy and Order in American Jewry

I

WE ARE now in the season when Americans of Jewish connection will be celebrating the three hundredth anniversary of the arrival of forbears of theirs on the mainland of North America. The Tercentenary theme is to be "Man's opportunities and responsibilities under freedom."

Within the period, the word *Jew* has acquired a variety of new, and in many respects, contradictory meanings, most of them entering social and historical discourse after the Democratic Revolution of the eighteenth century. Before that Revolution, whose momentous initiation was the establishment of the United States of America as an independent and sovereign nation, *Jew* meant a member of a historical people, unevenly distributed throughout the western world and on spots in Asia, but with customs, traditions, folkways and mores, rites and rotes very much the same everywhere. A Jew born and bred in North Africa or in France could make his way east to Muscovy or north to Prussia and break his journey anywhere on his road among groups whom he could join at prayers, at meals and at study, among whom he could marry and live or sicken and die, sure that he was violating no divine commandment, breaking no important custom. If their vernaculars of secular intercourse were different from his, their languages of worship and study, their codes regulating the relations between man and man or man and woman were not. If their meat and drink varied as their places of domicile, the rules of preparing them for consumption did not. As Jews, their minds and hearts were commonly conformed to "the laws of Moses and of Israel." By continual rehearsal and reinterpretation of the same Bible — Heine called it the "portable Fatherland" — the same Talmud, they shared patterns of faith and works and followed a way of life which together composed the cultural identity that the word *Jew* designated for them, rendering individuals who severally grew up and were instructed in it, jointly Jews. The culture associated their private lives into a communion which combined, and not infrequently coerced, personal diversity into organized commonalty. Until after the Democratic Revolution the world's Jews, however dispersed, did in fact live and move and have their being in established institutions whereby they lived as members of one another, their diversity joined into an inward unity, national, cultural, and not entirely normal.

The force producing the un-normality was neither Jewish nor inward. It was a factor in the Jews' non-Jewish environment without parallel in human relations. The conventional appelation of this factor is *anti-Semitism.* Since the Democratic Revolution it has become modish to deny any sort of social singularity to anti-Semitism. According to the deniers, both sociological and psychological "researches" demonstrate that anti-Semitism is one instance of the world-wide perennial war of all against all that can be observed wherever people who are different from each other have to struggle with one another over necessities of life and forms of living. The impact of the struggle, the deniers say, gives rise to reciprocal prejudices, aversions, and aggressions which are the direct consequences of the frustrations, the failures and the feelings of inferiority or guilt that the struggle must necessarily evoke. The doctrine of anti-anti-Semitism attributes the greater intensity and articulation of anti-Semitism among the "better" classes to indirect forces which compel even the mighty to require scapegoats. It pays little or no attention to the fact that the anti-Semitic sentiment is native to Christian and Mohammedan cultures and also highly visible in regions of those cultures where no Jews live to arouse it; while it does not occur among non-Christians or non-Mohammedan people — such as Hindus or Chinese — although they have Jews for neighbors, until it has been taught to them by Christians or Mohammedan teachings.

For anti-Semitism adds to the tensions and conflicts, which are of the normal weather of social life everywhere on the globe, a set of beliefs regarding the Jews alone. These beliefs started as differentiae of the Christian creed and were adopted in that of Islam. The two are supernaturalist schemes of salvation drawing for their accounts of the origin, the nature and the destiny of man and of his relation to the universe upon the Bible of the Jews. Both agree that God — to whom each assigns a character and designs contradicting the other — had chosen first to reveal his will and law to Abraham, Isaac and Jacob, and had elected their descendants to be his people. Thence they diverge. Christian creeds attribute to divine providence a cosmic plan of which the central concern is the creation, the sinning and the salvation of all the generations of Adam and Eve. The plan began to unfold with an angelic rebellion, in the uncreated supernatural world, which resulted in the defeat and banishment thence of the rebelling angels and their transubstantiation into the devils of hell. This was followed by the creation of the part of existence we call Nature, and of the perfect first man, Adam, who with his seed, was to take the places left empty by the rebel angels. Adam was made a being in whom the natural and the supernatural are commingled. God domiciled him in the garden of Eden and gave him certain commandments — the paramount one, not to eat the fruit of the tree of knowledge of good and evil. This commandment, Adam, tempted by Eve, who had been tempted by Satan, disobeyed, thereby committing the Original Sin, falling from his own perfection, and establishing his basic sinfulness as the heredity of all his seed. Because this sin is thus intrinsic to our human nature, we are all born under divine condemnation to a miserable life of labor ending in eternal death.

But the divine plan does not design eternal death for all of Adam's seed. Its justice requires that the Adamic sin should be atoned, and its mercy arranges that the atonement should be vicarious and achieved by the divinity's taking on the form of humanity and suffering the sentence laid upon humanity. It was to this end that God chose the Jews, revealing his will and his law to their patriarchs and Moses and their later prophets, finally appearing himself among his Chosen People incarnate in his son begotten of a virgin, and consummating his plan of salvation by dying a shameful death on the cross, in atonement for the sin of mankind. Of course it was only in his humanity that the divine voluntary scapegoat could sacrifice himself. As divine he is deathless and eternal, and so on the third day the entombed Christ resumed his immortality, left his tomb, and before returning to his supernatural realm reappeared among men. But by his crucifixion, the atonement had nevertheless been mercifully accomplished. Those who "believe on the Christ" and accept it, are saved unto eternal life; those who disbelieve and decline the grace of his sacrifice, are doomed forever; they will be only "resurrected unto condemnation."

And the Jews, whom God the Father had chosen to be the messengers and agents of this salvation, reject it, denying Christ the Son and refusing his sacrifice. Hence God rejects the Jews. He replaces his covenant with them by a new one with those who believe on the

Christ as the God who died for them in Thisworld to save them from eternal death in the Otherworld. Now these believers are the Chosen People; the Jews are now the Rejected People, outlawed from the fellowship of Christian mankind. The entire history of the Jews, their status and role in the cultural economy of the Christianized world can be understood only in the light of this creedal delineation of the Jewish being.

A similar conclusion is to be drawn regarding the history of Jewry in the Moslem culture. For Moslem anti-Semitism is analogous to Christian. But whereas Christian anti-Semitism had been devised, not by the observant Jew, Jesus, but by later alienated generations who had translated him into the hellenistic dying god, Christ, it was the Arab man Mohammed who himself initiated the anti-Semitic disposition of his own cult. Proclaiming himself the prophet chosen of Allah to supersede Moses, Jesus and all others, Mohammed found his asseverations concerning the Hebrew scriptures denied and made fun of by the Jews of Medina. At first he had tended to adopt the Judaist perspective in his singular revelation. Inasmuch as he himself acknowledged Moses and the Torah, why could not the Jews accept him and his Koran? Since they would not, he had them expelled from Medina, and extended his ban to the entirety of Judaism. Its rites and rotes, its Sabbath, its *kashruth*, its day of atonement, indeed its holy bible, made up a false religion. The true, final, faith is not that contained in the Jewish book, or for the matter, in the Christian one. It is that which Allah communicated to his last and greatest prophet, Mohammed, and which Mohammed revealed to be read by the sons of man in the suras of his Koran. It is the Koran which recovers and discloses the true religion that the patriarch Abraham had ordained with his sinistral son Ishmael. Its shrine is not a temple-site in Jerusalem but the Kaaba in Mecca, to which every true believer must make at least one pilgrimage. Its rites call for no dietary regulation, no seventh day Sabbath, no single day of atonement, but a month, Ramadan, of fasting and repentance. The way of God which it commands is to wage unceasing war for the true faith against all misbelievers. Among the misbelievers the Jews have a unique place. Mohammedanism does not distinguish them quite like Christianism but sufficiently for orthodox Mohammedanism to shut them out and cut them off from free and equal participation in the life and labor of the moslemized portion of mankind.

II

Christianism and Mohammedanism, the two major organized religions of the western world, both singled out the Jews by creed and code. Creed ordained theological condemnation, code enacted and enforced social, political and cultural exclusion. The isolation thus imposed has no historic parallel. The theological degradation and inferiority, by which it was rationalized, re-enforced the religious self-isolation of the Judaistic communions. It called out compensatory uses of the Jew's traditional definition of themselves as objects of special divine election. By setting up a wall of separation between non-Jew and Jew, it rendered the members of the Jewish community more than normally centripetal: institutionally it drove Jews in on one another; culturally it impelled the Jewish psyche in upon itself. With all the inevitable osmosis of doctrines and disciplines that no xenophobia could inhibit and no religious and cultural policing prevent, the ghetto was, during a millennium and a half, a self-contained and self-containing community with its own characteristic institutions and its own peculiar lifeways and thoughtways.

The Democratic Revolution opened the gates and breached the walls of the ghetto. It did not abolish the reciprocal isolation of Jew and non-Jew; but by repealing the laws which penalized people for their differences, by removing the disabilities imposed on the Jew for being Jew, it provided the opportunities and multiplied the occasions when the two could meet each other, with the integrity of their faiths and cultures intact, as equals in liberty and right. George Washington wrote to the Jewish congregation in Newport in 1790, "The citizens of the United States of America have a right to applaud themselves for having given to mankind examples of an enlarged and liberal policy, a policy worthy of imitation. All possess alike liberties of conscience and immunities of citizenship. It is now no more that toleration is spoken of, as if it were by the indulgence of one class of people that another enjoyed the exercise of their inherent natural rights. For happily, the Government of the United States, which gives to bigotry no sanction, to persecution no assistance, requires only that they shall demean themselves as good citizens, in giving it on all occasions their support."

The few Jews to whom this was addressed, being inhabitants of Roger Williams' Rhode Island, had certain liberties not allowed Jews elsewhere — in New York for example — among them, a synagogue and public worship. Immigrants from Poland and Germany as well as Holland and the West Indies, their diversities found ready reconciliation in the Torah and Mitzvot of their communion, with its rites of birth and burial, of circumcision and wedlock, of diet and worship. Weekdays, Sabbath and holidays, they together repeated much the same prayers, read the same portion of the law and the prophets, measured the year by the same calendar, looked alike toward the advent of a supernatural Messiah who should redeem them from their God-ordained exile and lead them according to divine promise under divine law back to the Promised Land.

But the Newport communion did not long survive. Its members emigrated, most of them to New York, where they joined a Jewry of even more diverse derivations, and among whom they found themselves as readily at home as with one another in Newport. Overwhelmingly, the social history of the Jewry of New York is the social history of all Jews of the United States. The autonomous core of their society consists of the folkways and the mores whose doctrines and disciplines were the Bible, the Talmud, the *Shulchan Arukh* and their implementation by the traditional institutions of communal life — ceremonial, cultural, charitable. Their conventional formations were the burial ground, the synagogue, the *cheder* or *talmud torah*, the *Chevrah Gemiluth Chasodim* and *Chevrah Kadishah.* Their traditional functionaries were the *rabbi*, the *chazan*, the *shochet*, the *shamash* and the *gabaim*. New immigration only repeated, it did not noticeably alter, the basic communal pattern. Nor did vernacular differences much affect it, for the language of communion was biblical and later Hebrew, or Talmudic. Communion maintained community. New generations grew up into the fellowship of their elders, the cohesiveness of the group being little affected by the American Idea until about the middle of the last century.

That there was a certain easement in the attitude of Christian Americans toward American Jews even in colonial times, the record of the Jewish settlement attests. But not until after the Civil War and the commencing of the great migrations did the reciprocal exclusiveness and isolation begin its over-all uneven and superficial relaxation. Since the nineteenth century trend toward democratization and secularity marked the entire Western world, the relaxation was to be noted in Europe as well. But in Europe the road to equality continued long to be *shmad* — the individual's deliberate repudiation of

Judaism and Jewry and his identification with the creed and conduct of his Christian milieu. This followed from the fact that it was synonymous to be a Jew and to live under condemnation, to be kept in an inferior status, to be denied full access to the arts and the sciences; to be shut out and cut off from careers in public affairs, the learned profession. As Heine, himself cynically a convert, had observed, "das Judentum ist ein Unglueck, es ist keine Religion." Conversion looked like the surest, quickest, easiest escape from that misfortune.[1]

Heine and Disraeli were converts whose conversion appeared to have freed them to exalt, each in his own way, that which they had converted from. Most converts, however, found it necessary to justify their turning, not by a freed appreciation, but by a greater than conventionally Christian hatred; and conversely, most Judaists regard *shmad* as the ultimate betrayal and the *meshumed* as the most corrupted of men. In the United States there was, by comparison, little conversion. From the beginning people could flee the misfortune of a Jewish heritage without repudiating and without condemning. One might speak of the formation of an American *Haskalah* channelled by the principles of the Democratic Idea. This Idea, establishing the separation of church and state, postulates the parity of all religions and guarantees to each the equal protection of the laws. Hence, the individual Jew came under no socio-political compulsion to seek freedom and a life more abundant by repudiating and attacking the creed in which he had been brought up and those who continued to live according to it. The consequences of free communication with his neighbors, of the new problems and tasks presented him by the new conditions of personal ambition and communal responsibility, might lead simply to innovating reformations and new constructions in both the ideology of Judaism and the institutions of Jewish living.

This is what happened. The Americanization of the Jewish community has consisted in a movement away from the traditional Judaic nucleus of creed, code and conduct. In the main it continued centrifugal without becoming wilfully separatist; however radical the mutation, however extreme the social and psychological distance from the starting point, Judaism, Jewish and Jew remained the distinguishing terms.

In theology, the movement has tended to transvalue the traditional supernaturalism with a naturalism which many contend is more

[1] See below "Albert Einstein as a Jewish Intellectual," pp. 160 f.

consonant with the common intent of the great prophets of Israel. At one pole, it became "Ethical Culture" which dropped the Judaistic identification; at another it became "Reconstructionism" which retained the identification and replaced the theology. In the wake of World War II has come, however, a resurgence of supernaturalism, articulate and vocal, in idea and aspiration a transposition into Judaistic terms of the neo-orthodoxy of the Protestants and the existentialism of the Roman Catholics, both responses to the impact of this war. Indeed, a denominational label of this new supernaturalism is "Jewish existentialism."

In worship, preaching, and the conduct of Jewish affairs, the process of Americanization has tended entirely to replace the sacred tongue with the profaner ones, with Yiddish first and then with English; to replace talmudic law with the law of the land, prescriptive eating and drinking with free diet, the seventh day Sabbath with the first day, the binary festival days of Passover, Pentecost, Succoth, Rosh Hashonah, with the only single ones, the many fastdays with fewer and fewer, and fasting even on Yom Kippur recessive. Christmas and Easter tend to supplement Chanukkah and Passover; January 1st to be celebrated as an orgiastic New Year's Day with no less fervor than Tishri 1st as a solemn one. *Bar Mitzvah* dilutes into "confirmation" and the female of the species is admitted to the rite on equal terms with the male. Indeed Americanization brings the Jewish woman from her inferior status in doctrine, religious discipline, and communal responsibility, to equality with her man; and she not only may become a functionary in a religious society, but may even be ordained a rabbi. Moreover, Americanization has given her the liberty and the power to form such unprecedented independent organizations of the sex as the Council of Jewish Women, Hadassah, the Woman's Division of the American Jewish Congress, and has made a place for her in such primarily male societies as the American Jewish Committee, the various denominations of Zionists and the like. Where she does not participate directly with her men, she may form "ladies' auxiliaries" of which the "auxiliary" of the Jewish War Veterans is a sample.

Among her men Americanization keeps increasing the number and variety of emulative echoes of gentile groupings — from social and country clubs to fraternal orders, labor committees, veterans' organizations, teachers' unions and the like. In terms of community establishments, Americanization has either supplemented or displaced congregational synagogue and *shul* with temples, synagogue centers and Young Men's and Young Women's Hebrew Associations and Community Centers; it supplements or replaces *chadorim* and *talmud torahs* with *folkshulen* and Sunday schools, weekday (miscalled parochial) schools and technical schools, all conformed as much as possible to the recommendations of educational science; Americanization refines *yeshivahs* into denominational theological schools or transvalues them into colleges and universities offering secular, liberal and professional education. It transposes rabbi from scholar into pastor, from expert in Torah into minister of religion.

Americanization both supplements and displaces the study of the Sacred Books and their commentaries by the production and elaboration of a secular literature in Yiddish, Hebrew and English; it has brought into being a Jewish Publication Society, an English version of the Hebrew Bible by Judaist authorities, a Yiddish daily press and a Yiddish literature and theatre. Since English more and more replaces Yiddish in the conduct of the daily life, Yiddish is joined to Hebrew as a sacred cultural value for whose conservation and cultivation societies are formed, schools instituted, contributions solicited and a bitter *kultur-kampf* waged. The Otherworldly ideas of Exile and Return under the providence of a divinely commissioned *Messiah-ben David* becomes transposed into secular Zionism, with its facts and fantasies; and a practical concern with the fortunes of Thisworldly Israel gives earthly meaning at last to the compensatory Otherwordly creed.

The necessities of financing all these diversifications and complexities have converted *zedakah* and the *Gemiluth Chesed* into elaborately organized Federations, Welfare Funds, Community Councils, other Appeals, and have transposed the *pushke meshulach* and volunteer collector of donations into the highpowered professional pressure-agencies which exact "voluntary" contributions toward the maintenance of their establishments.

And all the while these centrifugal transformations and diversifications of the original nuclear Jewish communion were bringing ever greater intentional and social distance between its formations and their members. Men and women of Jewish derivation quietly let loose their Jewish allegiances, and seek communion among their non-Jewish occupational and professional likes. As Havemann and West report, in *They Went to College*, most Jews who so went dropped all affiliation with synagogue or temple and assumed practically none with other Jewish establishments. The not inept conventional term for this extension of social distance has been "assimilation."

Concurrently, however, anti-Semitism also diversified. Its primal theological determination also was subjected to "assimilation." It was transposed from religion to political economy, from political economy to cultural anthropology, from cultural anthropology back to religion again. There is a marxist anti-Semitism whose first voice was the Christian son of a converted Jew, Karl Marx himself, and among the most articulate have been such "scientific" authorities as Werner Sombart and Leon Trotsky. There is the anthropological anti-Semitism which counts among its seers and apostles Count Gobineau, Richard Wagner, Houston Stewart Chamberlain, Alfred Rosenberg, Adolf Hitler, Charles Coughlin. There is the anti-Semitism of the Christian Socialists, and the Jewish and non-Jewish communists. Wherever ideology has been followed by action, Jews have consistently been made the scapegoats alike for the oppressions and teachings of the old masters of peoples and the incompetencies and the failures of the sadists that replaced them. So it was in the Affaire Dreyfus; so it was in the Bolshevik revolution and the Stalinist dictatorship, with its now liquidated *Yevsekzie*; so it was in the Hitlerian holocaust; so it is in today's Moslem world. What Lord Davies declared in 1942 remains a continuing challenge to the free world.[2]

His is a perception which brings to the rationalizations of the Jews' role in Western society a debunking perspective — particularly to the anxious rationalizations of those Jews in anxious flight toward a lasting de-Judaized security that fails as it lasts.

III

The terms I have been using mark a line of ongoing change. It is unnecessary to stress how much of the change came with the great immigrations which had begun in the eighth decade of the last century, how much of it was shaped by the anti-Semitic exigencies of the Jewish position in Central and Eastern Europe before, during and after World War I, and wherever in the world totalitarians took power and automatically exploited Christianity's chronic anti-Semitism as a decisive instrument of power-politics. Anti-Semitism in Europe, and to lesser degree in the United States, has been a persistent and all-comprehending stimulus to new forms of Jewish association and group action. It has provided the major motive for such formations as the

[2] See below "National Solidarity and the Jewish Minority," pp. 58 f.

American Jewish Committee, the French *Alliance Israélite*, the German *Hilfsverein der deutschen Juden*, the British *Board of Jewish Deputies*. Organizations of this type manifested how answerable, comparatively safe and prosperous Jews did spontaneously feel, for their endangered and underprivileged fellow-Jews abroad. Their intention toward those was far less fraternal than defensively paternalistic and philanthropic. Their care was more to put them under safe tutelage than to free them to care for themselves. Because of the geographical distance from them, little conflict over social distance could grow from that generosity and goodwill. The contemptuous German expression *Ost-Juden* could be applied and translated without any significant exacerbation.

The case was different where geographical nearness tended to challenge social distance. Hence, East European Jews who migrated in considerable numbers to Germany or France, and the great multitudes who settled in the United States soon became a thorn in the flesh of their earlier and more recent predecessors or their descendants. The motivation was not simple. If I am not mistaken, it turned largely on an anxiety consequent on the idea that a fearful evil, long left behind, had returned. Prosperous "assimilated" Jews — that is, Jews increasingly more distant from the original Judaic nucleus — felt, some consciously, most unconsciously, that they had largely rid themselves of the misfortune of their Jewish difference. True, certain of their rabbis, now transvested into "spiritual leaders," preached from the safety and comfort of their American pulpits that Jews are a "priest-people" charged with the "mission of Israel" to testify to "ethical monotheism," and that the divine truth of their testimony was signalized by the civil disability and physical crippling and spiritual starvation which divine election had brought.

But the followers of these spokesmen for God could no more than their leaders be expected to accept personal participation in the consecrated disasters of their "co-religionists." How, when once safe in America, the latter lived, what they believed, how they looked and bore themselves, constituted, their benefactors felt sure, the motivation of the theoretical and practical anti-Semitism of the Christians. If only, then, those Jews could cease to be thus Jews, if only the penalized Jewish difference could be assimilated into likeness with the privileged Christian superiority, they themselves might be entirely freed from the social penalties laid upon the Jew because Jew; the disabilities which were still their lot would fade away. Without their consummating assimilation in conversion, they might be accepted as the equals of, because they had made themselves the same as, their Christian neighbors. Inasmuch as the survival and cultivation of both the traditional and untraditional Jewish diversity tends to hold them to an identity they felt sure they had shed; inasmuch as it lays upon them cruel burdens and handicaps they know their innocence should not suffer from, their attitude toward this diversity became ambivalent. They felt they had to exert their influence and spend their money to save and heal it, while at the same time they scorned and condemned it. This sentiment tends to pervade the generations of the "assimilated," whatever their own or their ancestors' country of origin. Their deep-lying insecurities crystallized in the paradoxes of what has in recent years come to be called "Jewish self-hatred." An enlightening symptom of it has been the passionate resistance to calling, by the commonplace, diversely employed names "Congress" or "Assembly," over-all confederations of Jewish groups — each of which had the declared aim of securing to Jews equal rights as men as citizens — lest those terms suggest to the non-Jews, who use them freely without fear, some sort of "dual allegiance." An even more enlightening symptom is the violent animosity evoked by such an expression as "Jewish survival;" or by the idea that "Jew" stands for membership in an identifiable historic and social, as against abstractly religious group.

The formations consequent on the attitudes and activities just reviewed exhibit diverse structures and practically irreconcilable intentions. There are those who speak of a "fragmentation" of the Jewish community in the United States. This has no ground in the record. One might as well speak of the fragmentation of a family which is increased by the birth of twins and triplets and even quintuplets every year, each an individual struggling to obtain a satisfactory portion of the family income, in order to get on by himself amid the similar strivings of brothers and sisters. Of course the bonds that keep the family one family, strain, weaken, alter; of course, some members unite against others, some abandon the family to struggle on their own, some stay to look after the old-folks and to make sure they get decent burial and are correctly mourned when they die. At all events, all their progeny will remember them, and the common remembrance may be, on occasion, a bond of union drawing them together; it may even lead them arrange for some sort of mutual help, insurance, and action to preserve the family mementos — the letters, the papers, the photograph albums, the heirlooms and the like; it may even develop into a kind of ancestor-worship, as among the Chinese. The United

States is full of such family associations, whose diverse and incompatible members come together perhaps once a year at the house of one of them to make communion and to exchange fellowship and aid, emulation and envy. Their extreme limit is reached in such societies as the Daughters of the American Revolution, the Sons of the American Revolution, the Colonial Dames, the Daughters of the Confederacy, the Ku Klux Klan. And of course, among the nation's families are perhaps as many whose members hate and flee one another and would rather be with strangers than with their mothers' sons.

These latter are the truly fragmented. And it can happen that the aggregated Jewry of America may end up thus in fragments. But that consummation, devoutly desired by many Jews, even by some who join in celebrating the tercentennary of the Jewish settlement in America, is in no way foreshadowed by the record of American Jewish living. Rather the contrary. True, the singleness and simplicity of the original unit — call it *kahal*, call it *shtetl*, call it *chevrah*, call it *minyan* — are no longer so visible. But they are altered, not dissipated. They have multiplied and diversified. There is no longer Judaism; there is a sequence of Judaism*s*, with pretensions ranging from the totalitarian right of the Lubavitcher's to the totalitarian left of the American Council for Judaism Inc. There are no longer the few communal functionaries — the bearded *rabbi*, *shochet*, *mohel*, *shamash*, *dayan*, *gabbai*, *melamed* and the like. There have been added to them assistant-rabbis, professional Zionists, executive vice-presidents, center workers, bureau directors, hospital and "home" superintendents, club leaders, school principals, labor leaders, "defense" executives, research workers, publicity directors, journalists and publicists, fund raisers, and other functionaries of an English-speaking "Yiddishe Gass," all clean-shaven, each serving some one particular group or other with an organizational structure, and elective officialdom, a membership drive and an interest and propaganda, competitive to all the rest. Each strives to secure for his own group, either in goodwill offerings, or social exactions, or both, the most he can of the surplus earnings of the Jewish portion of the American people. The resulting configuration of activities impatterns the communal economy of American Jewry.

Now, ultimately, contributions from such surpluses are gifts, whether free or exacted. As exacted, they cease wherever the power to exact weakens or lapses. As free, they are a self-taxation motivated by the giver's conscience, by his commitment of heart and head to a working faith in the nourishing and strengthening relationship of

Jewish culture and ideals, as embodied in Jewish communal works and ways, to the American Idea and to the pursuit of equal safety and equal liberty for the different which the American way of life strives to embody in practice.

Currently, fund-raising has been built up into a hypertrophic profession whose devices tend to comprehend all contributions within reach of their squeeze, and to exploit or to challenge and displace the motivations of working faith. But the sentiment appears to be spreading that these practices are in the long run self-defeating and that there can be no substitute for a working faith; that not even the anxieties and fears responding to the ideas of anti-Semitism, which in recent years have been compounded into the most telling and persistent of the professional fund raisers' instruments, can be such a substitute. "Defense" has been the most evocative pressure-theme of organizational squeeze. On the whole and in the long run the emulative struggles of "defense" organizations with one another has together with the almost unanimous concern for Israel, overshadowed all the other interests — cultist, cultural, philanthropic, educational, Zionist —, which are currently soliciting money and members among American Jews by invoking dangers often more fictional than real.

IV

The right expression for the relationships to one another of the entirety of American Jewish groups is not "fragmentation." The right expression is "anarchy." Our Jewish scene presents a cutthroat competition between its manifold confederated local organizations of interest, each asserting its own unique rightness, each tending to claim exclusive authority for itself on the ground that it alone possesses the sole doctrine and discipline which in its field of operations can be good for the Jews. Thus, whatever any other might be doing, each is disposed to reduplicate the other's works, to denounce the other's ways, and to declare itself entitled to total support for itself, whether as a denomination of Judaism, a Zionist party, an educational enterprise, a cultural endeavor, overseas service, or "defense."

That this anarchy should evoke aspirations after order is a foregone conclusion. The centrifugal impulsion and the confusing diverse formations and movements, which that impulsion generated among the Jews of the United States, were accompanied by centripetal ideals.

Even though the new centre which their ideals envisioned might be antithetical to the original Judaic nucleus and the new pattern of organization it projected lacked genuine Jewish precedent, it tended to establish a gradient. The record contains a number of designs of order and of plans to conform diversities of "Jewish living" to these designs. Initially, the designers limited their blueprints only to single regions of the centrifugal Judaic culture complex, such as the "reform" congregations and the "reform" rabbis, the "labor" groups, the *landsmanschaften*, the Zionists. Confederations of societies with similar principles and practices continued to be formed, most only to disband.

But as the years passed, a certain order did become manifest. It can be described as an unstable hierarchy of prestige, power and influence, whose lower levels were in a state of active or passive resistance to the higher-ups. Since the turn of the century, associations of denominational groups — orthodox as well as "conservative," extremely fundamentalist as well as orthodox — have been added to the "reform" ones. Their rabbis have similarly combined, and the *shochetim* and kosher butchers have formed trade unions (outside the Jewish "labor" groups, of course). The center workers and the Jewish social workers have followed suit. There are now also unions of journalists, of Hebrew school teachers and others. None of these organizations of interest had also designed affiliation with different ones in an over-all association.

By intention and structure, these formations have, on the face of it, nothing in common with the American Jewish Committee, a voluntary society of Jews of wealth, influence and goodwill, organized during the early years of the century in reaction to the horrors of Kishineff and Gomel, under a charter entitling them to "defend" Jewish rights wherever they were endangered. This committee was an innovation in American Jewry, supplementing philanthropy with political and social action. Many of its members were Jewish notables, several with a *shtadlanic* tradition. Their prestige and influence brought the Committee they set up paramount standing in its endeavors *for*, as against *with*, their overseas brethren. In its membership neither representative nor inclusive, paternalist in its activities, the Committee could try to shape up an over-all order from without, but evinced neither a will nor a way to shape it up from within, all American Jewry.

The first group with such a comprehensive intention was the

abortive *Kehillah*[3] of New York City, whose one meaningful enduring consequence is the interest it awakened in the Jewish education of the American Jew. Later designs remained the speculations or fantasies they were born as. Some, that might have been practicable, could not win the men and money required to implement them. Even when men might be plentiful, as the Zionist very quickly found, money was scarce. And indeed, it was the need to find money for the ever-increasing diversity of Jewish needs and wants that led to the first planned shaping of the anarchy of "Jewish living" toward a type of order.

To meet the need, to eliminate the confusions and chicanery which accompanied too many appeals for gifts to too many undiscriminated good works, there were devised first "United Hebrew Charities," then "Federation." The principle of the latter is the establishment of a central fund to which everybody could make one single contribution and thus be freed from the annoyances and hardships of being diversely solicited by many different solicitors in behalf of different "causes." The allocation of the collective gift becomes the task of a board or committee which appraises the organizations of interest asking support and assigns them a place in a preferential order of worth. The definition of this order obviously gets determined not less by the allegiances and prejudices of the allocating group, and the power and influence of the petitioning interest, than by the urgency of the needs and the importance of the wants petitioning for satisfaction. In part because of the urgency of overseas needs, in part because of the heightened personal status of board members and the obvious functional gains through the federation method, the local federations were united into a federation of federations — the National Council of Jewish Federations and Welfare Funds. Since 1946, appraisal has been separated from allocation and made the specific occupation of a professional group, with some lay associates. More and more organizations to meet needs or serve wants were brought under an increasingly standardized conception of Jewish values, whether at home or overseas, such as the relatively recent Large Cities Budgeting Conference is developing. That the unit of measurement does not inhibit experimentation or innovation where Jews of initiative and understanding have the courage

[3] The *Kehillah* idea still has its aficionados. During the half century, less or more, since its formulation, it has passed through a number of mutations, each with its theological or sociological rationalizations, the most original being still those of M. M. Kaplan.

to undertake them is another story. What matters here, is that the anarchical competition for money was brought under rule, that a certain order was established in collecting it — however dubious still the methods; and in allocating it — however incommensurable the demands and invidious the decisions.

V

Concurrently there appeared, among the inarticulate commonalty of American Jewry, whose spokesman is the Yiddish press with its factions and doxies, formations betokening a widespread anxiety over the anarchy and disunion among organizations purporting to meet their needs and satisfy their wants at home and overseas. The unorganized majority, whom Yiddish writers refer to as *die breite massen*, did not then, and still do not, regard without fear and resentment, the anarchy among the organized minorities clamoring to be their representatives and leaders. Order brings feelings of security, even when it is imposed by an external authority, if that gives evidence of a paternal concern about the well-being of the ordered. But Americanization had rendered repugnant the idea of such a paternalist authority. There was manifest something like a consensus, in the Yiddish press — and among other spokesmen — for a "Jewish unity" which should have the form of a democratically constituted and democratically maintained order. Advocates of such an order — to be shaped up through a gathering of freely elected representatives — were acclaimed as the true voices of the unorganized, regardless of their sectarian or factional affiliations. With the outbreak of World War I and the acute problems of overseas salvage (marked at first by a rivalry between "labor"-sponsored "People's Relief" and "bourgeois" Joint Distribution Committee), which that brought on, the need for co-ordinated, orderly, planning and action became critical. New figures appeared above the horizon of the competing Jewish organizations — "assimilated" Americans of Jewish derivation and of national repute and stature, who had hitherto left unheeded Judaic concerns. They gave the Zionist endeavor a new turn, with new meanings due to its transvaluation in terms of the American Idea. As World War I came toward its successful close, order at home was recognized as indispensable to effective defense and salvage of endangered Jewries abroad. After long and often violent public debate and private conference, the warring factions agreed upon an order. It was to take the form of an American

Jewish Congress to be made up of delegates, both directly elected and organizationally appointed. The task of this Congress was, to designate, for the Peace Conference in Paris, spokesmen who should if they could, make sure that in every land equal liberties of Jews, as groups and as individuals, would become part of each national code under the law of nations to be established by the peace treaty. When the work had been performed, the Congress was to hear a report and disband. At the Peace Conference, President Wilson's project for the safeguarding of minorities, Prime Minister Balfour's Declaration for a Jewish homeland became, for the powers, initiations of new national responsibilities in international relations. They also brought to aggregate Jewry unprecedented socio-political responsibilities under the League of Nations and international law.

These, the need of vigilance over minority rights in foreign lands and the upkeep of the "Jewish Agency" for Palestine, imposed a certain degree of interorganizational order and unity in relation to overseas tasks; so did the altered situation of the Jewries of bolshevized Russia. But they contributed little to mitigate the anarchic disposition toward the handling of Jewish affairs at home. The first American Jewish Congress heard the report of its emissaries and was disbanded *sine die*. Soon the Zionists split over plans for Palestine, the great majority finding the economico-political realism and the practical wisdom of its greater American leaders alien to its passional and essentially Otherworldly exilic messianism.[4] As between Weitzmann's "diaspora politics" and Brandeis' Palestinian economics, the Zionist "masses" preferred the customary patterns advocated by Weitzmann. During the strange interlude of Harding's post-war "normalcy," American Jewry appeared to revert to its own normalcy of interorganizational anarchy of claims and counter-claims. Such flare-ups of chronic anti-Semitism as the Frank case, the agitations of the Ku Klux Klan, the overt application of academic *numerus clausus*, appear to have had little effect on this war of all Jewish societies against all. New group formations arose to compete with the established ones in the confederations and confraternities already noted, as "labor's" Peoples Relief competed with "bourgeois" Joint Distribution Committee. The Jewish Welfare Board became a firmly rooted

[4] The union of vision and wisdom was devalued as "Gentile." As the late Menachem Ussishkin told off one of the younger members of the practial American group: "You have a Goyish head but we have the Jewish heart." It has ever since been the burden of that head to save that heart from its headless follies.

institution. The B'nai B'rith, under new and bolder leadership, entered the lists for men and money. Its arm of "defense," the Anti-Defamation League, set up in 1913, moved toward complete independence of power and action. The conservative congregations and rabbinate initiated a forceful over-all organization of their ilk, and so on. But none of this relieved the persistent general feeling that something was basically wrong in American Jewry nor satisfied the continuing yearning after an American form of "Jewish unity."

Nor did the renewal of the American Jewish Congress — denounced by the Committee as a breach of faith. Although the new Congress' bylaws, structure and rule were democratic, and although its first form was like that of the American Federation of Labor, an association of diverse autonomous units (religious, industrial, cultural, Zionist, and the like) for the purpose of serving common ends, it was still but one more competitor for the support and allegiance of the unorganized, appealing to public sentiment and working on public opinion in order to accomplish its undertakings of "defense," salvage or construction, of which the World Jewish Congress that replaced the Committee of Jewish Delegations is a signal development. The new formations appeared to add to the discord rather than to bring harmony. They raised to a painful shrillness the disorder by disputation of the competing self-designated would-be spokesmen and benefactors of American Jewry. In point of fact a number of diverse over-all formations were in process of which the more conspicuous were the philanthropic, the Zionist, the denominational, the communal, the "defensive."

The coming of the great depression, together with the insurgence of new and diverse forms of totalitarianism among the European peoples and the penetration of their organizations and propaganda into the United States, brought to anti-Semitism at home a force and influence hitherto as unimaginable as it had always been un-American. High points of this anti-Semitism were reached at one pole in Henry Ford and his agents, at another in the Roman Catholic priest Charles Coughlin and his organization. The aggressions of these new incarnations of the ancient hatred again forced the apparently irreconcilable "defense" organizations to explore the possibilities of reconciliation and of orderly defense action. Agreements were reached which were first grudgingly implemented and then either allowed to lapse or consciously broken. On the face of it, no common understanding could be achieved *re* the foundations of order in Jewish relations, the strategy and tactics of defense, the source and nature of the responsibility of the "defenders." Public sentiment described the situation as a conflict between self-rule and *shtadlanuth*, democracy and authoritarianism, in the conduct of Jewish affairs.

At the same time, quietly, at Judaic grassroots and among men and women alert to the relationships between education and the upkeep of a culture and its ways and works, a new over-all organization in an old and basic area of conflict presented itself for the support and cooperation of the unorganized. This was the American Association for Jewish Education, into which are joined representatives of interests ranging from extreme religious orthodoxy to equally extreme secularist orthodoxy; from believers in Sunday schools only, to believers in day schools and even parochial schools, in *talmud torahs* and *yeshivahs*. Since its organization in 1939, this union of the diverse has been able to orchestrate the varied and conflicting organizations of educational interest into a growingly cooperative team; it has brought to the educational work of American Jewish communities all the available resources of the science and art of education in America; through the community Bureaus which it sets up, it enables the Jewish schools, whatever their ideological premises, to do their job better, and to bring together in reciprocal respect and understanding hitherto rival and mutually denunciatory groups. True, there still remain self-isolating and isolated educational endeavors, to which the Association is anathema. Nevertheless it has won, on its record, the appreciation and approval of the dispensers of the financial resources of American Jewry. Like no other Jewish organization of interest, it expresses the sense of community and in its own field realizes the craving for unity of the unorganized Jews of our country.

That, with a similar will toward cooperative union, other Jewish organizations, "defense" and service alike, many of them supporters of this Association, could similarly combine for the general Jewish welfare and their own better advantage, would seem a foregone conclusion. But the rich and powerful ones among them do not reach this conclusion. Not even the tragic urgencies of the Nazi concentration camps nor the defensive necessities of World War II, nor of the armistice wherewith a trusted ally turned treacherous foe, and the hot war waged by Hitler was only changed into the cold war waged by Stalin, could stimulate the consistent collaboration of diverse Jewish organizations of power which the crises so obviously pointed to. First, there was the abnormal disputation, already referred to, about what such an instrument of collaboration should be called — Assembly,

Congress, Conference. The issue was not semantic; it was emotional and burdened with many unconscious as well as conscious fears and anxieties about imputations of "dual allegiance," that perennial token of "Jewish self-hatred" among certain categories of Americans tenuously Jewish. After feelings were quieted by calling the all-Jewish gathering "conference," the anxious ones nevertheless withdrew. They chose rather to be bringers of salvation to their Jewish brethren by themselves alone. So, when the State Department had worked out a plan by which the Jews of America would send a consultant to the Conference of 1945 in San Francisco, they successfully used political pressure to have two Jewish consultants instead of one, the second to represent their faction as a peer of the representative of the Conference they seceded from. This made it necessary to provide for a similar reduplication for other group representatives. But so long as their isolationist pretensions were vindicated, the inconvenience thus caused for all others concerned could be only trivial. Certain Jewish journalists, however, did quote Zangwill:

> Hear O Israel, the Lord thy God is One
> But Israel his people is dual, and therefore undone.

VI

The year before this specific disruption of the endeavor after order, the restiveness of unorganized Jewry before organizational anarchy had led to the formation, on the initiative of the Council of Jewish Federations and Welfare Funds, of the National Community Relations Advisory Council. This is a meeting of men and women representing "national" organizations and local community councils across the country. The "national" organizations had been the American Jewish Committee, the American Jewish Congress, the Anti-Defamation League of the B'nai B'rith, the Union of American Hebrew Congregations, the Jewish Labor Committee, the Jewish War Veterans. These local community councils number twenty five. The meeting came to be known as NCRAC. Its mandate was, to satisfy "the need for effective national planning and coordination in the field of Jewish Community Relations." But the important word in its name turned out to be "advisory," not "need." Over a long period, the principle of order signalized by its associative purpose was a screen for the practical anarchy of the more powerful "defense" organizations among its members, each apparently holding that whatever the others did it could do better. Thus, no unified plan ever came to fruition; no determination and coordination of function was ever accomplished; no supersession of the gods of publicity by goals of performance was ever completed. The projects of the hypertrophic "defenders" were marked by emulative reduplication, overlappings, and elaborations, having less regard to the most efficient use of men and money in the improvement of Jewish relations, than to outshining the rivals. Practically NCRAC was more a field of rivalry than a pattern of cooperation.

Less powerful members of NCRAC were irked by this nullification of its mandate from the beginning. In due course their sentiment came to be shared by some of the more powerful ones, such as the American Jewish Congress. When this was reinforced by the mounting impatience of the Council of Federations and Welfare Funds and the frustration of the unorganized, it was agreed to have an objective survey of the purposes, the structure, the functions and the effectiveness of the labors of NCRAC, on the basis of which its anarchy could be brought to some semblance of order. The person chosen to conduct this survey was Professor Robert MacIver of Columbia University, a complete outsider and one of America's most eminent social scientists. After a year of study, the inquiry was completed and its findings were embodied in the now celebrated *MacIver Report.*

Dr. MacIver had not known what he was letting himself in for. Following the letter and the spirit of the directive under which he conducted the inquiry, he made, upon the ground and analysis of the relevant facts, recommendations for a functional rearrangement which would eliminate the evils complained of, lead to consensus concerning the tasks best suited to the powers and competencies of the associates in NCRAC, and thus to a division of labor which would bring the maximum total result for a minimum cost. He went somewhat out of his way (although in the creed and conduct of some Judaist denominations — their Christian parallels are the Roman Catholic hierarchy — who would isolate themselves as completely from others called Jews as from all called *Goyim*, there is justification) to deprecate a segregating, isolationist misinterpretation of "cultural pluralism" which every *bona fide* cultural pluralist naturally appraises as inimical to such pluralism.

If adopted, the recommendations would have required two of the "national" organizations, the American Jewish Committee and the Anti-Defamation League — estimated by Dr. MacIver's inquiry to be responsible for ninety percent of the duplications in the field — to limit their activities, on the basis of agreements reached, to those fields where precedence, experience, and efficiency were optimal and thus to effect corresponding savings of the communal energies and resources. Of course, both organizations reacted to this with a *non possumus*. In the two-year-long process of "evaluation" and debate which the submission of the report set off, the argument was shifted from the economy and efficiency of programs with the same ends in view, to the "voluntary" springs of all such endeavors; from the nature and uses of order, to the rationalization of anarchy; from the ineluctable conditions of free communication and cooperation to rejections of them rationalized by imputations of reversion to exactly that kind of pre-American ghetto life which the Report excoriated. To impartial observers all this could appear as only disingenuous justifications for the prolongation of un-American anarchy in inter-organizational relations.

To get the neo-voluntarists to agree to some semblance of order, Dr. MacIver's original suggestions, honestly voluntaristic as impartial students regarded them, came to be diluted beyond recognition. Nonetheless, the neo-voluntarists, like the Soviets in the Security Council of the United Nations Organization, persisted in their vetos. When their fellow members of NCRAC had voted for the diluted resolution in a ratio of more than three to one, this vote was stigmatized as an undertaking to displace "freedom" with "authority" and to "impose terms of unity." The two vetoing organizations seceded from NCRAC, thus imposing terms of disunity. Between the alternatives of reaching a consensus without counting votes, or reaching a decision by means of a count of three quarters or two thirds majority on the one side, and minority veto on the other side, the seceders chose minority veto; between self-isolation and continuing participation in the work of the team freely endeavoring to win the affirmative back to their views, the dissidents chose to isolate themselves and go it alone. Between democratic order and authoritarian anarchy, they chose anarchy and called it Americanism.

VII

Occuring in a democratic society of the sixth decade of the twentieth century, both the development and its rationalizations must seem unique. Only totalitarian semantics thus assimilates anarchy to liberty and equates organized liberty with undemocratic authority.

For what else can democracy be but the organization of liberty? On the record, the American Idea and the organizational patterns which implement it reject anarchy while preserving and strengthening freedom by means of order. Their intent is summed up in Daniel Webster's famous phrase *Liberty and Union, one and inseparable, now and forever.* The American Idea postulates that all association — whether political, religious, economic, cultural, educational — is a voluntary union of diverse persons and groups of persons who pledge to one another either service to a common end by their individual means, or the united upkeep and use of a common means on behalf of their individual ends — or both. The terms of association embodied in the pledges may be legal contracts, gentlemen's agreements or a general understanding. The laws provide redress for breaches of legal contracts, a sense of honor and the influence of public opinion inhibit breaches of agreements or understandings.

That the "voluntarists" were unsure of their decision seems indicated by the argument they addressed to public opinion. Here they were, men of goodwill who had voluntarily formed voluntary committees and leagues for the purpose of defending themselves and fellow-Jews from anti-Semitism and other forms of handicap and injustice. They took for granted the Jews' acceptance of their would-be protectors and of their arts of protection. They neither sought consent to their guardianship nor invited their unconsulted wards' participation in their own defense. They did not ask them, they told them, and at the same time employed the devices of the fund-raisers to elicit from their unaware protegés the costs of an insurance the latter had neither requested nor could require accounting for. Like certain businesses, American Jewry were to accept and pay for protection by protectors whether they wanted them or not. In sum, the "voluntarists" assumed authority over others which the others had not granted, and denied that as authorities they need account to those others for the manner and costs of its exercise. Arguments implied that it was essential Americanism to be self-chosen but not called, not representative; to take measures affecting the existence and interests of large numbers of people who are pressured into financing the measures' costs without being responsible to those who are affected and are footing the bill. The spontaneous centripetal turns, within the enclaves of Jewry, compensating the centrifugal, were translated into a myth that some notably secularizing rabbinical leaders were impatient of secular control; or the centripetal trends were attributed to a doctrine of "Jewish peoplehood" which as such has no dynamic impact on the Americanization of American Jewish communities as a social process, and which deprecates the process. The craving for unification was also attributed — and this in the light of the record, correctly — to a sense of insecurity.

Such attributions are not explanations of the social dynamics of American Jewish living but rationalizations of powerful components of the dynamics pressing to retain and enlarge their preponderance. Among other rationalizations was a factitious one justifying their anarchic intent on historical grounds, as if the import of history is that the future must repeat the past; that what was, will be, and by implication that anarchy and not ordered liberty in the conduct of Jewish affairs is rightly American because it had arisen in the American scene. Much turned on reading into Dr. MacIver's report intentions that were not there. I choose one instance that has come under my eye. This justifies the "voluntarists" by charging that "Professor MacIver's proposal would have given *the NCRAC predominant control over budgetary matters*." But an accurate reading shows that the Report had made an entirely tentative suggestion that representatives of the NCRAC be given *one-third* of the membership of a total allocating committee. It would hardly seem too much that the communities which contributed so much of the funds should have had that much say in how they should be distributed. Moreover, the Report nowhere denies the right to conscientious dissent and action. Nothing can be found in it to justify the strange charge that it would stifle dissent.

Again: "The Report provisionally handed over this area (of religious relations) to but one group of rabbis, those affiliated with the Union of Hebrew Organizations!" True, the UAHC had been, at the time of writing, the *only* agency representing the rabbinate within the whole group of agencies under consideration. And the MacIver proposal was that they should no longer remain the only group but that the other denominations of Judaism and their rabbinates should also be included, to form a unified system solely for the purpose of entering into and developing relations with other religious bodies for the promotion of a cause common to them all. Significantly, this has since happened; the United Synagogue of America and the Union of Orthodox Congregations have joined the NCRAC. So have a number of secular groups.

And finally, "the Report urges that all legal services be transferred to a single agency." The Report nowhere makes any such recommendation. This is falsely read into a statement that there is "no reason why two agencies should separately prepare briefs for the same court," which is a different matter altogether. Courts do not like to have separate briefs on the same subjects from agencies in the same field and some of them refuse to accept more than one in any case. But apart from that there was no designation of any single agency in the Report. It was left to the common sense of the agencies to get together, in each instance, to avoid an obvious waste of skilled service.

The argumentation made much of the event that the voluntarists "did accept some recommendations including the principle of joint planning." But, having "accepted" the "principle" they seceded from NCRAC rather than practice it.

VIII

The immediate consequences of this present phase of struggle over anarchy and ordered liberty looks like a victory for anarchy. As yet, the wealth, the influence and prestige of the anarchic organizations are all too great. The National Council of Federations and Welfare Funds reaffirmed the need for "effective national planning and coordination," and initiated endeavors to reconstitute the union known as NCRAC. The seceding organizations were both condemned and offered appeasement. But the allocating committees of local federations and welfare funds were not ready to refuse them subventions on principle, no matter how dishonorable they regarded the secession. On the face of it, the centrifugal trends in American Jewry remain preponderant.

But that they will continue so is a conclusion disregarding the redirective influences of the American Idea, the ongoing democratization of all sorts of Jewish groupings. The number and variety of centripetal formations by these groupings signalize a trend. Today the most comprehensive and practical is the Council concerning itself with funds, the most dramatic is perhaps the Synagogue Council of America, apparently modelled as an association upon the Protestants' National Council of the Churches of Christ. Like all other free formations in the world, these formations are in some respects as individual and singular as their member groups, and the member groups as the persons who compose them. On every level, each is different from the others; on every level, they pool their differences in a communion, not in order to suppress or abolish them, but in order to assure to them equally the liberty, the safety, the support and strength they could not acquire by isolating themselves in the lonely ways of the war of all against all. They embody the American spirit and follow the American way, which is the way of liberty and union, on all levels of association.

If American Jewry is to have a future at all, growing from a living past, it will make its future only as it follows this way. Otherwise its way will be from relative anarchy to absolute anarchy; otherwise the diverse aggressions of the mutative anti-Semitism of the non-Jewish milieu, the consequent fear and flight of Jew from Jew and war of Jew with Jew in the Jewish milieu, will displace Americanization with fragmentation and fragmentation with dissipation. Thus, with the celebration of the three hundreth anniversary of the settling of Jews in America, the most vital, most prosperous and strongest Jewry in the world today is clarifying the choice between social self-preservation and social suicide as a community of free men.

Book I: Modernity and Survival

"Of Them Which Say They Are Jews"

> I know the blasphemy of them which say they are Jews, and are not, but are the Synagogue of Satan.
>
> *Revelation II, 9.*

> They shall speak with new tongues.
>
> *Mark XVI, 17.*

IT HAS been my experience, during the present Hitlerian era, that in any company of Jews where the talk falls upon some matter in which a Jew figures, one of the companions sooner or later demands a definition of *Jew*. The demand sets off a discussion in the course of which some one of the disputants blazes out that some other burns him up, the whole event giving off much heat and little light. I have never known a definition to be accepted by all present. Each definer is charged with leaving out somebody or something that another wants to put in, or putting in something or somebody that another wants to leave out. All produce their definitions passionately, like prescribed articles of faith; with none is a definition simply a summary of observation and experience. As a rule, debate is cut off by a call to more liquid forms of spiritual intake or by the lateness of the hour; the discussion only stops, it does not end. The idea of what *Jew* means remains a formulation of desire, fear and belief, an upshot of wish-thinking, not a conclusion from the testimony of the record. The party breaks up with each of the symposiasts sure that he is a Jew and disagreeing with all the others as to what a Jew is. That which, to a sympathetic bystander, all of them certainly share is the label *Jew*, so that anybody is a Jew who of his own free will calls himself by that name or who feels compelled to answer to it when others call him by it. The rest seems to be a matter of selection, attitude and emphasis of apparently arbitrary differentiae as conflicting as they are numerous, and as variable as they are conflicting.

Consider the inner history of the people called Jews and you look

Reprinted from *Contemporary Jewish Record*, December 1944.

upon the record of what seems to be a centrifugal impulsion, of a process of variation, multiplication and conflict about certain modes of living and believing by which aggregations of men and women identified themselves as *Jews*. In their way's name they cut each other off and shut each other out, demanding as the token of fellowship in the congregation of Israel that the others should include *this* or exclude *that* in their faith and works. *This* and *that* are extremely diverse. In Harlem there are dark-skinned men and women who affirm that they are the true Jews because their skins are dark, and that people whose skins are not dark can at best be only Jews of the second class. On the other hand, most of their pale-faced neighbors called Jews hesitate to concede that the dark-skinned Jews of Harlem are Jews at all, even of the second class, though they would concede dark-skins to be Jews readily enough as Falashas in Abyssinia or Yemenites in Arabia. Where skin-color is not a differentia one or another item of doctrine or discipline is. To many, *Jew* is a synonym for *Judaist;* they cry aloud in the forums and in the market places that what is not of Judaism is not Jewish. To others, Judaism is not a necessary but a contingent component of a Jew's being: a Jew may take it or leave it; for them *Jew* has a secular, not a religious core of meaning. With some such secularists, the whole of Jewishness is the Zionist enterprise; with others it is the cultivation of Hebrew letters and the Hebrew language; with others of the ways and works of Yiddishism; with still others the combination of Yiddishism with socialism. With still others it is a compound of sentiment about the word *Jew* and philanthropic enterprise and "social work." And so on, from struggling variation to variation until you reach the loosed individual who is detached from all groups, like most of the eleven "Under Forty" who recently testified in *The Contemporary Jewish Record* — individuals like Clement Greenberg, who "has no more of a conscious position toward his Jewish heritage than the average American Jew — which is hardly any," or Howard Fast, to whom "a Jew is a man," and that's all. For these young people the greatest common denominator of *Jew* seems to be simply the word, together with an aura of emotional tensions — mainly vague unease and discomfort which the word and the images and concepts it suggests at once arouse, focus and enchannel. Their opposite number is Waldo Frank, a lone prophet of a secularistic Judaism singular to himself, crying against rabbi and radio for the audience of a stiff-necked generation.

Nor are those for whom *Jew* is a synonym for *Judaist* less diversified or less in mutual opposition. Within the two major sects of *Orthodox* and *Reformed*, there are any number of minor cuttings. The Orthodox diversify into Ashkenazim, Sephardim, Hassidim and Mitnagdim, and these into numerous specific variations of doctrine and discipline — Mizrachite, Conservative, Agudath-Israelite and what have you, until a last term is reached in the personal singularity of this or that Hassidic wonder-rabbi. The Reformite sects range from those for whom, as for the cultists of the American Council for Judaism, Inc., Torah is all doctrine and no discipline, to those for whom, as for the Reconstructionists, Torah is all discipline and no doctrine. The range is from theology without the *Shulchan Arukh* to the *Shulchan Arukh* without theology; in the language of the Christian neighbor, from faith without works to works without faith.

To most of the men and women who form the congregations of these Judaist creeds, the creedal differences are largely matters of indifference. They are members of their respective congregations because of habit, social pressure or social emulation. The creed offers them no genuine living option; when it does, it is because they have found themselves in a trouble from which natural means have failed to save them, and turn to the rabbi as their family specialist in supernatural aids. Only a very small minority is so concerned with the growth, the standing and the power of the sect as to make these a cause to live and work for. And they are fewer still to whom doctrine or discipline or both have that symbolic value and far-reaching philosophic significance which can be identified as "religious" in the most approved psychological sense of the term.

The active life of the Judaisms, like that of all other religions, seems to reside, not at the massive center, which is inert, but at the thin outer edges which are in flow, which are the locus of reformations and readjustments, of responses to the tensions of inward strife and outward assault. These changes are the operations of minorities to whom they have become living and momentous issues, forced options. For the most part, the majority passes by unaware; inertia holds it together; inertia crumbles it down as time flows on. But sometimes the majority follows along. This happens at times of deep general crisis like the present, when everybody reacts to the forces which under normal conditions only small numbers of sensitive men and women respond to.

Now, from the time that Constantine compelled the Christian sectaries to formulate a single, exclusive, correct creed, and to submit to a single, over-ruling, ecclesiastical organization, to the time of the Democratic Revolution, when a French nobleman declared in the

National Assembly of 1789: "to the Jews as a nation — nothing; to the Jews as human beings — everything," Jews, whether also Judaists or no, might be said to have been living in a state of chronic general crisis. The name for this chronic general crisis is anti-Semitism; people pay it something like adequate attention only when it is acute, as today. Pre-democratic anti-Semitism overruled the spontaneous centrifugal impulsion of the Jewish being. It was a centripetal force pressing from without in; it drove Jews back to the doctrine and disciplines of the Jewish tradition and confined variation and conflict to the lines of its ways and works. Anti-Semitism in the age of democracy has a contrary effect. The implication that a Jew, to receive his right as a human being must cut off his being as Jew, reinforced in a new and unprecedented way the handicap formerly imposed on the Jew because he chose not to become a Christian but to remain a Judaist. It brought in a kind of secular *shmad*, and some describe this apostasy as one of the maladies of Jewry of the present age. By a tragic but natural misinterpretation of the principles and purposes of the democratic revolution, there was initiated a liquidation of the Jewish being, not by anti-Jews but by Jews. And this liquidation stimulated anti-Semitism to branch out into new forms which added themselves to the old. To all, the label *Jew*, regardless of who bears it, is a disturbing symbol, a stimulus to aversion, hate and aggression. It unifies all to whom it is applied as targets of ill will and misprision. Let them differ and quarrel with one another as passionately as they wish, to the anti-Semite they are equally and identically Jews. Religionist and secularist, orthodox and reform, Yiddishist and Hebraist, Zionist and Judaist, Congressite and Committeeman, Federationist and lodge-brother — are to the anti-Semite alike members of one another, carriers of the same evil, meriting the same interdict and excommunication and punishment.

Of all them which say they are Jews, each may be the synagogue of Satan to the others, but all, whether they speak with the old tongues of Sephardi and Hassid or the new tongues of Zionist or American Council for Judaism, Inc., are equally the synagogue of Satan for the anti-Semite. The common enemy imposes on them a common identity and a common cause. Perhaps even without his coercion toward union they would suffuse and modify each other's being by the give and take of their conflicts as well as their friendships, belonging with one another in an intimacy more compelling than that which they achieve with persons not called Jews. But anti-Semitic pressure enhances whatever of such a process may be going on. Deny and condemn one another as they may, Jews are so members of one another that they are unable to let each other alone. In relation to other Jews, they cannot live and let live. They feel their fates so bound up together that a Judaist of the American Council for Judaism, Inc. must perforce protest to American officials about the reported organization by the British of a so-called Jewish Brigade. They feel their fates so bound up together that another of the same sect must perforce fail to mention the Jews whose heroic stand in the Battle of the Warsaw Ghetto he with thirty-six other notables is commemorating; he alone of the thirty-seven speaks neither of the Battle of the Ghetto nor of the Jews who fought it; for him the battle is "The Battle of Warsaw" and the fighters are "the unfortunate inhabitants of Poland."[1] To the psychologist this mode of expression signalizes an identification feared and rejected, a flight in which the fleeing carries along with itself that which is fled.

The psychological mechanism underlying episodes of this sort deserves more study than it has received among Jews. Their inner, often entirely unconscious revulsion against identification with one another underlies many an apparently unintelligible aspect of the effect of Jews and Jewish organizations upon each other and the strange rationalizations by which they are accounted for. They go with the disposition that limits *Jew* to some singular and exclusive meaning and cuts off and shuts out all that does not conform to this meaning. When the mind is free and the heart is secure this does not happen. Then principles and purposes of democracy prevail in the spirit of *live and let live, live and help live; Jew* is accepted as denoting an orchestration of all the diverse and diversifying meanings of the term; an orchestration such that the agonists of all the meanings, each different from the others, so live together with each other that their togetherness becomes the condition for the full and healthy development of the separate Jewishness of each.

Failing this orchestration, the prospects are good for a Jewish anti-Semitism of the twentieth Christian century which will reinforce and diversify the classical anti-Semitism initiated under somewhat similar conditions in Israel during the first Christian century. For the anti-Semitism which is a chronic malady of the Christian world is a non-

[1] See *The Ghetto Speaks*, April 1, 1944, p. 9, the message of Arthur Hays Sulzberger. The writer is a distinguished citizen who, in his vocation and in all but his Jewish relations had given signs of unusual courage and understanding. There is reason to believe that these qualities have since been unblocked for his Jewish relations as well.

Jewish elaboration and employment of Judaistic intolerances. The intolerances are recorded and their theological elaboration and employment are initiated in the New Testament. Of recent years various Protestant authorities such as James Parkes,[2] Conrad Henry Moehlman,[3] S. A. Campbell,[4] have called attention to them as such. But to my mind the process they involve comes out with even greater clearness and distinctness in a smoothly written and tactfully constructed study of the religions of the New Testament for an altogether different purpose. The study is called *The Varieties of New Testament Religion.*[5] Its author is the distinguished authority on the New Testament, Dr. Ernest F. Scott. The point of his book is that New Testament religion is diverse and diversifying religion, a Many and not a One, and that the unique vitality and appeal of the New Testament inhere in this protean mutation of its belief, which exemplifies a spontaneous power of self-renewal in different minds in different forms, enduring through the ages. The New Testament, Dr. Scott holds, is the Magna Charta of Christian liberty, the spring and matrix of all the heresies: "no book, indeed, could be less fitted to serve as touchstone of orthodox belief." Born of the inspiration of "the Spirit," which is free and speaks with any tongue it chooses, new or old, the New Testament is characterized by the division which freedom breeds and which testifies to the reality of the freedom which breeds it. "So long as men are free, they will follow the light within them and refuse to bow to any fixed authority. Division is involved in the very nature of our religion, and this is the truth brought home to us as we study the writings of the New Testament. They are inspired by one faith, but every teacher interprets it differently, as he has known it in his own soul. . . . There will be endless differences as each one holds fearlessly to the truth that is in him, but out of this division will come the only unity which is worth our struggle." The unity is that of the process, of the continuity, of variation. It is the creative unity, the one-in-many of life itself: "The divisions which have seemed from time to time to destroy the church are part of

[2] James William Parkes, *Conflict of the Church and the Synagogue: A Study in the Origins of Anti-Semitism*, Soncino, 1934. *Jesus, Paul and the Jews*, Student Christian Movement Press, 1936.

[3] Conrad Henry Moehlman, D.D., *The Christian-Jewish Tragedy*, Rochester, N. Y.: The Printing House of Leo Hart, 1933.

[4] W. A. Campbell, *The Crucifixion and Resurrection of Jesus*, London: The Pioneer Press, 1933.

[5] New York: Charles Scribner's Sons, 1943.

the life-process which keeps it secure." Indeed, it is not division that brings destruction. The differences, the innovations, the "heresies," in which the process adds new to old are as such enrichment and strengthening, like increases in population and occupation. Destruction enters in the attitude toward division. Destruction enters when the different is penalized for being different, when it is treated as an intruder, when it is required to submit and conform or else be cut off and shut out. In other words, destruction enters as arrest of the life-process.

During the first hundred years of Christianism, the years of the formation of the New Testament, destruction was only incipient, the life-process overruled it. The Christian faith began as a variation from Judaism. That it culminated with a theological anathema upon Judaism is not a consequence of its vital being but of efforts to arrest the process of this being, to unify from without, in creeds and organization, to believe on authority and not by the spirit. The Jewish society in which the Christian variation upon Judaism took form was itself a one-in-many of beliefs and ideas. There were Jews, also among the high Temple functionaries, who were not Judaists; there were Judaists who were by nationality and speech Greeks, Italians, Syrians, Egyptians, Persians, Babylonians. The Judaists themselves were divided — most commonly mentioned are the sects of the Pharisees, Sadducees and Essenes. All were in their way heedful of the Torah, but each had his own interpretation of the Torah, and each synagogue had its own interpreters and leaders. New Testament Christianity is an offspring of the Synagogue, and not the Temple; it was completely taken over by a priestcraft and sacerdotalized long after its books had been written. Most of the New Testament Christians — the disciples, Paul, the other apostles — were Judaists of different sects, adding the Christian difference to their Judaism. Jesus, of course, was a Judaist, a product of the Synagogue with a prophetic passion, teaching certain modifications of Judaistic faith and works by which the *Malkhuth Shamayim* might be established. The event of his execution and burial and the conviction of his subsequent resurrection made his person (in a world where the fear of death was mightier than the love of life) more important than his teaching. It led to a handling of his teaching which, save for that of the apostle James, gave it a meaning quite different from that which its author intended. This differentiating treatment was a work of synagogues both in Palestine and the Diaspora. The synagogues were the first churches. The diversity of liturgical, economic, social and intellectual conditions in which they existed occasioned a diversity of treatment of the good news of which Jesus was made the incarnation and carrier.

The addition of Gentile groups to Judaist congregations gave the Christian divergence from the Judaistic center still other channels. The paramount item of divergence was the doctrine that Jesus, who died and was alive again, is Lord. The validity of his teaching was turned into a function of his resurrection. The idea of his resurrection became the core of the continual reconstruction of his personality to which the Gospels and the references to him in the rest of the New Testament bear witness. Initially, the force behind these reconstructions was "the Spirit" inspiring believers to "speak with new tongues." But Hellenistic influences, the ideas and methods of Philo Judaeus, the interest and activities of sacerdotal converts, first channelled, then choked off the Spirit and replaced inspiration with theology and dogma, spontaneous worship with rituals, inspired leaders with indoctrinated priests. At first all these diversifications could live side by side in difference without enmity, conducting a friendly debate. There could be Judaists who did not believe in Christ; good neighbors of other Judaists who did. There could be Christians, such as the followers of James, to whom the inwardness of the Lord's good news was the prophetic gospel of righteousness; there could be Christians such as those who followed Paul, the Pharisee so exercised about resurrection, to whom the good news was the guarantee of resurrection through Jesus. There could be Christians to whom Jesus was the apocalyptic revealer of the divine will, the comforter of his churches in time of trouble, as those to whom Revelations was addressed; there could be Christians, such as those to whom Hebrews was addressed, to whom the good news was that Jesus was the High Priest of High Priests, who was at the same time the sacrifice by whose blood men are saved. There could be Christians for whom faith was enough; others, for whom works were indispensable. To some, works consisted in the sacerdotal rituals and sacraments; to others, in righteous conduct. Each disciple, each apostle — Mark, Matthew, Luke, John, James, Peter, Paul, Stephen, Apollos, Timothy, Titus — had his own new direction, guided by the Spirit speaking with a new tongue, from the spring of departure: *Jesus is Lord.* There were even Gentile Christians — Gnostics, Docetists — to whom the Lordship was not a fact of personal experience and historical record, but a metaphysical appearance. So, Jesus was in one place *Messiah*, in another *Lord*, in another *Son of God*, in another the

Priestly Sacrifice and Sacrificer, in another an *Aeon*, an *Earthly Appearance*, in another the *Eternal Word*.

However the Spirit caused Christians to think about their Savior, they came, sooner or later, to a dilemma of which Paul and his career were the embodiment. The early harmony of Torah *and* Christ was transformed by the impact of personal rivalries, group emulations, the conversion of Gentiles and other factors into the irreconcilable alternative, Torah *or* Christ. Paul, struggle as he would, could brook no harmony. He began by persecuting Judaistic Christians, he ended by excommunicating Judaism — "if any man insist on the law, he has fallen away from Christ."

A time came, especially after the year 66 — which saw the revolt of the Jews against Roman power — when the safety of the Christian could depend on his division from that power's enmity toward Jews and Judaism. The New Testament records the emergence of this attitude of destruction and its crystallization in dogma. In the First Gospel Christianism but fulfils Judaism. Later, it supplements, then it perfects, then it supersedes Judaism. The Fourth Gospel finally makes of Christianity the rejection of Judaism and of the Chosen People whose religion it revalues into the Rejected People. It makes of them utterly "the Synagogue of Satan." Later events hardened the process into the classical anti-Semitism of dogmatic theology and the consequent laws and customs of Christian society.

It is this hardened structure which the Democratic Revolution crumbled and somewhat liquefied. Because of it, the new process of division was initiated among Jews of which the diversifications of the nineteenth and twentieth centuries are expressions. I will not press the analogies between the various reform and other movements among the Jews of this age and those of the New Testament era; nor will I draw the moral they point up.

Judaism as Disaster

ALTHOUGH I use the term Judaism in the title of this address, I do not mean Judaism. Judaism is the name of a certain western religion. It is in the same category with other religious isms — Roman Catholicism, Presbyterianism, Methodism, or any of the other Protestant faiths. The adherents of those faiths might be Spaniards or Italians or Irishmen or Englishmen or Frenchmen or Danes or Norwegians or Swedes or Jews. Once, not so long ago, they might have been Germans. An adherent of any variety of Christianism, whatever his other associations, is a Christian, and similarly, an adherent of any sect of Judaism, whatever his other associations, is a Judaist. Although most Judaists are Jews there are Judaists who are not Jews and Jews who are not Judaists. For this reason I have long preferred to signalize the entire culture-complex wherewith a Jew may be identified as Jew by the word "Hebraism." In the tradition of English letters this word stands for the height and breadth of the culture or spirit of Israel, alike in its concentration and its diversity; "Hebraism" is an easier word to speak than "Jewishness' which has come to mean much the same constellation of group qualities, group memories, group attitudes, and group activities, but somehow it has not caught on, and "Judaism" as it continues to be employed, has acquired something of both the denotations and connotations of "Hebraism." So I am constrained to use "Judaism," meaning by it what I mean by "Hebraism."

As I think of this usage, there comes to mind a commentary on the effort at redefinition made a quarter of a century ago by the late Judge Mayer Sulzberger of Philadelphia. Addressing Jews of conflicting interests and opinions, he warned them:

> I do not trouble myself much about definitions of Jews and Judaism. I do not think very highly of the learned talk I have heard about race and nationality and a variety of other things. . . . I do not think that any of you can now or ever will learn to define Jews and Judaism. . . . The Jews are a fact and that is all; that is old. They are a fact thousands of years old and they need no definition, and if they did, your definitions

Reprinted from *Jewish Education*, Volume 13, No. 2, 1940.

> would be good for nothing. Nor is it your definitions that you are anxious about. It is the definitions of the others that are troubling you. The others are not troubling about your nationalism, or Zionism, or your conferences, or your congress, or your democratic representations — not a bit of it. For them you are one, indivisible, inside and outside, a Jew. The great world outside does not bother about your misunderstandings.

These remarks of Judge Sulzberger's impressed me deeply. I made them the text of the discussion of "Jewish Quarrels and Jewish Unity" which is the eigth chapter of my book, *Judaism at Bay*, and their import is as pertinent in 1940 as it was in 1916. What else is this import but the recognition of the fact that the force which drives Jews, willing and unwilling, in upon one another, toward a common life and a common fate, is far less an inward will than an outward compulsion — the compulsion of an environing society to which the differences between Jew and Jew are irrelevant, if not null; to which the word "Jew" names the same essential thing regardless of whom it names.

As the tradition of the non-Jewish world means it, this essential thing is not a desirable thing. The Christian meaning of the word "Jew" rests on the interpretations of the New Testament by orthodox sectarian theologies. The sects differ widely among themselves. But to all alike "Jew" conveys the idea of a being separated out and cut off, of a special people that had been first chosen and then rejected, a people cast by God for the role of villain in the drama of mankind's salvation.

You recall the plot of this drama. Adam and Eve were living happily in the Garden of Eden. Everything was open and free to them except the fruit of the Tree of Knowledge of Good and Evil. This, God had forbidden them to touch. Nor would they have touched it, but for Satan. Satan had been a mighty prince in heaven. Pride caused him to rebel against God's rule. In the heavenly war which ensued, he and his followers were defeated and driven out of heaven to the hell prepared for them. But defeat did not make Satan abandon his war against God. In due course he found his way to the newly-created earth, to Eden, and tempted Eve, who tempted Adam. Both having disobeyed God's commandment, God cursed them and expelled them from Paradise. Instead of immortal, they were now mortal; instead of enjoying the leisure and abundance of Eden, they were now condemned to the labor and scarcity of a world no longer made for them. The bearing of children was to be labor and pain to Eve, the earning of bread was to be painful labor to Adam. Their sin was to be hereditary and constitutive, and the destiny of their children and their children's children was to be eternal death — unless God's mercy tempered His justice, and the First Parents' sin could at one and the same time be both expiated and forgiven.

God's providence arranged human history toward this end. From among all the descendants of Adam he chose the seed of Abraham to be the vessels of His will. They only were to be His people; He only was to be their God. He revealed to them his commandments. He established them in the Promised Land. He raised up David to be King over them. Though they sinned much and were chastened much, He promised them a Messiah who in the fulness of time should save them from their enemies, end their misfortunes, and establish The Kingdom of Heaven on earth, with Jerusalem its capital, and Zion its crown. But the true Messiah came not in glory, but in humility. He came as the Lord's only-begotten Son, the Second Person in His triune oneness, to be born of a Virgin of the House of David, and in the shape of a Jewish man to suffer a shameful death on the cross, to be buried, and on the third day to rise again. This son, Jesus of Nazareth, was the true Messiah. His death on the cross was the expiation of the sin of Adam. Those who believed in it were to be saved from the eternal death which was the consequence of that sin. Those who did not believe were to be cast out from the fellowship of the Saved. God's Chosen People, the Jews, did not believe. They regarded Jesus as a false Messiah, they rejected him, they condemned him to the shameful death upon the cross. Thereupon God rejected them. They became the outcasts from the fellowship of a mankind that shared the belief in Christ's Incarnation and his Vicarious Atonement for Adam's sin.

The folkways and customs of the believers all turned, in their attitude toward the Jews, upon this meaning given the word "Jew" by Christian theology. The theological meaning governed the enactment of law and the attitude of priests, princes and people. Although, in certain sections of the Christian world it has been tempered by the impact of the natural and social sciences, by "higher criticism," and by a democratic philosophy of life, the original disposition remains. It is difficult if not impossible for any individual indoctrinated in childhood in the concept of Jews as deicides, Christ-killers, as rejected people, to think of the word "Jew" without discomfort and repulsion. In the enclaves of the more orthodox theologies, the original Christian definition prevails, and in times of stress is emphasized. Thus, the worst insult that the brave Martin Niemöller could level at the hated Nazis was to suggest that they were like the Jews who "brought the Christ of God to a cross." The Jewish people, Niemöller declared, "bears a curse because they rejected and resisted him to the death." This view of Niemöller's is accented wherever orthodoxy prevails, as in Russian and Rumanian Greek-Orthodoxy, in the Roman-Catholicism of Spain, French-Canada, Poland, and Austria. True, the rivalry of Nazism has made it a matter of policy for the Pope to declare: "It is not possible for Christians to take part in Anti-Semitism," but Dollfuss-Schuschnigg Austria, Franco Spain, and their defenders in free European countries and in the United States (such as the Detroit priest, Charles Coughlin), remain willful anti-Semites. So do Protestant fundamentalists, such as the Ku Klux Klan and Henry Ford. In contrast with the Federal Council of the Churches of Christ in America, they employ and exploit the traditional theological definition of "Jew." Official doctrine regarding the Jews stays unreformed.[1]

The emotion generated and sustained by that doctrine, and the attitudes which it establishes, provide them with a basis for blaming the Jews for every misfortune that may occur in a society without at the same time exposing the absurdity of such a blame. The emotion enables anti-Semites to charge Jews with such fantastic conspiracy against mankind as is set forth by the notorious fiction called the *Protocols of the Elders of Zion.* These fantasies, as psychiatrists well know, are in fact paranoid projections of the desires of their inventors and users which are fathered on the Jews. The anti-Semites employing them exploit the Jews as a screen behind which they believe that they can safely carry forward their conspiracy against freedom. The Tsarist Russians were such conspirators; such are their heirs the Bolsheviks; such are the Fascists, the Nazis and certain Catholic groups. It sometimes happens that this convenient use of the Jews as a scapegoat is admitted, even boasted of. Thus, Rauschning, in *The Voice of Destruction*, cites Hitler as saying that if the Jews were destroyed, the Nazis would have to invent them. "It is essential to have a tangible enemy, not merely an abstract one." Therefore "Jews are to be tortured but must not be destroyed."

During the nineteenth century, the doctrinal ground for treating Jews as a Rejected People was shifted from a theology of sin and salva-

[1] See, for example, a homily of the Bishop of Cremona on "The Church and the Jews" (*Osservatore Romano*, January 15, 1939): "It is not true that the Church has changed now her canonic legislation to favor Jews who remain such."

tion first to a theology of class and class-war, and again of race and race-corruption. But the essential import of the word "Jew" continues unchanged. Obviously, what Richard Wagner, Stöcker, H. S. Chamberlain, Spengler, Rosenberg, and Hitler practically mean by their formulation is the same that the Christian sectaries, the Church Fathers, the various Popes, the Inquisitors, and Christian princes meant by theirs. In this respect Mussolini follows Hitler.

Nor need anybody delude himself that communism does not inherit from and capitalize on the same tradition. Anti-Semitism may be illegal in Soviet Russia as a public doctrine, but it is condoned as a personal practice and communism's intent remains the liquidation of the Jew as Jew. Did not Karl Marx write in 1843, in the essay entitled *The Jewish Question:* "The emancipation of Jews is in the last analysis the emancipation of mankind from Jewry — the social emancipation of Jews is the emancipation of society from Jewry"? Marxists, like Hitlerites and Christian Fundamentalists, persist in defining the Jew as the villain of the drama of salvation. Neither, indeed, are ostensible liberals, who have become secularized, and pretend to think in terms of science and democracy, exempt from the initial bias. Thus, that well-known British literary scold, the Utopianist H. G. Wells, writes a book on *The Fate of Man* in which he takes the Jews to task. He says that they are thinking of themselves as a chosen people; that the orthodox way of life which is postulated upon this idea has made them "inassimilable and aggressive." He charges them with a social and spiritual isolationism that has brought on the intolerance and accusations they suffer from. He charges that the Zionists labor for a national home in Palestine so that Jews could elsewhere "be forever foreigners." He indignantly demands that Jews should stop trying to be different. But he makes no effort to say whom they should be the same with. He apparently wants them to stop being different without becoming the same with anybody at all; that is, he wants them to stop being. In this book, as in so many others, Wells is very impatient of differences. He cannot tolerate differences, whether in Americans, Frenchmen, Catholics, Italians, Hindus, Chinamen, Japanese, or Englishmen, but he takes his intolerance out most on the Jews.

In sum, all anti-Semitism, either old or new, roots in a philosophy of life, a scheme of salvation, whose soil is the emotion imparted by Christian theology and whose intent is to make the Jew the villain of the scheme.

II

Now the attitudes which anti-Semitism generates and sustains react on the Jews. The non-Jew's definition of the term "Jew" becomes an unconscious part of the Jew's definition. However it may be resisted and denied consciously, a tendency to acquiesce in the imposed status leads unconsciously to a second sort of anti-Semitism. This is the anti-Semitism of Jews toward Jews. Knowingly or unknowingly, so very many Jews feel their Judaism to be disaster, and the unity of Judaism to be the unity of disaster. Each group, each sect, each party, blames the others for its predicament. To the centripetal propulsion communicated by anti-Semitism from without, there opposes itself among Jews a centrifugal trend which expresses the mutual repulsions of the anti-Semitisms within. This is manifest in a disposition toward flight from Judaism which, ironically, the positive humanism and philanthropy of the democratic world enhance.

I say, ironically. For, of course, the intent and effect of the scientific point of view and of the democratic philosophy of life are the precise opposite. To science, differences are natural, spontaneous, and inevitable. Differentiation and variation belong to the inwardness of life and thought, and such progress as mankind can achieve depends on the freedom with which variations get a chance to prove themselves on their merits. The method of science and the achievements of science have depended on the liberation and encouragement of differences and on the competition and cooperation of differences.

The democratic way of life and thought may be described as a suffusion of religion and politics and economics with the attitude of science. In religion this culminated in the idea of the universal fatherhood of God and common brotherhood of man. It led religious societies from the ecclesiastical to the congregational form of organization. It led them from treating their revelations as mutually exclusive and jealous sovereignties, first to a sort of negative toleration; then, from negative toleration to the rule of *live and let live*, then from the rule of *live and let live* to the rule of *live and help live.* Its principle, though not yet its practice, is signalized by the association of the Federal Council of Churches of Christ in America and in the Universal Christian Council.

In politics the democratic principle was affirmed in the propositions of the American Declaration of Independence and implemented in the American Constitution, and from its American springs its fructifying vision had spread to the whole of the West. It was the impetus to the true "Rise and Expansion of the West." In the domain of the spirit and the intellect, it led to the recognition of what I have been accustomed to call Cultural Pluralism — to the recognition of the fact that the high achievements of the human spirit grow and thrive only upon the equal liberty of differences in competition and cooperation. As the late Mr. Justice Holmes once declared,

> . . . when men have realized that time has upset many fighting faiths, they may come to believe even more than they believe the very foundations of their own conduct that the ultimate good desired is better reached by free trade in ideas — that the best test of truth is the power of the thought to get itself accepted in the competition of the market; and that truth is the only ground upon which their wishes can be carried out.

So far as their attitude toward themselves is concerned, this philosophy does not seem to me even yet to have come home to the Jews. Democracy did not mean to them freedom *for* something. Democracy meant freedom *from* something. Fundamentally, it meant to them freedom from the disaster of being Jews. And the first and most enduring response of Jews to the democratic opening of the doors to all the unprivileged and oppressed — to workmen, to black men, to women, as well as to Jews — was flight from Judaism. Even in many of the arguments on behalf of Zionism this component of flight is evidenced. For however much the protagonists of Zionism reaffirm abandoned Jewish values, they insist that Jews never can and never will be Jews freely and completely elsewhere than in Palestine. Is it not significant that it was one of the first Zionists, Israel Zangwill, who thought up the image of the melting pot? This is obviously a defeatist image, an image not of freedom, but of flight. It is a somewhat sour entertainment to note the spirit of this flight and defeatism in the small emulations and imitations of the "melting pot" of the daily life. A recent, peculiarly ironic example, was an account in the press of a ceremonial Sunday "breakfast" given in New York by a lodge of the B'nai B'rith. It was the first thing of the kind on record. And it was arranged in a social setting of innumerable Catholic Communion breakfasts celebrated by different occupational and fraternal Catholic groups, after attending Mass . . . .

It may be plausibly argued that the entire history of the Jews during the nineteenth century — the religious, the occupational, the social, the cultural, and the political history — records a flight from Judaism.

All its ranges involve the form of behavior which is called "assimilation," that is, the effort of the Jew to cease to be Jew and to become Gentile. In one direction the effort exhausts itself in the type of amateur Gentile whom I have on various occasions described.[2] In another, it comes to a stop in the intransigeant nationalist jingo who shows himself as unadjusted and unadjustable in Palestine as anywhere else. Between these two psychological limits, we may observe an indefinite variety of types. Very few appear to be such as stand firmly on their own two feet as self-acquiescent, self-respecting Jews, free and at ease in their relationships with non-Jews.

Now it was toward the Jew thus normalized that the democratic way of life was leading. As the underlying philosophy of this way of life moved to its climax in the War to Make the World Safe for Democracy, more and more it became clear that the destiny of the Jews, as of every other oppressed and unfree group, was part and parcel of the destiny of this democracy. But, for reasons this is not the occasion to discuss, victory for democracy in the War was followed by the abandonment of democracy to a hazardous peace. The War had vindicated an ideal. The peace failed to protect the ideal's incarnation in the political economy which the peace-treaties ordained. Hence the subsequent history of peace was the progressive corruption of every democratic form of human relations set up as law for the peoples of Central and Eastern Europe. Through the inertia, the negligence, perhaps the cynicism of the victors toward democracy and through the chicanery and brutality of the vanquished, the tables were turned. The old assault on democracy was resumed on old grounds but in new forms and with an intensity of hatred unprecedented in modern history. To bear the brunt of the attack on it — the Jews were chosen. They were the obvious choice, for the reasons I have already discussed. The War which was being revenged on them had itself been disaster to them in Central and Eastern Europe. The peace had brought them a hope that never became a fact. Then the hope was in its turn made over into disaster. Democracy was assaulted by identifying it with the Jews; the Jews were assaulted by identifying them with democracy. "Degenerate Jewish democracy" is a Nazi cliché devised not only for home consumption but for export to all the free countries of the world. In America, the priest, Charles Coughlin, taking advantage of the discomforts of the rich during the depression, united anti-Semitism to enmity to democ-

[2] See *Judaism at Bay*, New York: Bloch, 1932.

racy. "Democracy," he orated, "a cloak under which hide the culprits who have built up an inorganic tumor of government which is sapping away the wealth of its citizens through confiscatory taxation." Various Fifth Column sects of the totalitarian religion, such as the Christian Front, which purports to follow Coughlin, the Silver Shirts, which exalts him, the German-American Bund, which praises him, and the Ku Klux Klan, made the cliché their warcry in the United States; and their compeers were to be found in every country upon which Hitler had designs. And on what country does he not have designs? Emissaries of the brutalitarian sadistocracy that used to be Germany were sent to carry this art of betraying democracy in terms of the Jews, and of persecuting the Jews in terms of democracy, into every class and institution of the community: the church, the school, the social club, the trades-union, the business office, the bank, the halls of Government itself.

And the reaction of the Jews was to suffer this assault with a characteristic confusion of counsel. Fantasies regarding doctrines and disciplines ranged from Mr. Max Lerner's Marxism in modern dress — he suggested that the way to save the Jews from the threat of disaster was to pay no attention to their feelings, their thoughts and their ways, and concentrate on such a reorganization of the national economy as would bring the people of the land the security they had come to crave — to the babel of programs and leaderships within the Jewish community which have become manifest since 1933. The older associations with the most powerful vested interests of money, tradition, and prestige dominate the scene. These are the American Jewish Committee, the B'nai B'rith, the American Jewish Congress. As you know, I have been associated with the principles and policies of the last and have had some part in shaping the Congress conception of Jewish life as an item in the democratic philosophy of the national life and of civilization which is my basic religion. Unfortunately, the men of the Congress do not seem to me to know how to establish their doctrine as discipline, their theory as practice, their faith as a way of being and doing. It tends to remain only a way of talking. The Congress is a melange of personal allegiances and local or nation-wide Jewish organizations of plain people. I have been reluctantly forced to conclude that the leaders of these organizations engage mostly in pulling each for his own organizational interest; that the entire structure and action of the Congress persists in keeping itself *luftmenschlich* and undisciplined; that its personnel are content to take professions for practices and protests for achievements. The record shows that in spite of this mentality, which keeps the Congress Movement in a state of adolescent daydreaming, pretentious and futile, the Movement is in aspiration, and — within the limits of its weaknesses — in method, closer to the American way than any of its competitors. Those, embodiments as they are of financial power, philanthropic disposition and rule, and the fundamental timidity which seems to accompany these qualities, have persisted in a negativism which rendered the idea of defense the equivalent of "Hush! Hush!" Because of their interests and attitudes, none of these organizations have been able — even though some have been willing — to heed to the bitter cry of the plain people of American Jewish communities for an effective union of their diverse forces. And because they were unable, a large number of competitors to the old established organizations arise, have their day, and pass on. The most dramatic of the latter, of course, was that sponsored by the late Mr. Samuel Untermeyer. Less dramatic and more enduring has been the Jewish Labor Committee, and there have been many others beside. In the name of defense, the effort of the American Jewish Congress to educate and to unify American Jews by means of a democratic referendum was frustrated. The Joint Jewish Council which was one consequence of that effort remains much what the Polish Sejm once was — a body where action can be paralyzed by the veto of a single member. And the people keep on demanding unity as before.

All in all, the organized groups overtly responsible for leadership in American Jewish communities seem to be interested in acting *for* those communities, but not *with* those communities. They appear to be afraid of what democracy calls for in Jewish community life: the widest possible participation by Jews in reaching the decisions regarding principles and policies that concern them as Jews. The leaders, like business executives everywhere, they do best which they can do on their own authority, without public discussion. And that best is often very good. But because it chooses to be neither representative of nor responsible to the men and women it purports to serve, competitive claims to leadership multiply and confusion is intensified; "defense" has the general character of an animal's reaction in its struggle for its animal survival, not of spiritual insight into *what is being defended* and *why it is being defended.* The defenders of the Jewish community against anti-Semitism appear to know what they are *against;* but they evince no clear idea of what they are *for.* If they hold an affirmative philosophy of Jewish values as a part of the general values of democracy and freedom, they keep it a secret. Yet only such a philosophy openly held and implemented can impart to defense a positive character, and orchestrate it with the general defense of freedom.

III

I have tried to sketch for you in broad strokes, and without attempt at scientific precision, the influences, Jewish and non-Jewish, which determine the climate of opinion in which the Jewish Centers work, the social atmosphere which envelops their endeavor to "preserve Jewish group life on the highest possible plane." That their thoughts and plans should be qualified by this atmosphere goes without saying. Ten years ago, speaking at the eleventh annual conference of your association, Prof. Miller, of Oberlin, characterized Jews as persons who are constantly analyzing their own motives and actions. This description seems to me to be not less but more true today. I have received the impression that the work of the Centers is little more animated by a fundamental activist philosophy of Jewish life than the behavior of the general Jewish organizations or the aggregate of American Jewish communities. Like the latter, the work seems to seek blind survival rather than growth and strength directed by faith and illumined by vision. Each Center appears to undertake this or that item of its program as occasion demands or circumstance suggests. In each, the aggregate of activities fall into a pattern conforming to no central theme and responding to no fundamental belief. Much of what any does could be ascribed to the same flight from Jewish values, the same assimilative emulation of non-Jewish ways and activities as is found in other sections of the community. In the main the Jewish interest continues to be served by a special department or institute of "Jewish studies," as it might be in any non-Jewish institution, a Y.M.C.A., a school or a college. But the bulk of the activity, athletics not excluded, could be described as anodynes or evasions rather than the democratic cultivation of positive values. And how dissatisfied with the situation are the officials of the Centers themselves is evidenced by the numerous and varied ways they find to make surveys and studies of the Centers and their performance. More than ever an outsider like Professor Miller would receive the impression that you feel unable to take yourselves for granted and let yourselves live and labor and grow. And if you do feel unable, is it not because you are not sure of yourselves, because you suffer from a sentiment of insecurity, a sentiment testifying to deficient faith? A positive and militant faith in what you are about and why you are about it would free you from the desire for justification by means of studies and surveys.

And the Center merits such faith and of all Jewish institutions seems to me best fitted to sustain and to vindicate such a faith. Among these institutions the Jewish Community Center alone possesses an adequate associative base and adequate material instruments of a dynamic integration of the value of the Jew as Jew with the total interplay of community values in the democratic orchestration of communities and cultures which is our country. The values, permit me to repeat, cannot be those of mere animal survival for any one, let alone, a Jew. They are the values for which animal survival is no doubt a ground and of which it can be made a means; without them, physical survival would be the same as psychological extinction. Now the Center is physically equipped to keep the psychological flame alive. Moreover, it is not distorted by the emotions that flow from the conflict and division characteristic of other Jewish organizations. Its very name, *Jewish Community Center*, suggests a place where Jewish groups different from each other come together with each other; where their differences seek, and may compose into, a one of many, a consensus *e pluribus unum*. Then, again, its basic membership is drawn from the rising generation. Of the 380,000 members definitely enrolled, none is more than 25 years old, or less than 13. Seventy-seven per cent of them are not yet 21. As compared with other organizations, the Center reaches Jewish youth principally, and perhaps, too exclusively. The equipment it provides them with is considerable and expensive, often luxurious — perhaps expenditure can be profitably diverted from plant, or mere means, to people whose activities alone can make a plant significant. But however this be, it is the Center which above all other Jewish establishments can provide a common roof for every Jewish interest — not only of youth but of its elders, not only the practical arts but the imponderable dimensions of the common life realized as Jewish. No other Jewish institution in our country holds in solution such powers to be effective as a conservator and promoter of Hebraic culture and ideals in, for and through the larger processes of democracy.

How make this potentiality actual? It needs no survey, no statistical analysis to recognize that the first step would be to take cognizance of what is enduring and fundamental in the climate of opinion where Jews live and move and have their being and Jewish Centers their function; to take cognizance of this atmosphere, to understand it, and to overcome its fear-arousing and repressive contagion. Bertrand Russell somewhere defined education as preparation for the good life and the good life as one "inspired by love and guided by knowledge." I should like to add courage to knowledge and to recall Plato's definition of courage as wisdom concerning dangers. Life today is dangerous enough, spiritually and physically, for all races and conditions of men the world over, but especially it confronts the Jews with dangers. And what other equipment for meeting this danger can serve them better than wisdom concerning it? This is why, a prime, an indispensable part of the education of Jews — young and old alike — must be a scientific insight into the intent, the way, the works of anti-Semitism. No other field of knowledge has a greater claim on the Jew's interest and powers. It should serve him and strengthen him, should immunize him against its virus as the virus of smallpox absorbed through vaccination serves and strengthens and immunizes him against smallpox.

From such an immunizing knowledge of anti-Semitism, the step is inevitable to a similar scientific knowledge of the positive Jewish values which the malice of the anti-Semite would destroy. Indeed, the first is meaningless without the other; meaningless without a re-definition of "Jew" to the Jew in terms of the *positive* role of his culture group in the history of the societies in which it lives and labors and suffers. The Centers need to initiate and sustain a reaffirmation of the vision and aspiration of the Jewish people which will also recognize and understand and master, instead of apologizing for, or fleeing from, their failures and deficiencies. And they are called upon to provide this not as a process of mere indoctrination, but as a fundamental activity program wherein Jewish perspectives can be made to suffuse every activity from typewriting to boxing, from metaphysics to mimicry; "Jew" should designate the intellectual and emotional atmosphere for every specific project or program, whatever it be. Such an activity program is rendered the more necessary in view of the fact that the Center supplements and does not replace the public school. The activities it enables should be a release from the confinement and sedentary habits of the schools. No young Jew should be excluded from them. They should be open to the entire youth of a community. For those who cannot afford to pay in money, another way, perhaps a payment in service, might be found.

Essentially the same policy would hold for adults. In recent years a whole literature has been produced about adult education, and there has been much learned talk about adult learning and adult interests and what not. But so far as I can see, the methods which are successful when adults learn are those which are successful when children in the kindergarten learn. In the old Danish folk school we have a model of both organization and method, which can be fruitfully adapted to the purposes of the Center.

One thing that might result from it is the coming together again, to pursue *common interests*, of young and old. Since the depression, fathers and sons, mothers and daughters have been isolated from one another, isolated practically, isolated ideologically. Scarcely a country in the western world but is overrun with youth movements, led by professional youths of forty and over. The totalitarian countries have especially stressed and exploited this artificial and dangerous separation of the generations. The practice is no less a menace to democracy and a contradiction of the democratic way of life than the stratification of economic classes, or other forms of the segregation of human groups from free contact and cooperation with one another. The Center should make it an essential task to reunite parents and children in common activities. Some might consist in the preparation and celebration of festivals and national holidays, others in common plays and work. An occasional "father and son evening" or "mother and daughter *Kaffee Klatch*" is an empty gesture. The program of bringing the generations back to community of feeling and interest must reach to the fundament of family and group.

Moreover, just as all activities in a Center require to be affected with the Jewish tone and Jewish perspectives, so the Jewish interest as a whole, although always to be developed as a clear and distinct unit, should never be developed as an isolated one. It should regularly be planned in such a way as to exhibit and clarify its dynamic link and interplay with other non-Jewish interests. The obvious fact is, of course, that even the medieval ghetto practiced a certain more or less free exchange of ideas and values with the surrounding culture, inimical though that was. In the democratic society of the modern world free exchange of cultural values is of the essence. Every culture, willy-nilly, orchestrates itself to every other. Each is part of a society where men and their communities differ from one another, and *therefore* live and labor and trade and play together with one another. Every culture is inter-cultural. Every culture is at once a product of and a contribution to the Cultural Pluralism which constitutes the spirit of civilized mankind. The times call upon the Center to be militant regarding the relations of the Jew to this Cultural Pluralism and regarding the bearing of this Pluralism on the growth and enrichment of Jewish culture. All cultures are most easily and directly communicated and most readily understood and appreciated through their arts. The Center should make the most of this fact. An essential of its program could be so to perfect positive, distinctly Jewish expression in the arts — in painting and sculpture, in music, drama, the dance — that the non-Jewish fellow members of the greater community will spontaneously look upon such expression as an asset and wish on their own account to preserve and strengthen it.

And, of course, the Center should cooperate with non-Jewish groups on specific issues involving the general principle of democracy — issues of civil liberties, for example, of civic rights and obligations. Since Jews are especially dependent for their status and right on democracy, they have a special obligation in defense of democracy, and democracy is concentrated at the moment in the Bill of Rights and conservation of civil liberties at home and in resistance to the assaults of totalitarianism abroad. An essential part of this resistance is to make sure that those who appeal to the Bill of Rights and employ its protection in order to destroy it shall not receive the shelter of that protection for the practice of their treachery. In these dangerous days of Coughlinism, communism, and other fascisms and authoritarianisms, there will be many such. The Center must be on guard against them; but it must also be on guard against allowing itself to be made either the unknowing or the knowing instrument of the violations of the Bill of Rights. The Community House of a minority, it must be ready to provide asylum to the minorities who are faithful to the principles of democracy but are subject to intolerance because their views happen to be unpopular. Its best guide could well be that wisdom concerning dangers to democracy which I quoted from the late Justice Holmes.

Well, I must have done. I have tried to indicate what the Jewish Community Center might undertake in order to replace the feeling that Judaism is disaster by a more positive emotion, a mood of courageous self-respect which will put fight for Judaism in the place of flight from Judaism. And all that I have said comes to community organization and community education.

Especially education. For organization without education cannot offset disaster: education is the *sine qua non*. Only through learning the background and conditions of his life as Jew, only through affirming the culture and ideals by which "Jew" is positively constituted, and only by putting them into active play in the common enterprises of free society as a brave, self-acquiescent, and self-governed soldier of that society can the young Jew's flight from the Jewish being be transformed into a free vindication of the Jewish being, and his elders' "defense" of the Jewish being be transformed from blind animal response into a warfare illumined by faith and guided by the courage which is wisdom concerning dangers.

The time to undertake this organization and education is now. Freedom is a way of life with its own discipline. Jews who more than any others, willingly or unwillingly, stand in the front lines of the war of democracy, cannot wait for freedom. We cannot both be in flight from Judaism and fight effectively as Jews for democracy. We cannot accept the benefits of democracy outside the Jewish community and reject its obligations inside the Jewish community. Bitter and terrible as had been the portion of our people in the history of the Christian world, this lot became disaster only when Jews began to evaluate it as disaster. For the martyrs who died in the *auto-da-fés*, for the men and women of the tradition of the Prophets and Maccabees, martyrdom was victory, not disaster; victory because they did not abandon their own vision and profess that of their persecutors. More than a condition of the body, disaster is a state of mind. Judaism is disaster only if you choose to think it thus, and you choose only as you flee the knowledge of its inner quality and outer values, of its nature and its significance to the Jew and of its role in the orchestration of the cultures of mankind. More than any other institution of American Jewish life, the Jewish Community Center has it in its power to transform Judaism as disaster into Judaism as the victory of freedom.

National Solidarity and the Jewish Minority

WHEN a community, whatever be its size, decides some issue, it divides into a majority and one or more minorities. Our habits of thought and speech lead us to imagine such division as permanent. In free societies, however, it involves nothing static or fixed. An individual who is a member of a majority in one respect becomes a member of a minority in another, and vice versa. Each occupational group, each religious denomination, each political party, each sex, each race, set over against all the others, counts as a minority; associated with the others, as of the majority. Majorities are minorities in combination; minorities are majorities in division.

A society is democratic when its institutions insure and facilitate a constant process of combination and division, free mobility of decision regarding all the issues of life. Difference and differentiation give it its characteristic form and go. Here in America, the freedoms of the Bill of Rights define our dynamic in enterprise, in faith, in thought and expression, and in association; the Declaration of Independence defines our goal, our means, and our method. And the consummation of all the definitions is, the right of men and groups to be different. Majorities are orchestrations of the different;[1] minorities are dissociations of the different. The "American way" is the order of these constant combinations and dissociations in all the enterprises of living.

Unfortunately, too many people habitually think of difference not only as status, but as opposition. They identify the different as the inimical. They feel what the sociologist calls "xenophobia," or fear of the different. Their feeling is embodied in customs and conduct

Reprinted from the *Annals of the American Academy of Political and Social Science*, Philadelphia, September 1942.

[1] "As many speakers and writers have begun to suggest, our American ideal should be expressed not in terms of a 'melting pot' with its somewhat mournful implication of uniformity, but rather in terms of an orchestra, in which each racial group, like an orchestral choir, contributes its special, different tone to the rich ensemble of the whole." Harold B. Hoskins, "American Unity and Our Foreign-Born Citizens," *The Annals*, March 1942, p. 158.

which make up the problems of national solidarity wherein resides the permanent challenge to the American faith and the American way. Sicknesses of democracy, they are problems of the majority, not the minority.[2]

Antagonism Toward the Jew

The "Jewish problem" is the classical instance of such a minority problem. In certain fundamental respects it is very different from other minority problems. Coextensive with Christianity, it is the oldest in the Christian world. The migrations of Christianism have carried it to non-Christian countries, while Christians who have rejected Christianism for Nazism or Fascism have not only retained but magnified the Jewish problem as a cheap and potent instrument in their conscienceless conquest of power.

While such words as Pole, German, Texan, Czech, Walloon, Serb, Fleming, Croat, Magyar, Slovene, Yankee, Welshman, Scot, Breton, Irishman, Basque, and the like would denote nothing much and nothing definite to the world's unlearned multitudes, the word Jew carries a singular and universal meaning. To identify any group or individual as Texan, Pole, Czech, Scot, and so on, would hardly modify the attitude of others toward such people. To call the very same individuals or groups Jews would shut them out and cut them off, draw an emotional ring around them, and fix them as a constitutive minority. This is what Hitler and his crew have aimed at with their notorious Nuremberg laws; but their act is only a brutally acute local heightening of a chronic and general disposition.

The feeling and ideas which the word "Jew" awakens in non-Jews have no relation to what people called Jews in fact are or do. They compose a sentiment intrinsic to the Christian beliefs regarding the origin, the nature, and the destiny of mankind. In these beliefs the term "Jew" has a central place and a characteristic meaning. As I have already pointed out,[3] the Jewish people, Pastor Martin Niemöller told his flock in a sermon that leveled the deadliest of all insults at the Nazis by identifying them with the Jews, "bears a curse

[2] Franklin D. Roosevelt to the National Association for Advancement of Colored People, June 25, 1938: "For it is evident that no democracy can long survive which does not accept as fundamental to its very existence the recognition of the rights of its minorities."

[3] See "Judaism as Disaster," above, p. 42.

throughout the history of the world . . . because it rejected Him [Christ] and resisted Him to the death. . . . the Jews brought the Christ of God to the Cross." [4]

The theological reformulation of Christian dogma under the stimulus of the philological, historical, and social sciences has not yet reached the point of altering the sentiments of anathema and rejection which the word "Jew" awakens in general Christian usage. Thus the same person, according as he is or is not labeled Jew, will be seen with very different eyes and meet with very different responses. The psychological effect of the label is like that of the direct perception of skin color or other stigmata of race. The person to whom it is attached is automatically shut out and cut off as by an ancestral trait, and though scientific anthropology denies that "Jew" stands for race, fantasists like Albert Nock and J. F. Brown purport to perceive Jewish racial traits, and J. O. Hertzler observes, rightly enough, that to plain people the intent of the word "Jew"; is something racial.[5] What it means, however, is nothing that scientific anthropologists find, but something that religiously set non-Jews project — a prejudice, not a perception; an ideological fiction, not an empirical fact.

The Jew as a Scapegoat

When the projection is elaborated and rationalized into a theory and practice of conduct toward its object, it is called anti-Semitism. Its root and origin may be, and often is, ignored or forgotten: to justify and account for the feeling aroused by the word "Jew," all sorts of secondary explanations are constructed — manners, morals, economics, and what have you, are invoked separately and together, some with a base in experience, most without. So easy and simple is it to awaken and to mobilize the unconscious negative bias attached

[4] Martin Niemöller, *Here Stand I*, Chicago: Willett Clark & Co. For the origins, development, and uses of this dogma, see Conrad H. Moehlmann, *The Christian-Jewish Tragedy*, Rochester: Printing House of Leo Hart, 1933; W. A. Campbell, *The Crucifixion and Resurrection of Jesus*, London: Pioneer Press, 1933; *The Corner Stone of Christianity*, La Salle, Ill.: Open Court Publishing Co., 1938; Edward Gibbon, *The Decline and Fall of the Roman Empire*, chap. 15.

[5] See Isacque Graeber and Steuart Henderson Britt (Eds.), *Jews in a Gentile World*, New York: Macmillan, 1942. See also J. F. Brown, *Psychology and the Social Order*, New York: McGraw-Hill, 122 p.: "Almost everyone however can clearly differentiate . . . between a negro and a white Indo-European and even between a white European and a Jew."

to the word "Jew" that Jews become the cheapest and most effective scapegoats in Christian history. There is no evil which enemies of mankind have not accused them of in order to screen their own deeds and purposes.[6] Rauschning reports that Hitler said to him:

> My Jews are a valuable hostage given to me by the democracies. Anti-Semitic propaganda in all countries is an almost indispensable medium for the extension of our political campaign. You will see how little time we shall need in order to upset the ideas and criteria of the whole world, simply and purely by attacking Judaism.

In *Mein Kampf* Hitler wrote:

> In the year 1918 there was absolutely no systematic anti-Semitism. . . . Only very slowly did things begin to turn for the better. Unsuccessful as was our Guard and Watch League, its service in again opening up the Jewish Problem was great nevertheless. Later, the National Socialists transformed the Jewish Problem into the ruling passion of our great nationalist movement.

When the British mass bombing began, Goebbels declared that for every such bombing Jews would be killed. Since the Nazi invasion of Poland, they have murdered a million Jews. And the seditious priestly defender of the Japo-Nazi assault on the democracies, Charles Coughlin, wrote in his now abandoned antidemocratic propaganda sheet that Germany is the innocent victim of a "sacred war declared against her nine years ago by the Jews."

The initiation of the Nazi aggression not only upon Christian doctrine but upon the total economy of the Christian establishments has brought into the foreground of attention the Judaist origins of the Christian faith and brought also to fundamentalist circles the realization that non-Christian or "pagan" anti-Semitism is an attack upon Christianism even more than upon Judaism. "Spiritually we are Semites," declared Pope Pius XI; "it is not possible for Christians to take part in anti-Semitism."[7] Some Protestant ministers like the Reverend Stanley High, and certain Jews — the great Sigmund Freud and Mr. Maurice Samuel, for instance — have flatly identified anti-

[6] Cf. David Riesman, *The Politics of Persecution;* Ralph S. Morton, "Semites and Samaritans," *Protestant Digest*, Summer 1941; Carl J. Friedrich, "Anti-Semitism: Challenge to Christian Culture," in *Jews in a Gentile World.*

[7] Where does this leave Charles Coughlin, Edward Lodge Curran, Francisco Franco, Henri Philippe Pétain, and Pierre Laval, with their Christian Fronts, their Falanges, and other gangs?

Semitism as a Christian aggression upon the Beatitudes, which to them are the moral inwardness of Christianity itself. Anti-Semites, said Mr. High, "hate the Jews not because they killed Christ, but because they produced him." [8]

Jewish Attitudes

Among the Jews themselves, the import given to the word "Jew" by Christian dogma has led to a variety of consequences. Shut out and cut off from communication with the non-Jewish world by being deprived of their Roman citizenship in the fourth century of the Christian era, they lived in compact, segregated communities called ghettos until the last decade of the eighteenth century. Those communities maintained and elaborated a characteristic social and cultural economy, a way of life, with a doctrine and discipline of worship and learning, production and consumption, which each generation took over from its predecessors, and, with additions, diminutions, and transformations, have kept up to this day.

The American and French Revolutions put an end to the enforced legal, physical, and social segregation but not to the psychological one effected by the Christian import of the word "Jew." Under the impulsion of the democratic ideal, the laws of one land after another made Jews once more eligible to the duties and privileges of citizenship. But faith and folkways denied the free communication and the full participation in the common life which democratic law affirmed. In 1791 the National Assembly voted emancipation for all the Jews of France; in 1941 Pétain's Christian government at Vichy introduced Hitler's Nuremberg laws in France. During the one hundred and fifty years between, the generations of the Jews of the world so worked and struggled to be free that, according to Mr. Stanley High, they have become the very incarnation of the spirit of liberty and therefore have every tyrant for their enemy. Liberty — liberty for everyone — is in their dominant tradition: "There is more in Jewish history to hearten the underdog than in any other segment of human experience."

[8] Stanley High, "Jews, Anti-Semites and Tyrants," *Harper Magazine*, June 1942; Sigmund Freud, *Moses and Monotheism;* Maurice Samuel, *The Great Hatred;* see also Carl J. Friedrich, cited in note 6. All three might have referred to Nietzsche, and to the perverse use of Nietzsche made by such Nazi theologizers as Paul Bergenhagen. See his *Judentum, Christentum, Deutschtum bei Friedrich Nietzsche*, Berlin: Verlag Paul Steegmann, 1934.

Many Jews, however, took their history and being not for heartening but for disaster — Heine called Judaism a misfortune — and where they could not escape, they made every effort to minimize the disaster: from religious conversion to reform scarcely distinguishable from conversion; from the abandonment of the ways and culture of the Jewish community to bitter denunciations of those who refused to fly from Judaism. "We are in no way different from you," they assured their non-Jewish fellow citizens; "give us time and you shall see that we are indistinguishable. Not we, but the Jews who persist in their Jewishness make the Jewish Problem. If they did not struggle as they do to survive as Jews, there wouldn't be any problem."[9] To these suffering souls equal liberty did not mean the free growth and orchestration of differences; it meant surrender to xenophobia, and the total liquidation of difference in similarity.

Some other Jews, no less sure that Judaism is disaster and equally in flight from it, but in the extreme opposite direction, to medieval Christian fundamentalism, took an opposite stand. They justified the anti-Semitisms, not on the Jew's acceptance of his right to be different, but on his use of his right to free communication and equal participation in the common life which the democratic way establishes and guarantees. Since, they proclaimed, the modern age, as against the age of faith, is characterized by the growth and spread of science, the mastery of nature, a developing economy of abundance in thoughts and things, since it is especially characterized by the democratic liberties which have made these possible and which these sustain, the modern world is materialistic and corrupt, and the Jew, leaving the spiritual scarcities of the medieval ghetto for the fleshpots of freedom, has taken on the age's materialism and corruption and improved on them. The Jew's liberation has been his degradation. He has become the most debased of moderns, godless, unrighteous, corrupting commerce, art, and youth.[10] Thus "the case against the Jews" is an aspect

[9] The latest exposition of this typical attitude from an authoritative pen is "Red, White and Blue Herring," by Judge Jerome Frank, *Saturday Evening Post*, Dec. 6, 1941.

[10] This position is expounded by a Jew not himself known to have departed from the ways of the Gentile for the ways of the ghetto, but identified as a partisan of dogmatic neo-Thomism and America First. See Milton Mayer, "The Case Against the Jews," *Saturday Evening Post*, March 28, 1942. For an exposition of the antidemocratic premises of the argument, see Sidney Hook, "Milton Mayer: Fake Jeremiah," *The New Leader*, April 4, 1942.

of the case against democracy; the prior and far more potent theological "case" is not even mentioned. That is the case of the authoritarian, the totalitarian, wherever he employs anti-Semitism as a smoke screen for his designs against human freedom.

Jews Identified with Democracy

The peculiar identification of Jews with democratic ideals and democratic ideals with Jews has been variously made at different times with different intent by friends and foes, both Jews and non-Jews.[11] Sound or unsound, it is made. Perhaps the verse from the Old Testament inscribed on the Liberty Bell is a symptom: "Proclaim liberty throughout all the land, to all the inhabitants thereof."

Certainly, the Nazi cult aggressively couples the Jews with the democratic ideal. "Degenerate Jewish democracy" is a phrase ever in the mouths of Hitler and his apostles at home and abroad, and their war upon the democracies is always a war against the Jews. "We know full well," Hitler said as late as January 9, 1942, "that the war can end only by the extermination of the German people or by the disappearance of Jewry from Europe. The Aryan folk will not be removed from Europe, and this war will see the annihilation of Jewry." And Lord Davies, writing sometime later in the *Manchester Guardian*, declared:

> In this tragic conflict we must be for or against the Jews: there can be no neutrality. Our attitude towards them becomes the test of our professions and the sincerity of our war aims. It strikes at the root of our morale, and if we abandon the Jews we abandon everything, because Hitler has chosen to make them his special target. Whether we like it or not, and however inconvenient it may be, the Jewish people has become the personification of the issues involved in this world struggle between right and wrong, between good and evil. If we desert the Jews it may result in our losing the war, because it is a betrayal of our avowed war aims. Surely it is the height of folly to repudiate our principles and to cold-shoulder our friends in order to curry favor with neutrals or potential enemies.

The Jews have become "the personification of the issues involved" because more than womankind, more than Negroes, more than

[11] Among the most recent are Waldo Frank's "The Jews Are Different," *Saturday Evening Post*, March 21, 1942, and Stanley High's and Carl Friedrich's articles cited.

workingmen, who no less than the Jews are beneficiaries of the century-and-a-half struggle of the democratic faith to make secure the equal right of different people to life, liberty, and the pursuit of happiness, the Jewish communities stand, for the reasons we have reviewed, as the symbol of this faith's victories in the Christian world. They have thus a moral and spiritual stake in democracy of which their physical and economic stake is only a faint expression. They know very well, from the horror of their fate in Nazi Europe from Russia and Poland to France, from Norway to Italy, that for them this world-wide civil war is indeed a war of survival.

What sort of people the Jews in fact are, how they live, what they live by, has, since the rise of the Nazi terror, been also the subject of a considerable objective study by both Jews and non-Jews, as well as the assaults and advocacies and the hysterical recriminations of the sort reviewed above. Here in the United States Jewish societies of diverse persuasions have launched careful researches into the life and labor of the Jewish community. Individual Jewish scholars have reviewed the Jewish past and present.[12] The magazine *Fortune* published a study in 1936,[13] and currently there is the collective work, *Jews in a Gentile World*, already referred to. The consensus is a portrait of a community with its internal conflicts of sect and party, growing and changing in response to the American faith and the American scene, doing its part, and, in view of its handicaps, something more than its part.

American Jews

Today, the Jewish community in the United States numbers about four million souls. Its small first settlements were pre-Revolutionary, but the multitudinous Jewish migration dates from the eighties of the last century. The order of entry was the order of entry of the non-Jewish Europeans into the continent — first the Sephardim with the Spaniards, Portugese, English, and Dutch; then the German Jews with their non-Jewish Germanic fellow liberals; finally the Jews of Austrian and Slavic Europe.

An urban people, with more than half their number concentrated in the metropolitan area of New York and more than four-fifths of

[12] See Cecil Roth, *Jewish Contributions to Civilization*, Cincinnati, 1940.
[13] *Jews in America*, New York: Random House, Inc.

them in cities of over 100,000, American Jews have the consequential frame of mind, interests, and occupations. Their birth rate is low (17.5 in New York in 1932), but they retain the familial intimacy and sense of communal responsibility which is their cultural inheritance. They are very far from the wealth and the power which anti-Semitic fantasy endows them with in banking, industry, the press, the motion picture, the theater, or the arts. Their role in international finance is negligible, their place in heavy industry too small to signify, whether as masters or men.[14] In the national economy they stand tangent to and are generally the victims of the great concentrations of wealth and power known as trusts, monopolies, and cartels.

The Jews are most in evidence, alike as masters and as men, in the production of consumer goods and services, and there they have served as pioneers, opening up and developing new fields of enterprise. As is the case with the motion pictures, they are usually displaced in these, after their enterprise has developed them, by corporate finance. They hold their own in both the production and the distribution of textiles, garments, and furniture, but, except in New York, not through department stores. Numerous in the law, they are in that profession small fry without power. Seventeen per cent of New York's doctors are Jews, many good but few great. Their numbers in the civil service, state and Federal, are not significant, nor do they readily find employment in the public utilities, the banks, the insurance companies, or the transportation companies. In the police, fire, and other technological services of cities their numbers are kept unduly low, their opportunities in the teaching profession are limited.

As plain working people, gainfully employed, Jews figure most largely in the independent trades and crafts. They like to own the precarious little stores they keep rather than clerk in chains, and chains rarely employ them. Their establishment in the needle trades is well known, but they are also numerous among the carpenters, the painters, the plumbers, the cleaners and dyers, and the independent seamstresses and milliners.

A reinforcement of economic accident, such as affects all immigrant communities, with purposive discrimination such as is directed almost exclusively toward Jews and Negroes, is said to slow up and distort

[14] Miriam Beard shows how throughout history the banner for economic ruthless goes to others than Jews: "Anti-Semitism — Product of Economic Myths," in *Jews in a Gentile World.*

what would be the "normal" occupational distribution of Jews. But what would be normal nobody knows, for the development of our industrial economy has brought with it an enormous increase of the clerical and service occupations: about one American in every seven is thus occupied. In view of the fact that, as J. Lestshinsky points out, upward of 65 per cent of the Jews of such areas as Detroit and New York are wage workers,[15] perhaps their distorted occupational distribution is only another myth.

Jewish Sentiment

In the industries where they are influential, Jews have set a standard of democratic solidarity and cooperation. The conspicuous instances are the fur trade, the hat and cap, and the men's and women's garment industries, and the other industries correspond, though laggingly. The garment trades have developed during the last generation, in the form of union-management cooperation, a genuine system of industrial self-government and a technique for arbitrating disputes which keeps conflict down to a minimum and consistently expands the area of collaboration. The trades unions have taken the welfare of the industry as a whole for their concern.[16] In their internal economy they have laid a good deal of stress on labor education, co-operative housing, and the service of other consumer interests.

The practical political alignment of the Jews has been liberal, not radical. Traditionally, they vote the Democratic ticket; in labor party politics they are prevailingly of the right wing. They have won bitter internal fights with their small Communist fractions, which have led to the practical elimination of those interests from the unions.

An analogous direction of sentiment is to be noted among American Jews everywhere. It is evinced in the selection of the themes and the speakers at the forums of the Jewish community centers and in the formal expressions of opinion by the Central Conference of American Rabbis. The objectives of philantropic foundations particularly identified with Jewish names express it: the Rosenwald Foundation with its concentration on Negro welfare; Edward A. Filene's Common-

[15] In *Jews in a Gentile World*, p. 414.

[16] Irwin Ross, "Labor, Capital & Co.," *Harper's Magazine*, May 1942; H. M. Kallen, *Education, the Machine and the Worker*, New York, 1923; "Responsibility," *Ethics*, LII, 3, April 1942.

wealth and Good Will Funds with their emphasis on consumer organization as a way in economic democracy; the Guggenheim Foundation with its encouragement to creative workmen in the arts and sciences. It is indicated by the service and attention which Jews give to the defense of civil liberties throughout the land. It is expressed in the very low ratio of crime and delinquency among Jews as compared with other folks and sects.[17]

These items present a fair sample of what emerges from the climate of opinion of the inner life of the American Jewish community as a whole. Lived among its neighbors in the social atmosphere due to democratic aspiration inhibited by chronic, and occasionally acute, anti-Semitism, this life has been a very dynamic one of sharp internal sectarian and secular conflicts, rapid modifications of old institutions and the creation of new ones, continuous assimilation of and adjustment to the influences of the American scene in religion, philanthropy, culture, education, and community organization. The usual word for this process is "Americanization," but it is Americanization as orchestration, in accord with the free patterns of the national life, into an integral solidarity with the spirit of American democracy — not a dilution into characterless indistinction.

Changes in Judaism

In the American scene Judaism has diversified, and the Sephardim, the Ashkenazim, and the Hassidim of the immigration have been challenged by the Reformers, the Conservatives, the Jewish Scientists, the Reconstructionists of the later generations. The synagogue has been confronted by the temple, the temple by the community center, each with its functionaries and officials, its societies of professionals and laymen, its training schools and colleges, its characteristic journals and books, its divergent architectures and decorative arts, working out in their long debate a union and consensus analogous to that of the Protestant sects associated together in the Federal Council of

[17] See W. Healy and A. F. Bronner, *Delinquents and Criminals*, New York; W. T. Root, *A Psychological and Educational Survey of 1916 Prisoners in the Western Penitentiary of Pennsylvania;* C. R. Shaw and E. D. Myers, *The Juvenile Delinquent*, Illinois Crime Survey, Chicago, 1929; C. V. Dunn, "The Church and Crime in the United States," *The Annals*, May 1926.

the Churches of Christ in America. America is writing a new page in the theory and practice of Judaism, of which the changed status of woman is perhaps the most dramatic present symbol.[18]

The change in philanthropic ideals and techniques is as striking. Although the Sephardim might despise the "Germans" and the "Germans" might be deeply irked by their "brethren from the east," to look after the "greeners" when they landed, to find them employment and facilitate their integration with the national life, was an obligation of self-defense as well as of piety and righteousness. The effort to discharge this obligation has led to definite contributions to "scientific" charity, the training of specialists, the collection of funds, and the organization of local federations which embrace every Jewish establishment supported by voluntary contributions. The local federations, again, recently confederated into a Council of Federations and Welfare Funds, which acts as a sort of clearing house and licensing agency for claims upon community resources, whether by hospitals, religious schools, loan associations, Palestinian or other transatlantic dependents, or "defense" agencies directed to combating anti-Semitism, like the Anti-Defamation League, the American Jewish Committee, or the American Jewish Congress; it is able to exercise the pressure of the funding power upon them all.

First attached to the synagogue, Jewish charity has become a manifold social service work operating as a characteristic, independent secular institution with a competitive life of its own. It is altogether a growth of the American soil, new, unprecedented. Among its units, the most vital and expressive survival from the past is the Hebrew Free Loan Societies, which continue the ancient practice of lending money without security and without interest or other charges, upon endorsement of the borrower's note by one or two reliable friends.

Competitive yet supplementary to the religious and philanthropic associations are the *landsmanschaften* and the fraternal orders — most with beneficiary and insurance functions, some like the B'nai B'rith, without; the associations of war veterans, the social clubs, the women's societies, like the National Council of Jewish Women, and the invidious Jewish Greek-letter fraternities formed because other college fraternities shut out Jews.

[18] See H. M. Kallen, *Judaism at Bay* (New York, 1932), chaps. II, XIV, XV.

The Zionist Movement

All such societies are secular diversifications of an initially religious communion, religiously toned. But the high place of secularization is the Zionist movement, which has tended to align the diverse sectarian interests toward its single aspiration. Expression, at once, of the urge to alleviate suffering and to vindicate the equal right of Jews to live like other folks as a free people upon the soil which the history and the religion of the West identify peculiarly with them, Zionism is the Jewish case of "the principle of nationalities" whose prophet was Giuseppe Mazzini. It is the Jew's extension of the democratic principle from the individual to the group. For many Jews disillusioned with Otherworldly Judaism, the idea of a just and free Jewish state in distant but earthly Palestine seemed an efficacious surrogate for the New Jerusalem in the even more distant, unearthly heavens. And it would serve the body and spirit of Israel, actually, practically; it would go a long way to solve the Jewish problem.

The controversy over Zionism became a major force in the process of Americanization. It stimulated community organization, theological re-orientation, historical and social research, and literary expression. It enriched the educational enterprises with new drives, new themes, new methods, new men, new standards. It brought both Hebrew and Yiddish into the dynamic foreground of expression, and it redirected the thinking about Jewish relations among Jews and non-Jews alike.[19] It also has come to a consensus in which, save among a few reform rabbis, ideological conflicts remain entirely compatible with united co-operative effort on behalf of Jewish Palestine.

One consequence of the controversy over Zionism which ran from high to low through the communities was to bring to the fore the issue of community organization and community control, in the tradition of the issue between Jefferson and Hamilton. American Israel divided, on inner community methods, into two camps, each with its own paradoxes. The elder is represented by the American Jewish Committee, whose tradition is to think of the community as a somewhat hierarchical body governed by its elders — elders by virtue of birth, wealth, power, station, and superior education — who

[19] See Salo Baron, *A Social and Religious History of the Jews*, New York, 1937; H. M. Kallen, *Zionism and World Politics*, New York, 1922; *Frontiers of Hope*, New York, 1929; *Judaism at Bay* (New York, 1932), chaps. IV, VI, X, XI; Arthur Ruppin, *Jews in the Modern World*, 1934.

would act *for* their fellow Jews on their own authority, according to their own judgment. The younger and later is represented by the confederation of Jewish societies of all sorts and conditions called the American Jewish Congress, whose aspiration is to reach decision on the policies and programs of the community via the democratic process, by means of duly elected delegates who shall be both representative of and responsible to the people for whom they act. Such figures as the late Justice Brandeis, Nathan Straus, Louis Marshall, and Jacob H. Schiff were protagonists in the controversy. It remains unsettled, but is also moving toward a consensus. Its impact forced the American Jewish Committee somewhat to democratize itself; and all the conflicting parties to make efforts at co-operation by trying first a "consultative," then a "deliberative," council.

The Jewish Press

The expression and intercommunication resulting from the play of these diverse and often conflicting interests that compose and define the American Jewish community call for a daily and weekly press and a body of literary publications in English, Yiddish, Hebrew, and Ladino. The community produces about two hundred organizational house organs, technical and learned journals, literary magazines, and the like, written in English; it counts a metropolitan daily Yiddish press with four papers and close to twoscore of other types. There are about a dozen Hebrew journals, and at least one Ladino. There is a newspaper wire service — the Jewish Telegraphic Agency. At least two publishing houses print books primarily of interest to Jews, and the attractions of the Yiddish theater, radio, and Kosher Kitchen need only be mentioned.

The entire journalistic and aesthetic achievement is the outer range of the culture-complex, with its definite character as one way of American life, which constitutes the American Jewish community. All nations are made up of such communities, and their life and growth consists in their free exchange of all values with one another. Their solidarity is conditioned upon the variety and multiplicity of the associations whose different qualities and performances make the team play of the national life. What is true of nations holds equally of all civilization. Personal distinction and service to the whole is a consequence of the impact of the community of difference upon the personal life. According to the somewhat sardonic Thorstein Veblen, this would provide the dynamic of such men as Louis Brandeis or George Gershwin, Albert Einstein or Benjamin Cardozo, as they pass from their community to the life of the nation, the life of the world.[20]

Jews and the War

The social forces which, in Lord Davies' words, have made Jews "the personification of the issues involved in this world struggle" stand in the way of their doing the most they can against the enemies of freedom. In Palestine there are a hundred thousand Jews whose one desire is to meet the Nazis in battle for the Four Freedoms; in Europe and in the Americas there are thousands of uprooted, stateless men eager to get at the foe. Yet, although he has singled out their community, they are kept, on various pretexts, from meeting him as Jews in their own name, in their own identifiable strength, as one unit among the many forces of democracy. They are required to keep from fighting or, if permitted to fight, to sink their identity in the larger group.

It is natural that the urge for an unmistakably Jewish fighting unit should find many voices among the American people, Jewish and non-Jewish alike. And it is significant of the Jewish predicament that many Jews should oppose the formation of such a Jewish army on the ground that it might provide the anti-Semitic fifth columnist with another argument to impugn their loyalty to their country. They insist on absolute concentration upon all sorts of war activities at home — the collection of tin foil, tin cans, rubber, and the like, the selling of war bonds, the services in civilian defense, educational preparation for and shifts of occupation to the defense industries. Many, on the grounds of national solidarity, want Jews to make this effort without identifying themselves as Jews. Then they are met with the situation that their omitting to identify themselves as Jews is treated as deception, while as self-identified Jews they are often shut out from the services they seek to render.[21]

[20] Thorstein Veblen, "The Intellectual Pre-eminence of Jews in Modern Europe," *Political Science Quarterly*, March 1919.

[21] Testimony along this line was given by representatives of all organized American Jewish bodies at Public Hearings of the President's Committee on Fair Employment Practice, New York, Feb. 16, 1942.

The country's essential war industries were denied, in their emergency, the services of many types of skilled workers because they were called Jews. Members of the Commission on Economic Problems of the American Jewish Congress hold that the practice continues, but, since the Presidential Executive Order 8802, is disguised; Jews are now rejected because of elsewhere nonexistent ailments, or they are assigned to foremen who are sure to haze them out. Some fifty-one plants manufacturing arms and other war material, one school of engineering, and six agencies of the Federal Government, including the Civil Service Commission, have been complained of since Pearl Harbor.

As for the armed services, it has been one of Hitler's anti-Semitic devices to spread the notorious lie that Jews will not fight, but induce Gentiles to spill their blood for them. The lie has been exposed many times,[22] but it is repeated, and fifth column anti-Semites serve the Axis by parroting the falsehood. Undoubtedly there are instances of Jews who try to evade service, seek soft safe spots, and the like. Every group has its share of such cases, but the situation suggests that the Jews' is less. The record of volunteers and draftees is in the Adjutant General's office, and access to it is at the present time not possible. But it is well known that there are Jewish men in every branch of service of both Army and Navy, volunteers and draftees. These, the Jewish unit of the USO — the National Jewish Welfare Board — is organized to serve, and all the diverse and opposed groups of the Jewish community are as one in its support.

There is considerable talk in some quarters that certain branches of the service are disposed to shut Jews out, especially candidates for officer training,[23] and a medical examiner has been said to reject a candidate with a Jewish name first on one finding and then on a different one after re-examination was ordered, neither finding being justifiable under the regulations. Many Jews in the services are said to be reluctant to identify themselves as such, and complaints are heard that officers with Jewish names, though honored for gallantry in action, are passed over in promotions, for no other reason.

[22] See Julian Leavitt, "American Jews in the World War," *American Jewish Yearbook*, Vol. 21, Philadelphia, 1919; Damon Runyon, in his syndicated column, "The Brighter Side," May 10, 1942.

[23] See Pearson and Allen's "Merry-Go-Round" of July 9, 1941, on the attitude of Naval Intelligence.

Solidarity Against the Foe

But in what concerns the relation of the Jewish communities of the United States to the national solidarity, such matters as these are irrelevancies. Even if anti-Semitism in the United States had been like anti-Semitism in Poland, American Jews, like Polish Jews, would without reserve join themselves to their persecutors in indefeasible determination to put an end to the common foe. So, in the face of what they believe to be British injustice and British stupidity in Palestine, all Jewry unites its fate to that of England. How much the greater, then, must be the solidarity of the free Jews of the United States with the free men their fellow citizens, in the struggle for the survival of the freedom whose symbol Hitler has made them! No greater honor has been done the Jews since the Western world adopted Christianity, no greater dedication has ever been made of them, their lives, their fortunes, and their honor, than this, upon the altar of human liberty. The tragedy is that in many directions they are first prevented from fighting and serving, and then charged with evading battle and service!

The National Being and the Jewish Community

I AM asked to make an "evaluation of American Jewish living." This is a peculiarly disagreeable and thankless task for a Jew, far more trying than simply to "look at the record," to describe and to analyze, and to draw a "composite portrait," as do the authors of this book. That, naturally, delineates the healthy inwardness of "Jewish living" in the United States. It calls attention also, as it should, to certain "evaluations of Jewish living" which premise considerable doubt of the value of "Jewish living" whether as something in itself and for itself, or as a cause having consequences to the living of people who are not Jews. Such "evaluations" assume a certain duress upon the Jew to justify his existence and thus question, if they do not challenge, his right to exist. Among individuals, potential suicides have such an attitude toward themselves; they are persons whose lives are so burdened, insecure and fear-ridden, that they have to argue themselves into keeping up the struggle to live rather than flee anywhere, even to death, for relief. They know what they do not want; but they do not know what they want. As consequence, instead of simply living and growing, they are constantly examining themselves, "evaluating." Jews, since the Emancipation, have evinced a considerable propensity toward such self-examination and self-justification both in their private lives and as members of their Jewish communities, the inclination increasing with distance from the psychic center and nearness to the psychic boundaries of "Jewish living." The more marginal the Jew — that is, the greater the number and variety of relationships, actual and probable with non-Jews — the greater his feeling of insecurity and his urge to "evaluate" his existence as Jew; the more deeply aware he is of "the Jewish problem." He may think of himself as merely the innocent victim of anti-Semitism through "the accident of birth" and refuse all other connection with his fellow Jews; he may associate himself with "Jewish living" in any

Reprinted from *The American Jew: A Composite Portrait*, edited by Oscar I. Janowsky, New York, 1942. Copyright, Harper & Brothers.

higher degree, from contributing to Jewish philanthropies, membership in a Jewish social club, membership in a reform congregation, membership in an orthodox congregation, membership in a Jewish fraternal order or other definitely Jewish secular association, membership in a Zionist unit, membership in the American Jewish Congress, to full participation, via all the forms of consent and dissent, in the entire institutional organization of Jewish interests. Whatever his degree of participation, he will be disposed to seek justification for his Jewishness as his relationships with non-Jews widen and multiply; more than a member of any other community, he will feel a compulsion to "evaluate."

Many, by no means reconcilable, explanations are offered for this state of things. The basic one, which seems to me alone indicated by the record, is sometimes denied and usually ignored, belittled or glossed over by emphasis on derivative, on secondary and on occasional causes. This is the effect on Jewish relations due to the singular and universal meaning of the word Jew everywhere in the Christian world. This meaning does not come from what actual Jews actually are, from what they actually do or say, or from where and how they live. It is the same where actual Jews are entirely unknown and where Jews are well-known; where there are no Jews whatever, and where there are millions. Indeed where Jews are numerous and are well-known, direct experience tends to modify this meaning which is the same for rich and poor, for educated and unlearned, for masses and classes. It sets men in certain attitudes toward persons to whom the word *Jew* is applied. As I have already indicated,[1] so long as such persons are called Poles, Czechs, Texans, Russians, Belgians, Scots or what have you, no particular emotion is aroused and no fixed denotation is communicated. The plain people of the Christian world might not even know what those words stood for. But call the very same Poles or Czechs or Texans *Jew* and they are shut out and cut off; the epithet draws an emotional ring around them; it bounds them as a "minority" and in feeling permanently excludes them from and stands them against "the majority." The feeling may be expressed in overt acts or it may not. The material and spiritual conclusion to which it is the premise are the notorious Nuremberg laws; its initiation is the system of Christian beliefs, acquired in childhood, regarding the origin, the nature and the destiny of man in which

[1] See above: "National Solidarity and the Jewish Minority."

the idea *Jew* has a leading role. You remember Pastor Martin Niemöller's very special way of insulting the Nazis.[2]

Among all Christian sects which are open to the influences of the philological, historical and social sciences, the dogma embodied in these expressions is undergoing revision. But the process has not yet reached the point of dissipating the sentiment of discomfort and aversion which the word *Jew* arouses in general Christian usage. Psychologically, it has the same effect as a direct perception of skin color or other traits of "race"— this even among pundits who know well enough that no scientific anthropologist can regard the Jews as a race. Thus a midwestern psychologist named J. F. Brown permits himself to write: "Almost every one can clearly differentiate . . . between a Negro and a white Indo-European and even between a white European and a Jew."[3] Such notions are projections of motor-sets established in childhood; not observations, not facts, but unconscious prejudices formulated in stereotyped ideological fictions. When such fictions are given a logical form which rationalizes the prejudice without identifying it as a prejudice, all sorts of secondary explanations are drawn into the rationalizations: race, manner, conduct, economics, politics. Now one is made the base, and now another, and in each case an argument is developed which regularly proves that the Jew is the source of whatever trouble a society encounters. So easy is it to arouse and to mobilize the avertive sentiment attached to the word *Jew* that Jews continue to be the cheapest and most available scapegoats in Christian history. I have already quoted Hitler on the subject.[4]

Events have shown that Hitler's judgment was not wrong. Everywhere, consistently, anti-Semitism has proved an effective "Christian front" for the assault on democracy. Hitler, as Lord Davies wrote some time ago in *The Manchester Guardian*, has chosen to make the Jewish people his special target, to identify the Jews with democracy and democracy with the Jews: he and his crew never stop prating about "degenerate Jewish democracy." They have made the Jewish people, as Lord Davies said, "the personification of the issues involved in this world-struggle."[5] This is the greatest honor which the Jews have received from friend or foe since Christianity was established as the prevailing religion of the Western World.

[2] See "Judaism as Disaster," above, pp. 42 ff.

[3] *Psychology and the Social Order*, New York, 1936, p. 122.

[4] See above: "National Solidarity and the Jewish Minority."

[5] For the full quotation from Lord Davies, see above "National Solidarity and the Jewish Minority," p. 64.

II

Nor are the enemies of democracy mistaken in making their assault upon the Jews the spearhead of their assault upon democracy. At the time democracy came into effective being, with the American and the French Revolutions, the Jews of the world were in fact living shut out and cut off legally, physically, socially and spiritually. The ghetto walls were the physical embodiment of the psychological alienation of Christian from Jew, which kept the Jews immutably an excluded "minority" and permitted no Jew to be a neighbor, no neighbor to be a Jew. The rise and growth of democracy did not, because they could not, put an end to the psychological alienation, but did make its embodiment in the structure of society more and more difficult, and its expression in human relations less and less substantial or approvable. The democratic principle is that Jews can be neighbors, neighbors can be Jews. The democratic faith opened the gates of the ghetto that had locked the Jews in and shut them out for thirteen centuries. And during the one hundred and fifty years between 1791, when the National Assembly of the French voted equal liberty for all the Jews of France, and 1941, when the fascist "Christian" government of France imposed Hitler's Nuremberg laws upon the French, the generations of the Jews of the world have been so identified with the struggle for liberty that they have become, according to Mr. Stanley High,[6] the very incarnation of the spirit of liberty and therefore have every tyrant for their enemy.

Be this as it may, in terms of the inner life of Jews and Jewry, liberty had far from an identical meaning. To many sensitive and articulate spirits, of whom Moses Mendelssohn was the early type, the roads it opened seemed to be all away, and if he himself did not wander far, his children and his children's children did. Willy-nilly his "evaluations" pointed to the Jewish being as the misfortune which Heine called it: the road to freedom was a road of flight; the road of conversion, of reform, of ignoring and forgetting, thus changing oneself from a Jew to a "non-Aryan"; then of a bitter hatred of the Judaism which one reformed or was converted from, or ignored and forgot; and finally an irrepressible animosity against those who would not or could not flee the disaster of being Jews and therein remain

[6] High, Stanley, "Jews, Anti-Semites and Tyrants," *Harper's Magazine*, June, 1942.

somehow so different from their neighbors that the latter refuse to accept them for neighbors. The whole purpose of freedom became to abolish the difference. The end and means of democracy was to be assimilation; whatever else "Americanization" might mean, it would mean the disappearance of the Jew as Jew. His existence cannot be justified. There is nothing in Judaism whose survival is worth the struggle. As I have noted elsewhere, Jews who minds are thus set believe that it is the task of the minority to dissolve itself in the majority.[7] Surer of what they do not want than of what they want, such Jews do not inquire, who, what, is "the majority" in which they hope to lose themselves.

To this question there is one answer whose moral and political significance is peculiarly symptomatic of the times. It is an answer which accepts the fundamentalist Christian interpretation of the Jewish being and rejects the tempering of that interpretation which is due to science and democracy. According to the answer, nothing can ever diminish anti-Semitism. It has a permanent case against the Jews of our own times. In seeking the fellowship of the men of these times, the wicked times of science and of democracy, the Jews more than ever reject God and betray man. Because of the democratic liberties of the body and soul of man, the world has abandoned faith and piety for free thought and scientific method, the works of the Lord for mechanical skills and machine production, the scarcities of the spiritual life which were the glory of the Middle Ages, for the economy of abundance in thoughts and things which is the degradation of our own time. Thus the western world is given over to unrighteousness, materialism and corruption. The Jews, in turning from the fasts and the fastness of the ghetto to these flesh-pots of freedom, have turned more than ever from God to ungodliness. They have taken on the age's materialism and corruption and improved upon them; they have become the most debased of moderns, who reject God, do unrighteously and corrupt commerce, youth and art. Spiritually and materially they would be safe, if not saved, in the ghetto.[8]

[7] The latest exposition of this typical attitude from an authoritative pen is "Red, White and Blue Herring," by Judge Jerome Frank, the *Saturday Evening Post*, December 6, 1941.

[8] This "evaluation of Jewish living" has recently received wide publicity in the *Saturday Evening Post* of March 28, 1942. The author is a Jew himself said to have found salvation, not in the ghetto he recommends, but in the fashionable neo-Thomism of the day. See Mayer, Milton, "The Case Against the Jews." For

With very little addition, this "evaluation" might also be Hitler's, or that of any totalitarian dictator who employs anti-Semitism as the spearhead of his attack against human freedom, and possesses as Sidney Hook showed, all the logical and moral stigmata of the totalitarian propaganda. Although it has a similarity to certain extreme forms of Judaist fundamentalism, its premise is a hatred of Judaism and its conclusion is a flight from it. Like its opposite, it postulates the elimination of the Jew from contact with the modern world, but by psychic segregation instead of assimilation.

III

That no American can accept such an evaluation of the national being goes without saying. That, if he is truly American, he must reject both the segregationist and assimilationist evaluation of the Jewish — or for that matter, any other — community's part in the national being, is not so naturally obvious, but logically just as inevitable. It is not so naturally obvious, because there often obtains among Americans a certain confusion of mind as to what the nation's being truly is, and how majorities and minorities are related to one another in the national life. Only when we have a clear and distinct idea of their dynamic in the doctrine and discipline constituting the American way of life can we rightly evaluate "American Jewish living."

Now so far as the American way is a doctrine, that is, a system of beliefs on which conduct is postulated and justified, we have it in a comparatively few documents such as the Declaration of Independence and the Constitution, Lincoln's Gettysburg Address, Emancipation Proclamation and Second Inaugural, Washington's Farewell Address, Jefferson's First Inaugural. These are the outstanding books

an exposition of the animus against science and democracy which this article rationalizes, see Hook, Sidney, "Milton Mayer: Fake Jeremiah," in *The New Leader*, April 4, 1942. For the actual facts regarding the impact of American Jews on the political and moral economy of the nation, see the *Fortune* magazine study, *Jews in America*, New York, 1936; Roth, Cecil, *Jewish Contributions to Civilization*, Cincinnati, 1940; Ross, Irwin, "Labor, Capital and Co.," *Harper's Magazine*, May, 1942; Healy, W., and Bronner, A. F., *Delinquents and Criminals*, New York, 1926; Illinois Crime Survey, *The Juvenile Delinquent*, Chicago, 1929; High, Stanley, "Jews, Anti-Semites and Tyrants," in *Harper's Magazine*, June, 1942; Kallen, H. M., *Culture and Democracy in the United States*, New York, 1924; *Judaism at Bay*, New York, 1932; "National Solidarity and the Jewish Minority," *The Annals of the American Academy of Political and Social Science*, Philadelphia, September, 1942.

of the Bible of America. They figure most frequently in the school texts, they are the most widely quoted and ceremonially read. They are the vehicles of the American faith. The future is likely to add to the list Woodrow Wilson's addresses defining the American purpose in the first World War and Franklin Roosevelt's, defining American purposes in the second World War.

The propositions of the Declaration of Independence are the postulates upon which all the later affirmations rest. To understand the ideal of human relations which these propositions are intended to convey, it is necessary to remember that, when the Declaration was made, the world was everywhere caste-dominated and class-ruled; that some men were free, but most were serfs and slaves; that some ways of life and thought were privileged; that all who differed from the privileged were penalized solely because they were different; that the ideal and the law were conformity and submission to the ruling powers in faith, in morals, in politics, in study, in occupation, and in all similar matters; that those who failed to conform were degraded, shut out and cut off, existing on sufferance instead of by right; that the Jews were of all the variant groups in the countries of the Western World, the most completely shut out and cut off.

To this state of things the Declaration enters an absolute and final *non possumus*. In affirming that *all* men are created equal, and that the rights of *all* to life, liberty and the pursuit of happiness are *unalienable*, it accepts human beings as they are, with all the variety and multiplicity of faith, of race, of sex, of occupations, of ideas, of possessions; and it affirms the equal right of these different people freely to struggle for existence. Emerson expressed this repudiation in another way when he declared: "As long as any man exists there is some need of him: let him fight for his own." The American way of life, then, may be said to flow from each man's unalienable right to be different, as this is enchanneled in the American Constitution, especially the Bill of Rights and the subsequent Amendments. If these forbid Congress to make certain laws, they forbid Congress to penalize difference.

The discipline which gives to this doctrine of equal liberty for different people body and movement as a way of life, an organization of doing, feeling and thinking, operates in the political order as equal suffrage regardless of faith, occupation, race or sex, as the base of government of the people, for the people, by the people: in the economic order as free enterprise: in religion as freedom of conscience: in the arts and sciences as freedom of inquiry, research and expression: in education, as the free public school from kindergarten to the university; and throughout these domains of the common life in freedom of association into sects, parties, corporations, trade unions, fraternal orders and whatever other groupings individual Americans choose to come together in. Each such group, if it be reasonably stable, tends to form, within the framework of the national being, a doctrine and discipline singular to itself, with its own characteristic vocabulary and habits of speech and song; its own tradition of competency, heroism, legend and tale; its own architecture, suitable to its purpose and function; its own preferred diet; its own ceremonial occasions and forms of play. That which interests a New Englander in New York, a New Yorker in Florida, a Floridian in Chicago, a Chicagoan in Texas, a Texan in the Northwest, the Northwesterner in New England, are these characteristic differences which make one region important to another. But occupational groups, like, say, the doctors and the lawyers and the teachers, the carpenters and the machinists and the plumbers, the musicians, the stockbrokers, the bankers and the actors, also develop and maintain the characteristic differentiae which identify them as a group — in the Middle Ages they were often called Nations — and which constitute the cultures of their group. These differentiae cross all boundaries, so that American doctors, for example, may as doctors have more in common with doctors in China or England or Russia than with men of other occupations in America; American painters and musicians *qua* painters and musicians may have more interests in common with musicians and painters in Mexico or India or Norway or Brazil than with floorwalkers or clergymen or what have you in the United States. And so on, to any organization of a group interest that can be named, including that of the national interest itself. For the nation obviously has more interests in common with democracies abroad than with organizations inimical to democracy at home.

Now the national being rests upon the cooperative and competitive relationships of these voluntary associations and consists in the free trade of goods and services between them. Their connecting links are their members. While each association — be it a state, a region, an occupation, a religious or cultural community, etc.— is an autonomous culture-complex with a way of being singular to itself, any or every member of the association is, as a rule, also a member of a good many others. The member of the Bar or of a Tradesunion is at the same time a citizen, a member of a family, a church, a political party, a fraternal order, a social club, a consumer society, an alumni association, a patriotic, a philanthropic, an athletic, a burial or other society. Each is a different way of his being together with other people. He is the bond which unites the societies with one another. His relation to each varies in firmness and intensity. Some, like those to his father and mother, are not easily dissolved; others are loose and tenuous; but ultimately all are voluntary, and like his citizenship result from his choice and rest on his consent. The freer the social order in which he lives, the smoother and simpler is his movement in and through the associations which combine into this order. His relations are not fixed by status; they are not coerced to any inevitable sequence or hierarchy, but are liquid and mobile. This mobility of relationships is what gives its characteristic quality to the national being. Of this quality the consummation is Cultural Pluralism. For its diverse and ever-diversifying members are united with one another in and through their differences, and the singularity of our culture is the orchestration of those manifold differences — *e pluribus unum* — into the common faith which makes Liberty the foundation of Union, Union the guarantee of Liberty, and Democracy the fusion of the two in the common way of life.[9]

Where this fusion tends to be efficacious and consequential, "majority" and "minority" have neither the fixity of form nor the continuity of existence which we are disposed to expect from our having used these expressions in connection with religious and cultural groups. It is exactly the overthrow of such fixations and permanencies that the Democratic Revolution won, and it is precisely the restoration of such invidious status that the Nazis and the Fascists have murderously accomplished. In their Servile State they permit parts but no parties. Whether in politics, economics, religion, science or culture, they war upon the right to be different; the differences they cannot destroy they degrade and penalize. Free societies, on the other hand, know that the free interaction of differences is the surest way to right and truth, and they make discussion and division the instrument of decision. Consequently, "majority" and "minority" mean to free men associative and functional relationships of groups and individuals, not constitutive organs of unchanging societies. When you take together *all* the people who are *we the people* as one Association, any

[9] See "National Solidarity and the Jewish Minority," above, p. 58, footnote 1.

and every lesser combination of the people, no matter how large, is a minority, and *we the people* is but the orchestration of such minorities into the singularity of the national being. Every individual by himself alone is a "minority"; every association of individuals by itself alone is a "minority." A "majority" comes into existence only as the combination of such "minorities." But the combination is meaningful as a "majority" alone in relation to some particular interest or issue about which there has been discussion and which has been decided by division. It always remains open to the "minority," to endeavor to win so many members of the majority to its point of view as to convert "the minority" into "the majority." Where there is no issue to be decided, "majority" and "minority" are either meaningless or carry a totalitarian implication.

Obviously there can be no sense in speaking of "the medical minority" or "the dancer minority" or the "baker minority" except in relation to a division of "we the people" on an issue calling for decision by all. So, when the experts speak about "the Jewish minority" they may mean that non-Jews are more numerous than Jews, which is no news; they may mean that in a division on an issue the Jews as Jews stand alone, which is news but not true; they may mean that groups whose members are small and powers few are somehow inferior and have no rights which groups consisting of larger numbers need respect. This expresses a point of view that had been general before the Democratic Revolution; it recurs not infrequently among democrats, and is a prime dogma of tyrannical societies which democracies must combat with all their hearts and strength.[10] Such a meaning of "minority" reveals nothing about the doctrine, the discipline and the dynamic import of "Jewish living" for the national being. These are as unrelated to size as is the practice of medicine or any other art to the avoirdupois of the practitioner. They are variable configurations of passions, principles and aspirations nourished upon custom, upon tradition, and upon education, and implemented in an economy which ranges from birth to burial and diet to divinity, and is embodied as a going concern in an indefinite number of varying associations whose emulative rivalries take the form of a number of struggles to win a majority in the Jewish group. The conflicts and agreements of these struggles emerge in the Jewish press and literature, in the Yiddish and Hebrew and sometimes in the English, theater

[10] See "National Solidarity and the Jewish Minority," above, p. 59, footnote 2.

and concert hall, over the radio, in the culture of the *kosher* kitchen, in the theological resultants of sectarian controversy, in the forms of philanthropy, in the confrontation of Zionists and anti-Zionists, "Congress" and "Committee," and the like. Within the boundaries drawn by anti-Semitism, participation in this Jewish living is voluntary. Those abandon it who will, those share in it who desire. And it is likely that, because of the challenge of anti-Semitism, the sharer's is the braver, hence happier part; at least, he chooses to affirm and to defend his integrity, and as a man and a citizen to vindicate the equal liberty of his Jewish difference. Certainly this is more consonant with the national being alike as doctrine and as discipline. They establish the existence and freedom of this difference as unalienable right, equal with that of non-Jews, calling for neither apology nor justification. Even without fruitful consequences to the common life, the mere fact that it is there, that it is one more variety in the dynamic whole, is, like the addition of another taste or sight or sound, an enrichment, a contribution to abundance, spiritual and material. If against the assimilationist the American spirit affirms the right to be different, against the segregationist it affirms the right of free association of the different with one another. But it points also to a certain prior community of the Jewish group with the national being. This community is established in and through the Old Testament, which contributes so largely to the singularity of the Jewish psyche: Lecky wrote that "the Hebraic mortar cemented the foundations of American democracy."[11] But furthermore, the Jewish community, like very other composing the national being, serves as a psychological locale for voluntary social experimentation, for invention and discovery, as such, involving more limited risks than a nation-wide adventure would. Thus the Jewish locale has been an area of trial and error in employer-employee relations, in philanthropy, in education, in literature and in the arts. What was started in the Yiddish theaters of the East Side more than once was perfected — or corrupted — on Broadway; what began as a protocol on relations between Jewish employers and Jewish employees in women's wear, has become the initiating precedent in the national growth toward industrial democracy; what began as an effort to help immigrant "coreligionists" cheaply and efficiently, has contributed to the formation of the theory and practice of scientific charity, and so on. And it is not possible to

[11] *History of Rationalism in Europe*, II, p. 168.

call these developments more an Americanization of Jewry — even of the Jewry of Palestine — than an enrichment of the American way by Jewish contributions. "American Jewish living" makes an impression of a healthy symbiosis with the diverse other forms of living whose interaction orchestrates the Union we call America, and whose combined utterance is the American spirit. Like its neighbors, the community of Jewish living has a character of its own, a singularity which works as a reservoir and a breeding place of the Jewish difference. This its men and women of genius carry beelike from the nest which nurtured them to the national scene, there to serve as a fertilizing contribution to the commonwealth of things and ideals. Louis Brandeis and Ben Cardozo; David Lubin, Nathan Straus and Julius Rosenwald; Sidney Hillman and David Dubinsky; Emma Lazarus; Robert Nathan and Sholem Asch; Edna Ferber and Gertrude Stein; George Kaufman, Elmer Rice, Clifford Odets, S. N. Behrmann; Aaron Copland and George Gershwin; Leon Kroll, Maurice Sterne, Max Weber, William Gropper — I mention only a few of the long lists of jurists and business men, playwrights, composers, painters, trades-unionists, who are figures of my lifetime. There are many others, in every walk of life — virtuosos and inventors, physicians and architects, chemists and psychologists, merchants, engineers, whom *Who's Who* counts — all children or grandchildren of a ghetto that has ceased to be a ghetto because its walls have been breached and its gates opened, so that the life of the nation flows through it, and its life flows and mingles in the national stream, in a confluence where the free flow of each is the expanding life of both.

So I close my "evaluation of American Jewish living." I have not studied to make it either "judicial" or "scholarly." I have been concerned first and last to set down the ideals which any evaluation I could make would have to use for measure, and to signalize what, in terms of the national being, these measures of the Jewish community would come to. I have done so. What I have said can be valid only for those Americans whose faith in democracy is a fighting faith, and for those American Jews who are resolved to stand up in the armies of democracy as the democratic faith requires, freely and boldly as Jews.

Jewish Right, Christian Power

Sept. 23, 1945: President Truman urges British Cabinet to admit 100,000 Jews to Palestine.

May 1, 1946: Anglo-American Inquiry Commission recommends immediate admission . . . Truman again asks action . . . but Prime Minister Attlee says illegal Jewish armies must be disarmed and asked the U.S.A. what assistance it would give.

May 9: Bartley C. Crum announces British Foreign Minister Bevin had told the Committee its recommendation would be put into effect promptly.

June 13: Bevin says 100,000 could not be admitted to Palestine unless he put another British division into the country to maintain order. "I am not prepared to do that."

June 29: Frederik Kuh reports from London the end of the year as a target date has been abandoned.

July 1: *Violence.*

IN THIS calendar we have a concretion of "the Jewish problem." "The Jewish Problem" is the agelong predicament in which, through no fault of their own, the people called Jews are compelled to live and die everywhere in the world. On the subject of relief from this predicament I know of nothing new to say. The things I am repeating here are not intended to bring forward anything novel but again to direct attention to a deteriorating condition and to challenge the courage which is wisdom concerning the present danger in this condition. As the body daily needs its bread, so the spirit needs its daily reawakening to the enduring realities on which survival depends. It is the unexercised that atrophies and dies. It is the unheeded that betrays and kills. Remembering and being alert to hazard is like eating meals: an

Reprinted from *Contemporary Jewish Record*, 1946.

act daily to be repeated if the people concerned are to live and not die. This is especially true when the people concerned are Jews in "Judeo-Christian civilization."

In the summer of 1942, S.S. group leader Werner Best, legal adviser to the Gestapo, told elite guard functionaries: "The Jewish problem is the dynamite with which we shatter the bastions where the last snipers of liberalism have holed up. When nations abandon their Jews they give up their former, Judaized manner of life which rests upon false ideals of freedom. Only thus and then can they take their places in our war for a new order."

That same year the British peer, Lord Davies, wrote to the *Manchester Guardian*:

> In this tragic conflict we must be for or against the Jews: there can be no neutrality. Our attitude towards them becomes the test of our professions and the sincerity of our war aims. It strikes at the root of our morale, and if we abandon the Jews we abandon everything, because Hitler has chosen to make them his special target. Whether we like it or not, and however inconvenient it may be, the Jewish people has become the personification of the issues involved in this world struggle between right and wrong, between good and evil. If we desert the Jews it may result in our losing the war, because it is a betrayal of our avowed war aims. Surely it is the height of folly to repudiate our principles and to cold-shudder our friends in order to curry favor with neutrals or potential enemies.

I have many times quoted this statement since I first noticed it. Now let us look at the record in the light of it.

Before 1933 anti-Semitism was a sentiment universal and endemic wherever the Christian theologian's interpretation of man and his destiny prevailed. It is the sentiment to which St. Chrysostom gave characteristic expression in the fourth century: "The Jews have crucified the Son and rejected the Holy Ghost, and their souls are the abode of the Devil. . . . It is not insignificant controversies which separate us but the death of Christ." Another way of expressing this sentiment is to call the Jews "the synagogue of Satan." Modern times transpose these theological fantasies into economic, racist and cultural terms, but all terms are dogmas rationalizing the same sentiment. In modern times, however, the redefinition of these dogmas into programs and laws, their incarnation in deeds, has been occasional only. The anti-Semitic sentiment existed in the mores of Christian states as a permanently available instrument of policy and interest which both the *Ins* and the *Outs* could employ in their power conflicts when a diversionary object of hate, or a scapegoat seemed useful. Against both the sentiment and its uses were set the spirit of free religion and scientific method, the growth of religious liberty and of democracy as a way of living and thinking. With the handworkers, the women, the religious and other sections of Christian society who were penalized for being different — penalized for being poor, for being laborers, for being Moslems or females or Indians or Negroes or Quakers or Catholics or Methodists or Baptists or just Protestants, and so on — the Jews as Jews were, here and there, affirmed to have under the law of the land equal rights to "life, liberty and the pursuit of happiness." In the course of time the affirmation came to include not only the Jew as a human individual but the Jew as a member of one of the many nationalities that lived in subjection only because they were different, small and weak.

Ultimately, that proposition became embodied in the law of nations as two different rules with complementary purposes. One was designed to establish the equality of Jews *as* Jews before the law in certain countries where otherwise that equality would be very doubtful indeed. The other was designed to give effect to the Jewish national aspiration of creating in Palestine "a publicly recognized, legally assured" homeland. It was hoped to accomplish the first by means of the minorities clauses of various treaties concluding the First World War. It was hoped to accomplish the second by means of the Palestine Mandate, to which fifty-two sovereign states were signatories, and to which the United States is a party by the British-American Mandate Convention of December 3, 1924. One of the tasks of the betrayed League of Nations was to assure loyal performance of the obligations assumed under these treaties. Its simple covenant provided for bodies to which appeal might be taken against violations of the law and other forms of injustice.

The end of the First World War appeared to have brought the peculiarly *American* ideals of peace and democracy to dominance in the general outlook of the peoples of the world. It appeared to have brought to triumph in the west the democratic revolution which was signalized by the American Declaration of Independence in 1776. Actually, however, it initiated the world-wide counterrevolution whose aim is to destroy modern liberty and to reduce the unshackled plain man, body and soul, to his ancient slavery. The spirit of that counterrevolution may be said to have had its birth in the Russian Civil War, and to have grown and expanded in the various forms of totalitarianism, which from its centers of infection in Rome, Tokio, Berlin, Madrid, Buenos Aires, Moscow, spread their anti-democratic contagion over the entire globe. Soon or late, all of them, in addressing their propaganda to Christian peoples, found they could exploit the Jew most cheaply and easily as the symbol of the ways of freedom against which they aimed to mobilize the hatred and aggression of the deceived peoples. From 1922 to 1933 they worked by means of indoctrination nourished on intermittent violence. After the Nazis took over Germany, precept and practice became indivisible. When, in 1939, Hitler unleashed his sadistic total aggression against mankind, he declared his war to be the occasion for the extirpation of the Jews from Europe.

Wherever Nazi power has reached, this annihilation has been carried out with the maximum of cruelty and obscenity. Today, of the nine million Jews, more or less, who lived and worked in the countries of Europe in 1939, more than half have been thus destroyed. The rest have been robbed of their property, driven from their homes, enslaved and put to work under conditions which, when survived, perforce has left the survivors without strength either of body or mind, their skills gone, their citizenship destroyed, broken wanderers without arms and without a defender on the face of a devastated earth.

All this has long been a matter of common knowledge. It has been referred to by the foremost official spokesmen for the United Nations. The United Nations made public a joint declaration denouncing the totalitarian murder of the Jewish people and pledging themselves to punish the guilty. It has been a major indictment at the Nuremberg trials. Churches, labor unions, men and women of goodwill everywhere, have joined in expressions of sympathy and horror. Ministers of religion have recognized that this "Jewish question" is a Christian problem. The Archbishop of York has stigmatized as "the greatest crime in history" this treatment of a people whose "only offence is that they belong to the race of which our Lord and his Apostles were members." Since 1933 all sorts of agencies, public and private, open and underground, have been formed to salvage Jewish remnants from Nazi immolation. Conferences such as that strange one in Bermuda met and adjourned without action. The total of achievement of all efforts in the entire period has been to bring perhaps two hundred thousand to some sort of safety. The fate of the remaining millions is signalized in the stories of the "Patria," the "Atlantic," the "Struma," and the events of the D.P. camps in Europe. With the most generous expressions of sympathy and goodwill, with the most reassuring promises of justice for their survivors when once the war shall be over, no positive step is taken to save them *now*, and they are inhibited from taking any positive step to save themselves. The decision of those who have the power is that nothing shall be done *now* to save them where they are, or to make it possible for them to save themselves in Palestine where, as Woodrow Wilson explained in 1919, "the allied nations, with the full concurrence of our government and our people, are agreed . . . shall be laid the foundations of a Jewish commonwealth."

That agreement is written into the law of nations. The purpose of the fifty-two sovereign states which underwrote it, chief among them Great Britain, whose government fully undertook to guide its attainment, was the gradual development of a Jewish Homeland under the protection of the British crown. Jews were to be free to enter Palestine as of right and not on sufferance.

Scarcely, however, had the right been established than its slow nullification took form. The first English rule of Palestine began a process which the White Paper was intended to conclude. As the late Josiah Wedgwood told the world from London in May 1942: "The whole administration in Palestine, from the top to the police, are against the half-million Jews of Palestine. They will never let them have arms, nor land, nor free immigration, nor a refuge, nor a home. Never!" If the great liberal's summary is true, then the tears and treasure, the blood and sweat which the Jews have spent upon the soil of Palestine have been the extravagances of a blind faith founded on a devilish lie. The case of the Jewish right in Palestine becomes one more item in the long, dark record of the cat-and-mouse method which the strong ever employ with the weak; one more item in the dark colonial phases of British imperialism of which England is reaping the bitter fruit in Burma and in Malaya and the Straits Settlements, where the people looked upon the Japanese as liberators and allies.

I cannot, however, accept this summary as the whole truth. British policy in Palestine, simple and obvious as are its consequences to date, has been governed by a complex of motives. One of these has been the more or less conscious anti-Semitism of army officers and of civil servants in whose education the first meaning of the word "Jew" was that given it by theological instruction. This has been further reinforced by the administrative master-race frame of mind acquired in Malaya and Burma, the Straits Settlements or Tanganyika. In consequence, what the Jews have achieved in Palestine has been achieved, not alone without the full cooperation of the mandatory, but against direct and indirect official obstruction and resistance.

This obstruction and resistance might have been considerably less if it were not for Arab interest. The Arab interest is not the interest of the simple fellahin of Palestine. Everything that is done to nullify the terms of the mandate also works to the disadvantage of the fellahin. The Arab interest is the interest of a small propertied class of great feudal landlords, government functionaries and their hangers-on whose standards and traditions derive from medieval Turkish imperialism which the Turks themselves have cast off. British colonial administration — and, ironically enough, there has been none better since the turn of the century — is disposed to hold the same view of the plain people as the people's native masters; it is at best likely to disturb vested interests for the benefit of the people as little as possible. Thus official disposition leads automatically to great complaisance toward Arab privilege, a complaisance reinforced by a certain conception of the policy of empire. The policy in Palestine has had necessarily to be a part of this policy of empire.

Now the British policy of empire, during the score of years between 1920 and 1940, was defined in an atmosphere of fear and insecurity — fear of "communism" at home, fear of fascism and nazism abroad; fears that eventuated in the betrayal of China to the Japanese, of Ethiopia to Mussolini, of the Spanish Republic to its totalitarian foes, of Czechoslovakia to Hitler. Those were the days when Neville Chamberlain could speak of Czechoslovakia as "that far away country" and of its citizens as "people of whom we know nothing." Palestine, of course, was not a far country, only its Jews were. On the border of the Suez Canal and the terminal point of a great pipe line, in a continental area of millions of Arab-speaking peoples, a link in the "life-line" of the Empire, Palestine's upper class Arabs were near as its plebeian Jews were not. The jittery British state of mind resulted in the creation there of the very conditions it intended to avert. Each act of appeasement was followed by greater "Arab" demands, finally by the rebellion — financed and armed in part with contributions made possible by the government itself, in part by Axis agents — which led to the MacDonald White Paper of May 17, 1939. The autocratic Arab Higher Committee, and its leader, Hajj Amin al Husaini, self-styled "Grand" Mufti of Jerusalem and Palestine's greatest landlord, were entirely creations of a policy which substituted surrender to gangsterism for a government loyally enforcing the law and guarding the peace.

The data on which this summary is based are not an enumeration of Zionist grievances. They are to be found in the report of the Royal Commission appointed to survey the situation in Palestine in 1936. This report is known as Command Paper 5479. It was published in July 1937. It comments on the "kind of mechanical impartiality which makes neither for good government nor . . . better relations between the races." The data are to be found in an analysis of this report by a British authority, Mr. H. J. Simson, in his book, *British Rule and Rebellion* (London, 1937). They are to be found in the observations of the Permanent Mandates Commission of the League of Nations which declared itself once in 1930 and again in 1937 (when it was commenting on Command Paper 5479): "The capacity of a government to establish peace and concord among those whom it governs is proportionate to its confidence in itself and its policy; and the likelihood of its being obliged to resort to force in order to impose its will is proportionate to the uncertainty of its intentions."

Some of the causes of this uncertainty of intention have been suggested. But any reader of the Command Paper can get the feel of them when he observes the discrepancy between the facts recorded and the recommendations made. For the report shows that even with the right established for them under the Mandate, the Jews immigrated into Palestine as into the United States or England, seekers of peace and freedom to live and to work, but with a different feeling and a different hope. The latter were due to the fact that the Koran as well as Western religion and culture peculiarly identifies Israel with Palestine and Palestine with Israel. Not since the days of the Judges, has there been a Palestine without Jews. Whoever may have been the ruling power in Palestine, Jews were always both native in Palestine, and migrating to Palestine. After the Balfour Declaration, which gave the force of international law to this religious, social and cultural bond between the people and the land, Jews began to immigrate into Palestine in greater numbers.

The land they bought to settle on was for the most part wasteland. The people among whom they settled was a stationary population, for the most part an illiterate, disease-ridden, pauper neolithic folk in bondage to feuding tribal leaders of wealth and power, such as the Husainis and Nashashibis. More than a fifth of the children born to them died, while babies and old people were not numerous. Most of them worked the soil, some were Bedouin nomads. Very few owned the land they tilled. The bulk worked for the effendi landlords. What tillable land Jews were able to buy was sold by these effendis from their non-productive surplus, and sold at extortionate prices. The larger proportion of the land which was sold to Jews was untilled swamp and sand for which they were required to pay "uneconomic" prices, as an Arab "notable" testified to the Royal Commission. The Jews own nothing in Palestine they have not paid for many times over. Their labor with that land caused a desert to bloom. It set going a democratic society on principles of free association in cooperative effort — the only center of democracy as a way of life anywhere in the Near East. It raised the standard of living of the Palestinian fellah. It increased literacy. It improved social and personal hygiene and reduced infant mortality.

As compared with the fellah of Syria, of Egypt, of Transjordan, of Iraq, of slave-holding Sa'udi Arabia, and Yemen, the fellah of Palestine is today much better off; so much better off that, whereas before the Jewish settlement, Arabs had been *emigrating*, they now began to immigrate. Immigration and natural increase have multiplied the 600,000 Arabs of 1920 into the over 1,200,000 of today. The Jews, on the other hand, have not been so fertile as the Arabs. They average only one child to a family while the Arabs average four. Their increase to the 500,000 of 1943 from the 60,000 of 1920 is due mostly to refugees from the abominations of European anti-Semitism.

The natural conclusion from the record would be that the Jewish homeland is a boon to the plain people of Palestine. But the Royal Commission did not draw this conclusion. Having heard a few effendis and functionaries and reviewed the journals in the control of the latter, the Commission declared that the demands of the ambitious Hajj Amin al Husaini and his party involve "a conflict of right with right." Examination of the demands alike by His Majesty's investigators and by the Permanent Mandates Commission of the League of Nations reveals no ground for such an assertion, whether political, historical or any other. No "right" has been found, either in fact or in law, unless the power of Amin al Husaini and the Higher Arab Committee to intimidate and coerce his Britannic Majesty's government constitutes a right. And that power consisted in the state of mind of British officialdom, not in the actual might of its pseudo-Frankenstein, the Grand Mufti and his Higher Arab Council. Officialdom's state of mind made the Mandate unworkable. As M. Rappard of the Permanent Mandates

Commission declared, "the mandate has become inapplicable because it has not been applied."

With the ukase of the MacDonald White Paper, under the impact of a war brought on by sell-outs in order to "preserve peace in our time," the Mandate was entirely nullified. It was Mr. Malcolm MacDonald's cynical contention that the Jewish Homeland had been established and the undertaking of the Balfour Declaration accomplished. In Parliament the Labor Party opposed the government proposal. Leopold Amery, Winston Churchill and a score of other Conservatives voted with the Laborites. The government got only 268 out of its usual 413 votes. Mr. Churchill said of the MacDonald paper: "What is that but the destruction of the Balfour Declaration? What is that but a breach of faith?" He may say it again of the words and deeds of Messrs. Bevin and Attlee.

Nevertheless the breach of faith to the weak and helpless became the program of the imperial British Government. If its purpose was only to secure and hold the loyalty of the Arab during the greatest danger the Empire had ever faced, it failed. It was a purpose built upon what could have been only a stupid illusion of judgment. If the makers of British policy did not know, they should have known that the rulers of the fifty million Arabic-speaking peoples thinly spotting an area three-quarters the size of Europe have neither the traditions nor the ideals of constitutional European society; that their emotions and conduct are focused on considerations of personality and power, not of law and contract. In their ideals and methods they are the psychological kinsmen of the Nazis and the Fascists, whose *führerprinzip* is natural to their ways, in which there is little distinction between wish and fact or lusts and achievements, while democracy is only a word. So with "Arab nationalism," especially in Palestine. To the landlords and functionaries who are the nationalist leaders, the intent of the Four Freedoms and the Atlantic charter or the Social and Economic Organization of the United Nations is something entirely beyond comprehension. National freedom and self-determination have meant and continue to mean only their continued exploitation of the fellah without let or hindrance. Thus, Hitler could proclaim himself "Descendant of the Prophet" with less violence to the sheikh and effendi mentality than Wauchope's attempt to set up representative government. Mussolini could announce himself as "Protector of Islam" with greater assurance of sympathy than MacDonald could get for exploiting the Jew on behalf of the effendi. English gold might outweigh Axis gold, but Axis religion was more acceptable and convincing than democratic faith, and Axis might proved that Axis religion could be nothing but right.

Hence the British appeasement at the cost of British treasure, British prestige, British authority and British honor as well as Jewish rights, was foredoomed to failure. Hajj Amin al Husaini's war of espionage and sabotage was soon waged with Axis money, Axis arms and Axis guidance among all the privileged classes in the Arab-speaking world — in Egypt, in Sa'udi Arabia, in Yemen, in Syria, in Iraq. Ibn Sa'ud sent Khalid ibn al Walid to Hitler in 1939. Hajj Amin al Husaini's rebellion in Palestine was repeated in Iraq and took a month to quell. The Egyptians did not even undertake to defend their country when it was invaded, and the Inspector General of the Egyptian army tried to carry its military secrets to the enemy. Wendell Willkie called attention to the Egyptian overlords' "fundamental indifference which side wins." As Franco's falangists joined Nazis against the Russians, so Arab effendis joined the Nazis against the Allies in Tunis.

For the Jewish community of Palestine, as for Jews everywhere in the world, there could be no question as to where their allegiance belonged. It belongs with every power that fights for those liberties which are the most important part of what Thomas Jefferson called "the inherent and inalienable rights of man." The British knew that however deep and just the Jewish grievance, the Jews were committed by the logic of the situation to oppose the Axis with everything they had. So, while Jewry gave blood and sweat and tears to the war, the High Commissioner proceeded to implement the MacDonald White Paper. He undertook to prevent the buying and selling of land and to exclude Jews from Palestine while admitting non-Palestinian Arabs. He was instructed to do this because, as MacDonald sardonically argued, it would help strengthen the position of the British in Trans-jordan, Iraq, Sa'udi-Arabia, Egypt and India. The record shows that MacDonald was either woefully ignorant of the social realities in those areas or that he was saying what he knew to be false.

While the masters of those lands identified themselves and their subjects with the Axis, the 500,000 Jews of Palestine sent more than 25,000 of their youth into the Allied armies in the Near East. They eagerly put their hospitals, their doctors, nurses and technicians at the disposal of the armed forces. Although their available manpower was thus much reduced, they expanded greatly the production of foodstuffs, and they launched upon a program of manufacture of those war materials whose import was cut off by the closing of the Mediterranean. They contributed about $2,000,000 to a war fund for the soldiers of the British army.

On the record, the masters of the Arabic-speaking peoples have from the beginning aligned themselves in faith and in deed with the enemies of democracy. On the record, they oppose the Jewish Homeland because that is a center of democratic influence making for higher wages and a higher standard of living for the fellah whom his masters wish to continue to exploit as it pleases them. On the record, what is called Arab nationalism is a cynical Arab fascism exploiting the poverty, the ignorance and the religious fanaticism of the enslaved multitudes of the Arabic-speaking peoples of the Near East and Egypt. On the record the manipulators of this nationalism deserve from the democracies exactly what Quisling, Laval, Pétain and other betrayers of the people received.

Now, the Near East has been cleared of the Axis. The overt fascist danger has been liquidated. The Arabic-speaking peoples are freed from the menace of destruction and death which overtook every Jew on the continent of Europe as Hitler revenged himself on them for his defeats. Not without the consent and the cooperation of the British power, fascist-minded, Arabic-speaking rulers are now making public announcements of their claims and demands, calling conferences to formulate their proposals for a postwar Near East, proposals which threaten destruction and death to the Jewish Homeland, and contain not a friendly thought for the exploited fellahin of the Arabic-speaking lands. In Palestine, in 1943, the Mandatory Power had announced a program of reconstruction and appointed a Reconstruction Commissioner, to work according to the directives of the MacDonald White Paper, thus further implementing the breach of faith which Winston Churchill denounced. In the United States, agents of Near Eastern Arab wealth and power and American oil interests have launched a propaganda of lies about Arab democracy, and rumors have been thick that certain officials of the State Department were not unsympathetic to the White Paper. Now the British Government has succeeded

Hitler and his companions of evil in making of the Jewish people more than ever "the personification of the issues involved in this world struggle between right and wrong, between good and evil."

What do the Jews ask?

Only that an honest effort shall *now* be made to save as many as possible of their brethren from the abominations of living death and the obscenities of cruel destruction which the Nazis perpetrate upon them. Only that Palestine, the one place of refuge guaranteed them by solemn treaty and the law of nations, shall not be shut to them. Only that, when the war ends, they may at long last live their lives in freedom and earn their bread in peace wherever they may be among the peoples of the earth, or in the Homeland of the Jews, the Homeland which they have earned a hundredfold with their blood and treasure and sweat and tears. Two-thirds of that Homeland, because of the jitters of the Mandatory, has to this day been suffered to continue as the uninhabited wasteland that it has been these hundreds of years. The Jews ask only the assurance that their lawful right to redeem it, established by treaty and covenant, will be respected and that their laborious sacrifices will not be frustrated and nullified. They ask that, as democrats who not only fight and die for democracy but live their lives out building it up, the democratic community of their building shall not be sold into bondage to the fascist Arab, nor reduced to a mere tool of the imperialist Briton. This the Jews ask. This the Anglo-American Commission of Inquiry unanimously recommended. This, British power refuse, and, refusing the Jews, betrays the Arab multitudes.

For fundamentally, the cause of the Jewish Homeland and the cause of the Arab fellah are one cause. I do not think that Zionist spokesmen have made this fact sufficiently clear to the enlightened opinion of the world. What the Amir Feisal, spokesman for the Arabic-speaking peoples, declared in 1918, and repeated many times thereafter, remains true in principle and, had the manipulators of British power so willed it, could have been developed in practice to the great gain of the plain people in the Arabic-speaking countries. Agreeing with the proposals of the Zionist leaders as laid before the Peace Conference, Feisal declared: "We are working together for a revived and reformed Near East, and our two movements complement one another. The Jewish movement is national and not imperialist. There is room in Syria for us both. Indeed, I think that neither can be an actual success without the other." And for the common Arab man in Palestine this has in fact been the case. From the record, the inference is inevitable that a basic anti-Semitism, reinforced by the traditional attitude of the British military and civil functionaries toward the plain people of the colonies, undertook to frustrate the complementation and pooling of interests. Believing apparently that the prosperity of the plain people of Arabian lands would endanger the Empire, those carriers of the white man's burden gave a sanction of their own to the Imperial German-Turkish propaganda of the First World War. For this British honor, the British reputation for fair-dealing, British prestige and the safety of the British Empire have since paid heavily.

If, however, the British Empire is an assemblage of crown colonies managed by Colonels Blimp, it is also an association of free commonwealths with a mother country whose government is a political democracy. Canada, Australia, New Zealand are on the whole freer, juster societies than the mother country. To the peoples and governments of these commonwealths, the Jews must bring a full knowledge of the record and an appeal for the fair play due them.

A part of that record is the fact that at no time in the course of its shameful faithbreaking did it go unchallenged. So long as they did not hold power, the Labor and Liberal parties have consistently opposed and denounced it and continue to do so, as have the wiser and braver heads among the honorable Conservatives, such as Winston Churchill. They knew then that "representative government" can go with authoritarian feudalism. They knew then that democracy is effective as political form only when it is first a way of life. They knew then, that the safety of the Empire is not assured by the security of its privileged classes but by the freedom and well-being of its plain people. For them the Four Freedoms were then not a slogan but a program, and the equal freedom of Jews to live and grow in Palestine, and thereby to help the life and growth of the Palestinian fellah, was necessarily a part of that program.

Imperial government, in view of such honorable Englishmen, is required loyally to enforce the law and to guard the peace which condition the freedom and well-being of the plain people. It is conceivable that the condition could receive great strength if British rule in Palestine should do there, as an essential part of its announced program of reconstruction, what the Japanese had done in Burma and Malaya and the Dutch Indies and what cannot be safely undone now that the Japanese are driven out of those lands — break up the great estates and divide them into freeholds among the fellahin who cultivate them. Let the Nazi Grand Mufti and his fellow "notables" at last restore to the common man a little of what they have sweated and swindled out of him. Let the government, as a part of its program of reconstruction, also open up as we Americans did by means of the Homestead Act the great stretches of uninhabited and uncultivated land of which both Palestine and Transjordan consist. This would explode the myth of the "landless" Arab, and nail the lie that there is any real connection between such landlessness and Jewish settlement. To date, the fact that "landless" Arabs are numerous in Transjordan from which Jews are excluded, and very few in Palestine where Jews have built up the economy, has not had much influence in nailing that lie. The fact is that no Arab need at any time be landless who does not prefer to be.

If the common Arab multiplied and prospered with the growth of the democratic Jewish community under the obstructive condition of the past, how much greater could be the expansion of his life and freedom if the obstruction were removed. This, the Jews must continue, so far as in their power lies, to make clear to the Arabs individually and collectively, by practice and precept, through every possible form of communication and participation. They must never relax their efforts to fulfil their part of the conception of the community of interest formulated by Feisal. Then, if they fail, the guilt is not theirs.

During the generation of struggle to preserve and to implement their lawful right in Palestine, the Jews themselves divided on means and methods. One party came to the same conclusion as the late Josiah Wedgwood, and sought a solution of the problem in the proposal that the British should give up the mandate. This was an idea favored also by Mussolini — he had not yet needed to resort to the Nazi's sadist use of the Jews as scapegoat — and he fancied his fascist corporative state as Britain's successor. The idea was welcomed also by a number of Englishmen who regarded the situation in Palestine as a distasteful impasse. But the character of imperial communications — although obsolescent as lifeline in wartime — is such that it is not presently conceivable that the British can withdraw from the strategic sea and air approaches to the Suez Canal. But it *is* conceivable that the British might want to change the conditions of their overlordship from those of a mandate to something else.

These conditions, insofar as they are not the preponderant power of British arms, are established by treaties constituting international law, whose enforcement was subject to inspection and judgment by the

League of Nations through its Mandates Commission. The decencies require that the British should make answer to the United Nations when that calls, as it must, for an accounting of the discharge of the task entrusted to them as Mandatory. It might then be possible, under the law of nations, to demand either the loyal execution of the terms of the Mandate and thence a "new deal" in Palestine, or the surrender of the Mandate.

Among the suggested alternatives to the latter have been the conversion of Palestine into a Crown Colony or into one more Dominion in the British Commonwealth of Nations. Should the British, however, prefer, as they assuredly will not, for reasons of empire, to withdraw entirely from the government of Palestine, then the government, and the enforcement of the law of nations on which it is based, could be extrusted to an International Commission of our new world organization. Commissioners should be citizens of the smaller countries such as Switzerland, the Scandinavian countries, Czechoslovakia, or Mexico, countries not involved in the complications of empire, outside the struggles of power politics, and aware through bitter experience of the tragic menace in both. Adequate sanctions should be provided to guarantee the effectiveness of the Commission's tutelage, until such a time as the Jewish Homeland and the Arab peoples can be admitted to the family of nations as self-governing societies all of whose institutions have been established in enduring forms of the democratic way of life.

The Jews must needs consider thoroughly and bring to the widest possible public discussion this and other alternatives to British rule in Palestine.

Nor should the Jewish people at any time be permitted to forget the ultimate and ever-present alternative pregnant in their tragic situation. This is that British power "for reasons of empire" will go the way it has hitherto gone, regardless of treaty obligations and the right of the powerless. It may hold that it is in Palestine to stay, and on its own terms. By concentrating, as it can, the force necessary to make the MacDonald White Paper effective, it may stop immigration, immobilize real estate transactions and thereby other economic enterprise, freeze the Jewish Homeland into a Palestine ghetto, that in the course of time must deteriorate into what the Jewry of Jerusalem's Old City had been before 1920, and worse.

The Jews then will find themselves compelled to choose between passive acquiescence in the strangulation of the Jewish Homeland or killing it and dying themselves by resisting the strangulation. For in the present stage of Jewish despair and of the development of Jewish Palestine, the alternative to growth is extinction. Should the British decide upon extinction — whether via the White Paper or the directer delivery of the Jews to the fascist Arab League, whose leaders would more than welcome such a classical insurance of their privileged status, — there is no escaping it. The Jews are a small and weak people who have rights but no power, and are the traditional scapegoat of the powerholders of the Christian world. The right they have is acknowledged, but it is an empty right, since they lack the might which, in the political economy of the world, gives rights their force and validity.

It must be obvious to everybody who believes in the dignity and worth of the human spirit, that the Jews, as self-respecting heirs of a great tradition, as present lovers and builders of freedom, will feel bound to accept only the martyrdom of resisting the strangulation. Confronting overwhelming power, they will mobilize whatever might they do have, alike more perfectly to build the Four Freedoms into the bone and marrow of their community and to fight for the integrity of its being with all their strength and all their will, to the last stone and the last man. The prisoners of the ghetto of Palestine will not acquit themselves less worthily than the prisoners of the ghetto of Warsaw, and when the last one is dead, the land that they have brought to life will have died with them and revert to the sand and swamp from which they had brought it up.

I cannot however think that the free and just men of Britain will endure that this shall come to pass.

I cannot think that the wise and brave statesmen of the British Commonwealth of Nations will fail to recognize today what Winston Churchill, then Secretary of State for War, recognized in 1920 — that a Jewish land on the banks of the Jordan which might comprise three or four million Jews, would "from every point of view be beneficial, and would be especially in harmony with the truest interests of the British Empire." I cannot but think that they will recognize that the assurance of this benefit and this harmony, which is the salvation also of a broken and crucified people that has no helper, is one among those "solemn but splendid duties which are the crown of victory," and which, Prime Minister Churchill declared on March 18, 1941, "the British Empire and the United States will share together." As Mr. R. H.

Crossman, friend of Mr. Attlee, member of the British-American Committee, replied to his friend the Prime Minister during the parliamentary debate on Palestine "in this action of the Government we are drifting into war. We are drifting first into war with the Jews, and after that into war with the Arabs."

"There is only one way I know of smashing a resistance movement and that is liberating it — smashing the conditions under which the movement has grown, giving the people the things for which they are willing to die."

I cannot think the decent people of the free world, who are this day still spending their blood and their strength on the fields and in the factories for the salvation of the human freedoms, will endure that anything else than such a Jewish homeland shall come out of this people's ordeal of suffering and death, to be their refuge and their restoration.

Is There a Jewish View of Life?

IS THERE a Jewish view of life?

Albert Einstein says that there isn't, "in the philosophic sense." He may be right. But also, he may be wrong. The question does not admit of a single, unambiguous answer.

For the Jews are an ancient people, and their history is long and varied. Their religion, Judaism, is not so old nor so varied as the history of its creators and adherents, yet its own life-history is marked with at least as many crises and alterations as the life-story of the Jewish people. And it could not be otherwise. For Judaism, like Hebraism, is an indefinite manifold. Its existence consists of the coming together and the moving apart of great numbers of diverse and contradictory items of thought, feeling and conduct. Each and every one of these items has a claim upon the consideration of any person endeavoring to establish what Judaism is or what Judaism is not.

But this claim is hardly ever honored. The definition which any citizen gives Judaism depends on his loves and hates, on his wishes and frustrations. Those cause him to react selectively to the entire shifting aggregate of which living Judaism is composed. They will lead him to affirm qualities which others deny, and deny qualities which others affirm.

To this rule, Einstein is no exception. In science, a specialist in astronomical mathematics; in human relations, a democrat, an internationalist and a pacifist, the loyalties and rebellions these terms imply determine in advance what items from the manifold of Judaism he will choose in order to make up an exclusive definition of "the Jewish view of life."

With Dr. Einstein's selection I have no quarrel. On the contrary, it is quite in harmony with the type of selection I myself make, as those well know who have read my works on this subject, especially my *Judaism at Bay*, where I have endeavored to show why some such view of Judaism may be held as peculiarly representative of the high place in the rise and fall of the Jewish tradition.

But demonstrating and establishing this definition call for the simultaneous recognition that there exist other opinions, other views of Jewish life, other and quite contrary definitions, each one of them an alternative demanding to be refuted and cast aside. Refuting them and casting them aside meant acknowledging that they had a place in the aggregate which is Judaism. Some of them include Maimonides and shut out Spinoza. Others include the Bible and exclude the *Siddur*. Some include the *Shulchan Arukh*, but exclude Maimonides, Spinoza, the *Siddur* and the Bible. Others combine them all with the *Shulchan Arukh*. Still others exclude the *Shulchan Arukh*, mutilate the *Siddur* and include a "mission of Israel" an "ethical monotheism" and at the same time glorify Maimonides and patronize Spinoza.

Who is right? Who is wrong? The answer does not depend on the intrinsic character of the definition nor on its historical correctness nor its religious sanctions. The answer depends entirely on its *consequences* to the strength, the enrichment of Jewish life.

Now in life, quite otherwise than in mathematics, consequences belong to an unpredictable future. They can not be established in advance. They are not foregone conclusions.

History, which can be written only by survivors in the struggle for life, is the judgment which the survivors pass upon both their struggle and their opponents'. Thus, Jewish history as written by Jews embodies the judgment of the victorious Elohist upon the defeated Yahwist, the victorious priest upon the defeated prophet, the victorious Pharisee upon the lost Sadducee, the persisting rabbi upon the transient dissenter, the effortful nationalist upon the sentimental religionist, and so on. Contemporary parties in Israel employ or reverse these judgments in order to rationalize their own ends and to justify their own struggles. For example, the very reverend Dr. Cyrus Adler, President of the Jewish Theological Seminary, President of Dropsie College, President of the American Jewish Committee, etc., etc., will put together and invoke one set of historic judgments to justify his mortuary policy and attitude in Jewish life. The less reverend Drs. Albert Einstein or Stephen Wise will invoke another set to justify their vital ones. Their compositions, their invocations, their demonstrations, their arguments are not revelations of the facts. Their compositions, their invocations, their demonstrations, and their arguments are only invidious uses, special applications of the facts. The facts themselves remain everlastingly neutral to all the causes that employ them, stubbornly elusive to all the meanings which are imposed on them.

We may get some inkling of the character and implications of the facts when the observer who studies them has no passionate concern about their use.

Thus, we may take it as being pretty close to the truth when George Foote Moore tells us, in his magnificent *Judaism*, that the Judaistic tradition owns no theology in the Christian or Greek sense of the term; that its dynamic essence was the rule of life or the system of observances which were finally codified in the *Shulchan Arukh* and were the same wherever in the wide world Jews could be found; but that "basic human relations are without measure or norm and left to the conscience and right feeling of the individual"; that they are *masur lalev*, committed to heart.

But Moore was writing of what has sometimes been called "normative Judaism." He had also made a selection. He paid attention to nothing outside of this traditional historic complex which the generations kept on reliving until the middle of the last century. He ignored the variant, the new, the heretical, which had arisen and struggled to establish itself within the complex. But he knew he did so, and he did not endeavor to have anyone take the part for the whole. A complete science of Jewry cannot ignore those things. A complete science must include everything that any Jew has ever identified as Jewish in life and quality. But Jews laboring in their struggle for a life and a living, are prevented from dealing with this all-inclusive total. The time and place and circumstances of their struggle, its passions and its ideals dispose them to seek one item and reject another, so that their passions may be gratified and their ideals realized.

Thus, it is Dr. Einstein's necessity and his right to select from the Jewish inheritance that which seems to him pertinent to his struggle and his ideals. His opponents have the same necessity and right to make their own selections. But both he and they would be wrong if they treated their selections as accounts of the entire Jewish reality, as descriptions of the historic content of Judaism and Hebraism. In the nature of the case, such selections can be nothing of the sort. First and last, they are personal and class valuations, special pleas made by means of data lifted thus out of their original contexts, and employed to express the feelings and to realize the ideals of those who have so lifted them. Judaism or Hebraism is not any one of them by itself. It is all of them together — and then some.

Is there, then, a Jewish view of life? No. There is not *a* Jewish view of life. There are Jewish *views* of life. The views are many. Life, with all its conflicts and antagonisms and hates, indeed through them, makes itself somehow one.

1938.

What Price "Jewish Living"?

I

MOST of what I read or hear about modern Jewish living seems to me sad and out of this world. Alongside of how people called Jews do in fact live wherever they live — say in New York's Bronx or Brownsville, its East or upper Broadway, its Hester Street or Park Avenue — either together or alone, the verbiage seems as tangent as it is plangent. Its esoteric nature becomes more telling when I think of persons, living and dead, who are classed together as Jews, and how different are their ways of life. Pick only people who have been in the public eye, pick them at random out of the cyclopedias and journals — men and women of mark such as Louis Brandeis and Julius Rosenwald, Abe Cahan and Adolph Ochs, Martin Buber and Morris Cohen, Max Nordau and Max Naumann, Kaufmann Kohler and Milton Steinberg, Henri Bergson, Edmund Husserl, Hermann Cohen, and Emile Meyerson, Solomon Schechter, Felix Adler, and the Lubavitcher rebbe, Judah Loeb Peretz and Jakob Wassermann, Joseph Fels and Jacob Billikopf. Join in your fancy Sigmund Freud, Harry Friedenwald and Barney Baruch, Albert Einstein, Benny Leonard, Benjamin Disraeli, and Benny Goodman; Fanny Brice and Edna Ferber and Henrietta Szold; Ahad Ha'am and George Gershwin and Jacob Gordin; Israel Zangwill, Leon Trotzky, and Judah P. Benjamin; Fanny Hurst and Hannah Solomon; Heinrich Heine, Sholem Asch, Sholem Aleichem; Samuel Gompers, Sidney Hillman, and Solomon Guggenheim; Karl Marx and the Marx Brothers. . . . These so scattered and diverse personages have all variously lived. That is, each has had to eat and drink and sleep and work and play and love and fight. Each got sick, got well; married, raised a family, made a home — or didn't; survived wars as soldier or civilian, joined many societies or few. Each probably went on journeys. Each spoke, read, or wrote some one of a variety of languages which had become the intimate voice of his needs and urges, his perceptions, demands and aversions, his fears and his hopes; had

Reprinted from *Judaism*, Vol. 1, No. 1, Jan. 1952.

become the sure voice of his beliefs and feelings and fantasies and reflections, articulating all the experiences of his day's round and his view of the matter and meaning of the human struggle and of his own part in it. Many had undergone schooling and attended college, *cheder*, or *yeshivah;* had worshipped in *shul* or temple or church. Our contempories had probably seen motion pictures as well as plays. Most had read poetry and novels and journals. All must at one time or another have played at cards or chess or more athletic games. All had probably given thought to death when some friend or relative died, and the remains were simply or ceremoniously buried or burned . . .

Well, most of the random list of men and women are themselves now among the dead; nor does anything in the record suggest that any of us the living can be denied the salvation of that ultimate Ingathering. All, whether it pleased them or not, are called Jews. What, now, from the days they were born to the day their remains are disposed of, qualifies their personal history as "Jewish living"?

Meditating the answers, I remind myself that every human's day, as it is lived waking and sleeping, is an indefinite streaming of countless trivialities; that the requirements of a job, or of some other succession of processes and products, draw items from the stream to fuse into composites which we remember only as singular, simple, stable, wholes; that they stick out upon the vague, unstill background of their streaming source, no longer its stuff, but its markers and pointers. I think: These wholes are what novelists note and probe and explore, what saints and sinners confess to, journalists report, and social scientists purport to define and account for. And if the day they impattern is a Jew's day, then, let him be Bontche Schweig or Jud Süss, let him make his home among other Jews or among Gentiles; it is in these wholes that he realizes "Jewish living."

There is, however, little evidence that agonizers over Jewish living are thinking about such specific psychosomatic actualities as compose the living of Jewish groups and individuals. Actualities are diverse and diversifying. All contain incommensurables. Alike in a personal existence or a group's history, some confront each other in irreconcilable conflict — the conflict is their life, and their Jewishness is the same as its mutual repulsions. Others are reciprocally indifferent. Others are aggressive and still others submissive. Others embody common ends set to conflicting means; still others common means seeking conflicting ends. Not many are so united in competition and cooperation as to be hopefully orchestrated to one another. Whatever orchestration they do in fact attain does not seem to be an action applying "the moral, ethical, and religious concepts [of Judaism] to contemporary problems." Neither the individuals and associations, whose relations provide the problems for the would-be reformers, nor the reformers themselves, yearning to resolve the problems by means of the concepts of Judaism, seem to share any consensus about what these concepts are or what using them is to accomplish. Indeed, it is not clear that any of the reformers aim at consensus and not at establishing their own doctrine and discipline as supreme in "Jewish living." It is not clear that they would forego the control of education and the open or secret censorship of the different, together with its suppression, its persecution, and its defamation, which have been in all history the devices for conforming a mobile multiplicity and variety into a single mode always and everywhere the same.

Now, as I see it, what is alive in Jewish living is manifest as multiplicity and variety, not as sameness. Change and multiplication are attributes of traditional Jewish modes no less than of untraditional ones. The dynamic which patterns them consists, most times, of interactions between parts within, and some times of spontaneous variations among them; consists continually of responses to forces from without. Since Christianism seized power in Europe, the outer forces get shape and purpose from the meaning given the idea "Jew" in Christian doctrine,[1] and its resonance in the religion of Mohammed. Their over-all effect was to make of Jews Christianism's untouchables, to erect a wall of separation around the Jewish being, a wall both visible and invisible, designed to shut Jews away from all material and mental communication with non-Jews. It did largely retard the movement of persons, things, and ideas from either to the other and render it both burdensome and hazardous. The democratic revolution breached this wall. The democratic idea, in transvaluing Christianism, transvalued also the Christian conception, "Jew." Affirming the brotherhood of man under "the laws of nature and of nature's God," the idea restored to the concept "Jew," the human meaning which follows from the idea's own humanist affirmation of the parity of the different and of the equal right of different individuals and groups, as different, to the freedom and abundance that their diverse natures need to live and grow on. The shape and direction given outer forces by the democratic idea was such as to encourage the free movement of thoughts, things, and

[1] For a recent exposition of the record, see Malcolm Hay, *The Foot of Pride.*

persons between the non-Jewish and the Jewish life-space. They were such as to unburden the Jews from the penalty laid upon them by Christendom for being Jews. They were such as to stimulate modifications by Christians in the Christian idea "Jew," itself.

To date, the effects of the democratic idea are still sharply circumscribed by the aggression of its deniers, and the indecision of its proponents. It is still far from having become the fighting faith that could release its power to enable men everywhere to grow toward equal liberty. The classical Christian definition of Jew persists either in its pristine form or as reshaped according to Communist, Nazi, Klanist, or Falangist dogma. These, in their characteristic ways, continue to disregard the inner diversities among the people called Jews, to declare each as the same with all, and to inflict upon all identical penalties for being Jews. The penalties range from the (by comparison) mild social and occupational discriminations they experience in relatively free societies, to the sadist excommunications, outlawings, expropriations, tortures, and mass-murders to which Jews have been treated in totalitarian dominions. In all, being thought a Jew and being condemned to degradation, suffering, and sorrow are variously synonymous.

Before the democratic revolution, this was the universal Jewish condition. The lifeways of Europe's ghettos then kept shaping themselves as defenses against life's acerbities, and endeavored to transvalue them into strengths. The transvaluations came to their high point in the thoughtways which both rationalized the lifeways and projected Otherwordly compensations for the Thisworldly condition. To the dogmatic Christian postulate that the Jews were a people first chosen, then rejected and cursed by God, the Jews opposed the proposition that they were God's permanently and only chosen people, scattered by Him among the nations of the earth that they might testify to His exclusive divinity and proclaim His commandments until the day when Messiah, son of David, shall lead them back to Zion. Then, as Zephaniah the prophet had last foreseen it, "many a people and mighty nation shall come to seek the Lord of hosts in Jerusalem and to propitiate the Lord. In those days, . . . ten men from nations of every language shall grasp the skirt of a single Jew, saying: 'We will go with you, for we have heard that God is with you.' " Both this world of illusion where the living die, and the other world of truth where the dead live were means toward the predestinate grand consummation when "the law shall go forth from Zion and the word of the Lord from Jerusalem."

This is the traditional consummation of "ethical monotheism." The countertraditional one identifies divine election with the mission of Israel and the mission of Israel with everlasting exile from Zion, thus transvaluing exile as punishment for sin into exile as evidence of divine favor, and contradicting both traditional Judaism and orthodox Christianism. The creation of the State of Israel is a challenge to all three.

Into the quite compact and durable configuration of Jewish ways and their institutions, the democratic idea penetrated like fire. In breaching the walls of separation between Jew and Gentile, it also breached the mores within the walls. Its effect upon them was the opposite of its intent. It did melt down the rigid boundaries of faith and form into fluid ones. It did vitalize traditional stasis into swift and sometimes sudden movement. But for the most part the movement was centrifugal. In one pattern it became Haskalah, in another Reform, in another assimilation, in another socialism, in another Zionism, each with its own singularities of doctrine and discipline. On occasion, it became a variable confluence of these different patterns. All of them could be characterized as secularization. But whatever name the movement went by, whatever its shape, tempo, and direction, its going was toward the common goal — so to reduce the social and cultural distance between Jew and non-Jew, so to replace with likeness one, some, or all aspects of Jewish unlikeness, so to liquidate difference into sameness, as to remove the burden laid upon Jewish existence and put in the place of the inequitable handicaps, intrinsic to living as Jew, the equality and freedom non-Jews were believed to enjoy.

The frame of mind is intelligible enough. Given the Jewish situation, what, at first, could freedom mean for Jews but flight from the situation? What could flight consist in, but the varied and varying changes in the economy of doctrines and disciplines which make up Jewish living? Changes in habits of speech and diet, in the forms of marriage and divorce, in modes of worship, in rites of initiation and burial, in modes of remembering the dead and educating the living? Changes in occupations, and in esthetic and intellectual pursuits? Changes mediated, above all, by an expanding alteration of the range and variety of contacts with Jewish and non-Jewish interests?

In the United States conspicuously, traditional communal establishments altered and diversified, while new structures, set to new functions, and making new demands upon the institutionally unaffiliated, were devised to meet new needs. Some were intended to retard or arrest movement, others to reverse it, others to diversify and speed it up. Certain traditional functions atrophied, and those responsible for them either lost their roles or devised variations on them. *Kelei kodesh* such as *rabbanim*, *shochetim*, *chazanim*, *mohalim*, *shamashim*, *dayanim*, and *melamedim*, entered into new relations with their employers, with one another, and with the residual Jewish population. *Kahal* itself became progressively more amorphous and impotent, its place being taken by an ever-growing number and variety of fluid voluntary associations. New categories of functionaries appeared, such as social workers, youth leaders, charity executives, money raisers, to form new hierarchical bureaucracies and to struggle for place, prestige, and power with the older ones. Occupational formations, similar to guilds or craft unions, developed as an aspect of the struggle both as insurers of common interests and as weapons of war.

The changes were, of course, forms and functions, goods and services, of "Jewish living." But the gradient on which they moved was one of recession from the fulness of the *terminus a quo*. In their persons and in their associations, more and more Jews became marginal people, without roots in the communion of their nativity and without power to take root in any other community. They made the impression of divided souls, yearning not to be Jews, unable at best to be anything else than amateur Gentiles. There was — there is — no way for them to delete for today whatever had been Jewish within their yesterday. At most, they could suppress it, but thereby they rendered it the dynamic of inner insecurity with all this involves. Nor were they permitted outwardly to live and move and have their being in equal liberty among non-Jews. They were always wary of anti-Semitism, which, breaking ever so often out of the chronic into the acute stage, kept pressing them back into the unwanted communion of the children of Israel.[2]

The process is a sustained and notable component of modern Jewish living, currently being called "Jewish self-hate." But "self-hate" is a misnomer. The hater and the hated are not one and the same. That which he hates he does not hate as Jewish, but as being inseparable from responsibilities, burdens, and disabilities which he cannot bear and knows to be unjust. He then identifies them with the Jewish *quale*.

[2] For recent specification of the process, see John Knight, *The Story of My Psychoanalysis*; Rudolph M. Lowenstein, *Christians and Jews*; Malcolm Hay, *The Foot of Pride;* J. P. Sartre, *Reflexions sur la Question Juive*; Isidor Chein and Jacob I. Hurwitz, *The Reactions of Jewish Boys to Various Aspects of Being Jews*. See also Sidney Hook's account, in his address to the fortieth annual meeting of the American Jewish Committee, of his polling students in philosophy on whether they would choose to become Jews: "No Jewish student ever wanted to be born Jewish."

But never with this *quale* as a trait of his own person, always as a trait of some other Jew's person. In his philosophy, it is regularly the *other* Jew, the *other* Jewish denomination, cult, or society, the *other* Jewish philanthropy, defense organization, *landsmanschaft*, educational establishment, political movement, or economic enterprise that is guilty of the ideas and behaviors by whose attribution the anti-Semite rationalizes his prejudices. The projection is a conspicuous trait of "defense" against anti-Semitism, and let me repeat, a persistent as well as pervasive datum of modern "Jewish living."

II

It is now more than a quarter of a century since I published in the *Menorah Journal*, a study calling attention, among other things, to the processes I have here referred to, to their dynamic, and to its implications for "Jewish living." I called this inquiry *Can Judaism Survive in the United States?*, and some years later reprinted it, with revisions, as Chapter XV of a group of essays regarding the relations between Judaism and modernity, under the general title, *Judaism at Bay*. Summing up the changes of the quarter of a century of Jewish living in America that the essays envisaged, I wrote:

> ... Judaism has been alienated from the Jewish people. Its upkeep is today the concern of a class above a certain income level, and by and large this class is concerned only to the point of supplying the cost of the plant and of the "spiritual leader" through whose professional expertness they may discharge their religious obligations ... They practice Judaism by proxy ... *Gabbaim* and *rabbanim* to the contrary notwithstanding, the Jewish way of life is no longer a religious way of life. Judaism is no longer identical with Jewishness, and Jewishness is no longer identical with Judaism. Jewishness — I prefer to say — Hebraism — is a focus of modernity. It is the Jewish way of life become necessarily secular, humanist, scientific, conditioned to the industrial economy, without having ceased to be livingly Jewish. Judaism will have to be reintegrated with this secular, cultural form of community which is Jewishness if Judaism is to survive.[3]

Since these lines were written, all mankind has lived in crises, one following another with no respite in sight. Humanity has suffered contamination and assault from communist, fascist, nazi, and falangist

[3] *Judaism at Bay*, pp. 4, 25.

totalitarianism. It has been a perplexed witness of the betrayal unto death of the League of Nations. It has lived through a global economic depression. It has been wilfully plunged into a second world war among whose results are: loosening the British colonial empire into a commonwealth of equal nations whose new members threaten each other with war; upsetting British rule in the Near East; thrusting upon the United States the British preeminence among free nations; Communist Russia's advancing its bid for global empire by every means of force and fraud. Mankind has seen this taking place within the framework of a United Nations Organization designed to keep peace just and secure, and against the background of the organization's Universal Declaration of Human Rights, intended to reaffirm, now specifically and in detail, the propositions of the democratic idea which as the American Declaration of Independence, embody the fighting faith of the democratic revolution. These are the propositions of the global religion, of that one faith which the entire miscellany of mankind can freely share. They are the battle cry of freedom wherever humans confront totalitarian tyranny, in hot war or in cold. Nevertheless, the peoples of the world saw such a tyranny impose dominion on its neighbors little and big, west and east. They also saw its bid for rule contained in a few places. They also saw the Jewish communities of Palestine counter mortal danger by reconstituting themselves as the State of Israel and betting their survival on strengthening and protection from peoples committed to the democratic idea.

Their wager is, of course, ultimately every Jew's wager. Jews, throughout this entire period, had been chosen by the foes of human liberty everywhere to be its avatars and scapegoats. Antisemitism has been inherent to totalitarianism, whatever its mode, whoever its missioners. In the concentration camps of the Nazis and the Communists, in the Warsaw Ghetto, on the Moslem deserts and on Palestinian sands, and in the refugee camps of their reluctant helpers, upward of six millions of them had been martyred to death in obscenity and abomination. Alone the free Jews of the United States of America had stood, as they continue to stand, sure redeemers to these lost; and the Americans had redirected their entire communal economy in order to meet the exigency, distorting the structures and dislocating the functions of its institutions, straining its strategy, tactic, and logistic to a point where liabilities are being felt to outbalance moral and cultural as well as material assets. Now American Jews are again in one of their recurrent moods of self-scrutiny and self-justification. "Research" is on the march among them. Communal organizations and establishment are having themselves surveyed and appraised by "social scientists." The self-acquiescent "Jewish intelligentzia" are joined by marginal intellectuals of Jewish parentage sweating to reconsider what "Jew" means to them and to redefine their personal relations with that meaning in terms of faith, works, and "belongingness"; in terms, if you prefer, of responsibility for future "Jewish living," hence for Jewish survival.

"Research" is being grasped as a magic key opening the door of the Jewish future in the United States. Is it survival or extinction? "Survival" is currently a term as blindly controversial as in former years "congress," "assembly," used to be. There are Judaists who see no good in survival and turn to research yearning that it guarantee the so desirable release from the burdens of being a Jew by some infallible demonstration that, even though Jewishness, like the old soldier in the song, will never die, it will nevertheless, like General MacArthur in public life, fade away. There are the "survivalists" who count on research to reveal for them an eternal ground for "Jewish living" and an unalterable structure to erect on this ground. Both are turning to social science for the gratification of their irreconcilable desires. They want a scientifically established "law" to guarantee that what they fear but cannot themselves overcome will perish, and what they desire but cannot themselves produce, will nevertheless surely come to them. If their frame of reference is also theological, they shape the ends for Providence and count on its omnipotence to shape the means for them.

Thus all are able with a good conscience to rationalize habitual inertia and drift, to avoid both choice between alternative actions and orchestration of them, and to call it relying on the laws of nature or of nature's God. They are apt entirely to disregard the fact, if they know it at all, that their reliance on "research" is itself a choice of means to an end they desire, and that it is first and last an act of faith on which they bet their Jewish lives. They refuse to heed that no known suicide has ever relied on fate or fortune to kill him, but must needs have taken his own life according to plan by the ways and means he has himself devised and implemented. They ignore the event that survival is an ongoing struggle against both fate and fortune, that it has no guarantees, that its means and ends commingle, and that it requires of the struggler resistance to natural necessity and divine providence, perhaps even more than reliance on them. Resistance and reliance, when and how and with what to direct them, are equally choices, and are either blind risks, or reasoned, calculated ones. Such risks are the primal subject matter of the social sciences, and their statistical averages and "laws" are but their composites or summations. Let those choices change, and change in the "laws" will also occur.

Thus, neither the survival nor the extinction of the American Jewish community follows inevitably from the nature of things or the will of God. Nor does it follow inevitably from the community's own will to survive or perish. But that will is a necessary precondition, whereas the others are contingent. On the record, man's arts and sciences are his achievements in altering the nature of things; his religions, with their prayers and sacrifices, their confessions and vows, and all their other rites and ceremonies, are his methods of influencing the will of God. The human enterprise is the knowledgeable determination to harness fate and fortune to the service of human living, either unto life more abundant or unto death. Jewish living is one unit of this ongoing determination, with its own singular compenetrations of works and ways. Where this determination holds, it can invoke "research" to explore the matter, means, and methods best suited to living on and growing, or to dying out. Jewish living *in toto* will consist in using those for both ends or choosing them for either.

The question *Can Judaism survive?* was, and continues, an inquiry into matter, means, and methods. Most answers to it seem to me to have been devised either as special pleas for, or as rationalizations of, some one Judaist interest abstracted from the aggregation of diversified ones which together give the words "Jewish" and "Jew" their concrete meanings. Occasionally, findings appear which derive from an objective conspectus of the aggregation.

Within the past year, there has come to my attention one such conspectus which seems to me of prime importance. It is called *Agenda for American Jews*. Its author is Eli Ginzberg, a Jewish intellectual of the younger generation, who, continuing integrally a Jew, has orchestrated his cultural heritage of Jewishness with his occupational interests as an economic scientist of unusual eminence in his chosen field. Reading his *Agenda* was a heartening experience to a mind confirmed in its disillusions by more than a quarter of a century of disappointing scientific observations and organizational effort. While I find myself doubtful of Professor Ginzberg's hierarchy of values in American Jewish living, I find myself giving ready assent to his appraisals of its leaderships, its matters, its means, and its methods; to the techniques of inquiry wherewith he comes to his judgments, and to his suggestions how Jewish living in our country might be brought to greater excellence and abundance.

In the twenty-five years since the publication of *Can Judaism Survive in the United States?*, the problems and prospects there called attention to have reached a critical poignancy. English has become basic to the vernacular of the American Jewish community. Secularization has moved apace and brought new institutions and functions. The rabbinate has itself secularized, and Zionist and other secular organizations draw leaders from its members. The number and variety of Jews by profession, clerical and secular, has increased, and with them the alienation of Judaism from the Jewish generality, who in many ways pay more for its upkeep but care less, leaving decisions regarding the collection and disbursement of funds, and the ends for which they are disbursed, to fewer and fewer people, mostly professional Jews who care less and less about Jewish living as a whole. And so on. When read in the context of the global crises of which World War I was the first, Eli Ginzberg's *Agenda* makes me feel, *plus ça change, plus c'est la même chose.*

I feel the same regarding what must needs be done to redirect and repattern this change-without-alternation, to turn it into a truly *different* process. It is to educate and reeducate. As I have reiterated so often, survival is education, education is survival; and Eli Ginzberg's *Agenda* brings another, and a very significant, confirmation of this truism. The first and last condition of Jewish living is Jewish education, but education with its entire economy of plant, program, and personnel so reorganized as to enable the growing child and grown adult to accept the realities of the Jewish condition "in good cheer and without illusion," to enable him to live positively and freely as Jew, "vindicating the integrity of his Jewish being according to the democratic rule of equal liberty for all men, proclaiming that liberty 'to all the land all the inhabitants thereof.' "[4]

That is, if the Jewish education of American Jews is to succeed in preserving Jewish living, it would need to be transformed from indoctrination in a Judaism only, confined to religious schools and ending for non-professional Jews at *Bar Mitzvah*. It would need to be shaped as an inquiry into the values of the entire Jewish cultural heritage, and as such extended to the secular educational establishments. It would need everywhere to be fused with the humanities of the liberal educa-

[4] See *Jewish Education and the Future of the American Jewish Community.* Publication No. 12, American Association for Jewish Education.

tion. It would need to convert the records of the Jewish past from inert remembrances to contemplate into living roots of future growth owning a dynamic relevancy to the dangers, the problems, and the tasks wherewith the changes and chances of the time confront the Jewish present. In this way, it might convert the centrifugal trends of contemporary Jewish living into an expanding spiral process in which a cultural enclave and its leaders endeavor, with some success, to realize, *e pluribus unum*, the democratic idea in American Jewishness.

But who will risk the hazards from such a revolution in Jewish education to the *status quo* of Jewish living?

Book II: Appraisals and Memories

Julian William Mack

NO ONE person's recollection, no, nor the rememberings of the thousands whose lives touched the life of Julian Mack can ever approach the substance of this high-minded being or recapture the zest for life or the impartiality that was yet all sympathy, which his presence communicated. From 1911 to 1941 — during thirty years — a judge on the federal bench, by universal consent one of the most hard-working, competent and judicious of his time, he refused to imprison the citizen in the judge, or to let the bench contain him. He went all out for applied democracy in one or another field of community life, and there is hardly a major social cause which he did not illumine and defend.

Born in San Francisco, grown to manhood in Cincinnati, he came to be known and cherished not only in those cities and in Chicago, New York, Washington and Miami, but at Versailles and Vienna and Geneva and Jerusalem. His life and works are an outstanding testimony of how freedom releases Jewish men and women to put distinguished powers and unyielding democratic faith into the common hopper of the American way. His story provides an outstanding testimony of how championing equal liberty for the Jew as Jew inevitably calls for strengthening the civil liberties of every human being.

The outer man, especially to those who knew Judge Mack only from his public appearances, gave little hint of the inner spirit. A stocky figure, short and stout, whose voice had in later years become a little plaintive and a little strident, he gave, in his prime, an impression of great drive and vital force. Chief Justice Stone of the United States Supreme Court writes of him as he was in 1917: "He had great intellectual vigor and physical endurance. He was a practical-minded man because of his long experience in the courts. He had a good understanding of human psychology. While he was not a man who could be easily taken in he was a man of broad sympathies, high intelligence, and was tolerant enough to know that men could be conscientious in beliefs which were wholly foreign to his own."

Reprinted from *American Jewish Year Book*, Vol. 46, 1944.

Later, and especially as deafness crept on him, he appeared inattentive, often seeming unconscionably to sleep while others were talking. But when it came to dealing with issues, people who counted on these appearances speedily found how deceitful they could be. There are many who have reason to remember his outraged roar, and more who still must smile as they recall the mighty ring of his laughter.

It is true, however, that Judge Mack exercised upon people seeing or hearing him for the first time no particular attraction. It is in working with him that they came to admire him and to love him. In fact, his smile, his zest, his directness, his outgivingness, made him one of the most engaging persons in public life. Not by any means an orator, Julian Mack held his own at meetings, in conferences, in committees, against masters of all the rhetorical tricks, by the extraordinary lucidity of his thinking, the sincerity and force of his spirit. People discovered in a very brief time how rare were their fellow-worker's qualities of mind and heart. Justice Stone, who served with him on President Wilson's Board of Inquiry on Conscientious Objectors writes, "his vitality and vigor, his lively interest in everything worth thinking about, and his enlightened intelligence, attracted me from the start." No one else could find the dynamic core of a problem so rapidly, or expound its nature and implications so simply, with such unusual clearness, and with such justice and sympathetic understanding for the aspects to which he himself might be even passionately opposed. Because of this generosity of spirit — which is commoner in science than in law, and is indeed the point of departure of scientific method — one felt Judge Mack's own views to be all the more compelling. "The great thing about him," writes his colleague, Judge Augustus N. Hand, "was his ability to act with judgment and detachment whenever he had to resolve contested issues in the courts, plus a kindly nature and warm heart that were guided by a high intelligence." These are the attributes of a just mind, that held it to be a part of the sportsmanship of equity, which legal justice achieves at its best, never to leave anyone in doubt what its own views were. Though he presided over many great trials — notably those of Harry M. Daugherty, Attorney-General during the Harding Administration, and Col. Thomas W. Miller, Alien Property Custodian of World War I — often involving much prejudice and the most complicated and confusing issues, he never once lost the confidence of the Bar and the respect and affection of the Bench. In 1935, when he sat in the case of the reorganization of the notorious Associated Gas and Electric

Company, counsel for this holding concern took recourse to charging Julian Mack, then the oldest Federal judge in the District, with personal bias and prejudice. Judge Mack at once asked Robert P. Patterson, the youngest judge, to pass on the charges, volunteering, although the final decision was lawfully his own, to accept Patterson's opinion without question. Patterson found the charges false. He declared in his memorandum: "There is not a trace of bias or prejudice against the debtor in any of these [Judge Mack's] remarks or rulings." And he dismissed the complaint as "frivolous."

And what else, indeed, could the finding have been? Unfairness was as foreign as obscurity to the spirit of Julian Mack. Whether in the practice of the law, the judgment of the court, or the handling of the problems that came before him from the various causes of human freedom and human welfare that he served, he invariably transformed the most confused and obfuscated matter into an issue simple and clear, with its scientific and ethical bearings unmistakable. Judge Mack was roused to anger not so much by ill-will as by deceit and hypocrisy. These traits would bring forth his roars; on these he would crack down with righteous indignation. Nevertheless his bitterest foes and most obstinate opponents — and his life-long service to the welfare and freedom of men brought him many such — fought him without hatred and opposed him without rancor. Insisting that he was wrong, they also conceded that he was generous and just. Many who opposed him, as I can testify, loved him.

The causes to which Julian Mack gave himself are extraordinarily varied, yet extraordinarily consistent with one another. His career as a liberal jurist and a democratic humanist began with the conventional participation of a not poor young man blessed with a social conscience in the charities of Chicago, the city where he chose to make his home. He had gone from his high school in Cincinnati straight to the Harvard Law School, and thence, with his degree of Bachelor of Laws and the Parker Fellowship, to the Universities of Berlin and Leipzig, where he spent three years in graduate study. When he returned in 1890, at the age of twenty-four, he took his bar examinations and settled in Chicago to practice law. Within five years he became professor of law at Northwestern University, and seven years after was called to the University of Chicago. In the interim he had married that lovely and charming lady, Jessie Fox of Cincinnati; he had been drawn into the service of the Jewish Charities of Chicago; he had begun to concern himself with the social implications of the law and the moral implications of municipal government. In 1903 he served for five months on Chicago's Civil Service Commission. The same year he ran for election to a Circuit Court judgeship of Cook County, Illinois. He was elected, and thus began a career on the bench of city, state and nation which stopped only with his retirement in 1941.

Judge Mack served on the Circuit Court of Cook County for eight years. Three of those, from 1904 to 1907, he presided over Chicago's famous Juvenile Court. Although Denver, with her unique Ben Lindsey, disputes its priority, this Court and the law which established it signalize a new vision and a new method in the treatment of youthful "lawbreakers" which, initiated by Americans in Chicago, have been imitated and emulated everywhere in the world. They owe their creation to the persistent social conscience of the members of the Chicago Woman's Club. Lawyers and clergymen everywhere were well aware that the population of the prisons of the world averaged under twenty-five years of age. With the common law, they were content to attribute this fact to original sin, to natural perversity, to deficiency in grace; they looked upon the "juvenile delinquent" with a hostile eye; they were concerned not to save but to punish. So, in England, children of nine used to be hanged.

But the members of the Woman's Club looked at the matter differently. They felt that family, church, and State as well, might be accessories to delinquency before the event, and the State could at least supplement and, where necessary, replace, family and church where they fail. From 1883 the clubwomen labored to implement this view, drawing to their side jurists and politicians, until at last the Juvenile Court Law was framed and passed and the Court established. Judges were assigned to it annually from among the members of the Cook County Circuit Court, on the basis, in part at least, of the recommendation of the Club's Juvenile Court Committee. Among the male collaborators of these humane and wise women had been Julian Mack. He had served on the Circuit Court but a year, when they asked him to go on the Juvenile Court. "He gave up," says Mrs. Joseph T. Bowen, describing the early days of the Juvenile Court in 1927, "most complicated and interesting legal work in order that he might help with the Children's Court. How well he did it! We look back with the greatest pleasure and thrill of pride not only to his decisions but to the educational campaign which he conducted at the time in order that the Juvenile Court might be interpreted to the people." As an instrument of this campaign he organized the Juvenile Protective Association which in 1907 absorbed the Woman's Club Committee. He helped secure the collaboration with the Court, of Chicago's Psychopathic Institute. He insisted that for the community the question regarding any child is not *Are you guilty?* but *How and why have you become as you are? What can best be done to save you from ever being brought to court at all?*

Among Judge Mack's fellow-workers were Jane Addams, Julia C. Lathrop, Graham Taylor, Florence Kelley and other Chicagoans who were laboring to make the democratic way more effective in the Middle West. Mack held court on Halsted Street, across the way from Hull House. The children who came before him were never charged with crime. He handled them as wards of the state under his powers of Chancery. He brought to bear on their problems the then new working conceptions of the psychologist and psychiatrist, of public health, of probation and of education. The precedents he set endure, and, in spite of much obstruction, his tradition grows.

Concurrently, he carried his share of the load as a member of the Jewish community of Chicago. A member of Temple Sinai, thinking of Jewish life and Judaism in the manner of its brilliant and temperamental rabbi, Emil G. Hirsch, he listened to sermons and served on charitable boards. Nor was his service limited to the Jewish needy and the Jewish immigrant. It embraced the entire miscellany which was pouring into Chicago. He helped Grace Abbott found her Immigrants' Protective League and was its president while he remained in Chicago, and at its call always thereafter. To the newly-formed profession of social worker his leadership was encouragement and inspiration; in 1912 he was chosen president of their National Conference. He was a founder of the Survey Associates, a board member since their organization, and the board's chairman from 1927 to his death.

But perforce the Jewish tragedy in Europe gave the Jewish need there and at home a special urgency. Jewish social workers formed a National Conference of their own and made Judge Mack president of that. In 1906, when, following the pogroms of Kishineff and Gomel, the American Jewish Committee was organized, Judge Mack was among the original fifty, who elected him vice president, and thus a member of the Executive Committee of fifteen. During the twelve years of his membership on the Executive Committee, he participated in all the major undertakings of the Committee,— its legal and educational work in favor of a liberal immigration policy, its diplomatic efforts to safeguard equal rights for all Americans regardless of race or religion; its studies of the general condition of the emancipation. He resigned from the Committee over issues of the internal organization of the American Jewish Community and the philosophy of Jewish relationships. It was as a spokesman for the American Jewish Congress that he labored to coordinate the Committee's endeavors at the Peace Conference to achieve "full rights for the Jews in all lands and the abrogation of all laws discriminating against them" with Zionist purpose and Diaspora aspiration.

For his studies of the situation of Jews tended to shift the direction of his thought, and gradually to bring his sense of the meaning of democracy away from the prevailing assimilationist conception of Reform Judaism to that of the older, somewhat overlaid one of which Thomas Jefferson was the avatar. This led him to Zionism. The symbolic expression for the Judaist conception was "the melting pot"; the symbolic expression for the Jeffersonian one became "cultural pluralism." As was the case with Louis Brandeis, it was no more Julian Mack's sympathy for the Jews as pitiful victims of injustice than his revision of his idea of democracy that made a Zionist of him as well. "We ask no more" he told the peacemakers at Versailles, "for the Jew than we do for any one else." Nor, as a loyal servant of freedom and justice, would he stop with less. To his conversion to Zionism, Judge Mack's intimate friendship with that brave, romantic Palestinian man of science, Aaron Aaronsohn, was an important contributing factor. Others were the ideas and example of Louis Brandeis, discussion with Felix Frankfurter.

When Julian Mack felt persuaded that instead of a "melting pot," democracy consists in the cooperative union of the different on equal terms, that a civilization is free and fertile in the degree that differences are neither suppressed nor penalized, but liberated, encouraged, and pooled in the common enterprise of the community, whether local or world-wide, he gave himself to Zionism with the same unflinching, lucid and realistic devotion as to his other causes. He labored to apply the rule of *e pluribus unum* to the special tasks which, with the coming of the first World War, fell to the Jews of America, as Jews. During a considerable part of that period as a member of the governing bodies of both the American Jewish Committee and the Zionist Organization of America, he labored to harmonize the two sects of opposed interests. After the Balfour Declaration, because of his efforts (seconded by those of Louis Marshall and Cyrus Adler), the American Jewish Committee called a special meeting and adopted a resolution welcoming the opportunity "to aid in the realization of the British Declaration, under such protectorate or suzerainty as the Peace Congress may determine, and, to that end, to cooperate with those who, attracted by religious or historic associations, shall seek to establish in Palestine a center for Judaism, for the stimulation of our faith, for the pursuit and development of literature, science and art in a Jewish environment, and for the rehabilitation of the land." In the first American Jewish Congress which resulted at last from the efforts at unity, Judge Mack sat as President of the Zionist Organization. A unanimous vote designated him as one of the seven spokesmen of American Jewry at Versailles. There he was the choice for chairman of the *Comité des Délégations Juives auprès de la Conférence de la Paix*, and Louis Marshall took over when Judge Mack had to return to the United States.

At home, during World War I, his duties had been diverse and heavy. Early in 1917 he had been called by the Committee on Labor of the Council for National Defense to serve as chairman of the Section on Compensation and Insurance for Soldiers, Sailors and Their Dependents. The plans he worked out and put in force were a new departure in the method of paying the state's debt to the citizen soldier, fundamentally more democratic, more regardful of the self-respect of the citizen, than the pension system. In face of potential industrial disputes dangerous to the war effort, he was also assigned the task of umpire for the War Labor Board, as an arbitrator acceptable to workers and managements alike. But his most signal task was his assignment, with Dean (now Chief Justice) Harlan F. Stone and Major Richard C. Stoddard, to review the treatment of conscientious objectors. For this there had been no provision in the Articles of War, the Draft Act, or by other Congressional action. The treatment of the conscientious objector had, until then, often been characterized by blindness, brutality and stupidity. President Wilson's directive to the Board, of which he appointed Judge Mack chairman, was to sift the bona fide objectors from the dubious ones, and to assign them to non-combatant service if they would accept it, or to "farm-furlough." The tasks called for visits to all the Army camps, for interviewing all the objectors, and distinguishing the true from the untrue. Later, the President requested the Board to examine the court martial records of all conscientious objectors who had been tried. "For the successful prosecution of this important work," writes Justice Stone, "there could not have been a more ideal man than Judge Mack." The principles developed and the policies initiated by the Board, experimental and tentative as they were, represented a concrete step forward in the realization of the "democracy" men were then fighting to make the world safe for. Without its precedent, the decenter mode of dealing with the few conscientious objectors of World War II could hardly have been implemented.

Julian Mack's labors in the Zionist Organization, in the American Jewish Congress, and in all the other societies, philanthropic, educational and humanistic, which drew upon his generous spirit, were neither stopped or diminished by this public service. He made time for everything and did five men's work. In 1918, when it became clear to him that the democratic unity he sought for American Jewry was unattainable, he had resigned from the Executive of the American Jewish Committee, but had retained his membership in the general body. With Louis Brandeis, Nathan Straus, Felix Frankfurter, Stephen Wise, he was the dynamic center of the American Zionist enterprise. He became the organization's president during its critical years. He was still its president when, in 1921, "the Mack-Brandeis group" resigned in a body from the executive of the Zionist Organization of America over a fundamental issue of *method* in developing the National Home in Palestine under the terms of the Balfour Declaration. Taking as its directive Louis Brandeis' statement of 1920—"the whole of politics is to proceed efficiently in the building up of Palestine"—this group, led by Judge Mack, proceeded to the formation of the Palestine Development Council, the Palestine Cooperative Company, the Palestine Endowment Funds. He gave great sympathy and understanding to the second American Jewish Congress after it was formed. He was Honorary President of the World Jewish Congress from its organization to the day of his death.

Judge Mack's service on the Chicago Juvenile Court had brought home to him the central import of the problems of education. They remained one of his deepest concerns the rest of his life. When, for his fiftieth birthday, his friends insisted on making him a special gift, and he finally agreed, he asked that it consist of a fund on which he might draw for loans or stipends to able but needy students working their way through college. It is a fund that ought to be kept up in his memory. The philosophy of education that had come out of his thinking and doing on this subject was the progressive one identified with John Dewey, and it governed his attitudes and actions whether as a Trustee of the Hebrew University in Jerusalem, as staunch supporter of the New School for Social Research from the very first, as a founder and later Chairman of the Board of the Jewish Institute of Religion, or as a thrice-chosen member of the Board of Overseers at Harvard College. To this last post, it is significant that he was twice nominated on petition circulated by the members of the Harvard Liberal Club,— first in 1927 and again in 1937. In 1927 he got a majority of the votes cast and the largest vote of any candidate. In 1937 Charles Francis Adams and George Peabody Gardner, Jr., polled not many more votes. Julian Mack's service to the University in the capacity as Overseer was varied. He was on the Visiting Committee for the Law School, the Germanic Museum, the German Department, and the Semitic Department. He helped largely in the establishment of the Kuno Francke professorship in Germanic Art and Culture, and the Nathan Littauer Professorship in Jewish Literature and Philosophy. But to Harvard liberals his most significant service to their Alma Mater lay in the stand he took in 1922 against President A. Lawrence Lowell's proposal to set up a *numerus clausus* for Jewish students. Without his sharp intervention, this expression of snobism and prejudice might have won out by default.

Perhaps the most characteristic, the most expressive fact of Julian Mack's conception of education is the one Palestinian institution to which he expressly gave his name. This is the Julian W. Mack School and Workshops in Jerusalem. It owes its birth, its growth, and its survival to Judge Mack who, in 1920, arranged that an American educator bring to the service of the children of Jerusalem what was most functionally democratic in the American theory and practice of education. The school was first known as "The School of the Parents' Education Association." It was a cooperative undertaking which brought together Jewish children of all classes, sects and origins, and sought, by adapting progressive methods of education to the vital needs of Palestine, to unify their diversity into a free, harmonious Palestinian Jewish type. It employed what Henrietta Szold describes as "an ethical method of acquiring knowledge," and the hope and wish of the school's principal, of Judge Mack, and of the people who joined him in its support was to extend its type of service to all the underprivileged and marginal children of Jewish Palestine. It was seventeen years before this could be undertaken in Jerusalem alone, and when it was, Julian Mack gave it his name, and the Julian W. Mack School and Workshops in Palestine stand as the unique symbol of his first and most lasting interest in education.

Take the record of Julian Mack's achievement as a lawyer and a judge, take the tale of his services as a democrat, a public servant, a humanitarian, a Jew and a humanist, and you have a record large enough for half a dozen lives, not only one. Yet throughout the days of his maturity Julian Mack was not a well man. With the most discriminating taste in food and drink, with a knowledgeable zest unusual even in a gourmet, he had to follow a diabetic's regimen, and once or twice suffered illnesses that brought him close to death. Nobody would have known it from him. His life was, through its long last illness, right up to its contracted last moment, one brave, willing affirmation. He took what he had to take, and he stood up, without flinching, saying *Yes* to life. Thinking of him, one thinks of the words of another great Jew, Baruch Spinoza: "A free man thinks of nothing less than death, and his wisdom is not a meditation upon death but upon life." Julian Mack was a free man.

The Faith of Louis D. Brandeis

LOUIS BRANDEIS was a very small boy in Louisville, Kentucky, the year that Abraham Lincoln warned his fellow citizens of the State of Illinois that slavery enslaves the slave-owner. "Familiarize yourself with the chains of bondage," the President-to-be said, "and you prepare your own limbs to wear them. Accustomed to trample on the rights of others, you have lost the genius of your own independence and become fit subjects of the first cunning tyrant who rises among you."

I cannot say that the Jewish boy who grew up into the mature American, whose look and whose speech kept reminding the nation of Lincoln, ever read these words of the Liberator's, although it is unlikely that he would have missed them. But I can say that the life and labors of Louis Brandeis embodied the vision these words communicate and the vigilance they enjoin.

The vision is that men are united in an equal liberty; that the genius of each man's independence is secure for that man only as it is secure for all other men. The vigilance is against the menace to that equal liberty from the human disposition toward invidious distinctions and special privilege. Let the front of freedom be broken by the entry of either at any point whatsoever, and both the soul and the body of freedom are threatened. The life-story of Louis Brandeis is yet to be written. The records which have been available are neither as complete nor as authoritative as they will be, and what is based on them is naturally subject to revision. But as they stand today they show this vision and this vigilance as an ideal of life purposefully chosen and undeviatingly held to. They do not figure as unconscious habits spontaneously formed of reflexes conditioned to the ways of living and thinking in the abolitionist, liberal household where Louis Brandeis grew up; they do not come out of automatic consequences of the matter and method of his early schooling, nor of the ethics of the legal profession as taught at the Harvard Law School or as practiced by the brethren of the bar whether in Boston or anywhere else in the land.

No; as I read the record, Louis Brandeis' self-dedication to freedom

Reprinted from a pamphlet published by Hadassah, N. Y., 1943.

was an act of deliberate choice, breathing the spirit of religious conversion. His career began like that of any other bright, ambitious young lawyer; his practice, because of his extraordinary abilities, far outdistanced his competitors'; the firm which he headed in Boston, where he chose to live and work, soon did the most important business of the Massachusetts bar. It brought them great wealth, and the record shows the young, prospering Brandeis going in the ways of the prosperous Bostonian; member of a boat club, a polo club, secretary of the Boston Art Club.

There was also, however, another Boston than the Boston of big banks and big corporations, the Boston of bondholders and coupon-clippers, whose accomplishments and culture rested upon an unsuspected foundation of financial oppression and industrial mismanagement, whose crash Brandeis early foresaw and repeatedly foretold. There was the Boston of the Abolitionist tradition, the Boston of the free, critical, non-conformist intelligence of which this young lawyer's friend, Oliver Wendell Holmes, Jr., was the most powerful incarnation at the Massachusetts bar. In that Boston lived and moved the person and spirit of Emerson, of William Lloyd Garrison, of Henry Demarest Lloyd, of William James. From that Boston, the rising young corporation lawyer learned about the multitudes of the little people whom the corporations rule or crush; about the struggles of the little people to establish and maintain their equal liberty by means of trade unions, cooperative societies, the public regulation and control of big business; about the dynamic role, in the life of each and in the general welfare of all, of the liberties guaranteed by the Bill of Rights, in so far as those could be practically implemented and enforced.

Confronted by a Choice

During many years, the corporation lawyer, made also by the problems of his clients into an expert of accountancy and an efficiency engineer, conformed to the forms of professional behavior prevailing at the bar, considering alone the legal import of his cases and turning the law to the best advantage of his clients, be its social and moral consequences what they may. Such public services as he happened to render — and they were many — figured much like a banker's philanthropies, rather acts of grace than of justice, issues of generosity, not works of righteousness. But slowly, during the third decade of Louis Brandeis' life, the alternatives were shaping to a momentous option in his heart. The time came when he could not refrain from making his choice. It was the time of Homestead Riots. He was preparing to lecture on the common law, and he found the law inadequate to that tragic reality. He threw the lectures away. He made his choice between legalism and morality, human rights and property rights, the liberties of the many and the privileges of the few. Its moral is expressed in an anecdote that an old client reports. The client asked his lawyer to pass on a contract which his firm was making with its employees. Brandeis pointed to a clause likely to mislead and injure the employees. The client retorted: "Whose welfare are you hired to represent, mine or my employees'?" "Will your welfare," Brandeis answered, "be promoted by swindling your fellowmen who are trusting you?" The client got the point and has since been a leader in the employer movement toward justice and democracy in business.

With Alice Brandeis as his sustaining comrade by his side, Louis Brandeis made his choice. That choice is the center of being of the warrior for freedom whom our generation has known and reverenced as Louis Dembitz Brandeis. It is the initiation of his faith, the final establishment of the spacious nobility, the simplicity, even the austerity, of his way of life; the combination of curiosity with patience, of deference to social facts against legal fictions — so much more in the spirit of scientific inquiry than legal disputation — of his way with the law. "In the past," he said, "the courts have reached their decisions largely deductively from preconceived notions and prejudices. The method I have tried to employ in arguing cases before them has been inductive reasoning from the facts." Following his choice, Mr. Brandeis' very considerable private fortune became to him a public trust, and all his income, save for the minimum he and Mrs. Brandeis required for their highly simplified plain living, went back to the service of the plain and simple people. With his death the capital has also gone to that service. "I have only one life," he once told an interviewer, "and it's short enough. Why waste it on things that I don't want most? And I don't want property or money most. I want to be free." "Property," he said elsewhere, "is only a means. It has been a frequent error of our courts that they have made the means an end."

To the businessmen, his one-time clients, to the attorneys, their hirelings, Brandeis' choice was a challenge and a threat. Since it raised uncomfortable questions about their privileges and profits, they took it for "a betrayal of his class." Much of their former world turned against Louis and Alice Brandeis. Louis was making the public interest his private duty; he was assuming the brief for the little men in the litigations of private business and the disputations of national affairs. When his sense of duty required that he should condemn an action he himself had taken, he condemned it. Where it required that he should fight an organization he himself had set up or a technique he himself had devised, he fought them.

Thus, when it became clear to him that however legal the leasing system of the monopolistic United Shoe Machinery Company might be, it was immoral and iniquitous, he resigned as counsel for that company, and after a certain time took the brief of an association of competing small manufacturers against the trust. Long before, in 1897, he told the members of the Senate Ways and Means Committee holding hearings in Washington on the extortionate Dingley Tariff, that he had come there "to represent those who form a larger part of the people of this country than any who have found representation here."

That declaration defined Brandeis' subsequent career as attorney and as citizen. Whether in his battles for the people's interest over charters to public service corporations in Boston, over railroad rates to shippers in Washington, over the stealing of the public domain in the Northwest, over savings bank insurance in Massachusetts, over the rigging of bank accountancy in Washington, over monopolistic incompetency of railroads in New England, over the exploitation of women in Oregon, he was representing the little people — the helpless, the unlearned, the unorganized people, who else would remain forever unrepresented.

Often, the enemy, unable to meet him fairly and without favor on their very own field, afraid to let the issue between him and them come to decision on its merits, resorted to the vilest methods of "abusing the plaintiff's attorney." Since his record was impeccable, they employed whisperings and insinuations. Once they hired Elbert Hubbard for their own ends. But Brandeis kept his watch and held to his vision disdaining to reply, undistracted from his chosen task, jealous for the genius of the plain American's own independence. The nation began to know him as "the People's Attorney."

The Fight Against Him

It is because he *was* in spirit and in truth the People's Attorney that Woodrow Wilson nominated him to be the Attorney General of the United States, and those who preferred that the United States should be without such an advocate were able to prevent his confirmation to that post. It was because he *was* the People's Attorney that Woodrow Wilson thereupon named him to a seat in the Supreme Court, and those who preferred that interpretations of our fundamental law by the nation's highest court — did not Mr. Chief Justice Hughes once bear witness that the Constitution is what the judges say it is? — should not be contaminated by the judgments of such man, determined to prevent his appointment, too.

During six months the great employers of legal talent and their employees fought the nomination by all the means, regardless of honor, that they could gather up. Brandeis' Jewish origins were invoked against him. It was doubted if "the Oriental mind could successfully interpret a system of law which was the product of Occidental minds." From every quarter the privileged ganged up on his reputation — his opponents, besides all the former presidents of the American Bar Association, included ex-President Taft, Elihu Root, Joseph Choate, Senator Borah, President Lowell of Harvard. They only stopped when Oscar Underwood threatened to bare their own records to the Senate. Said *The New York World*: "His public services have won him the hearty detestation of certain powerful corporations and financial interests. They hate him not merely because he is a radical, but because he is enormously able and efficient. To them it is indecent that a lawyer with such extraordinary ability should wantonly and deliberately use his talent to promote the social welfare of the American people when he might command princely fees in the service of privilege." Later Taft — and even Borah — apologized to Brandeis. But Lowell, whose immorality is defined by his contribution to the judicial murder of Sacco and Vanzetti (Sacco's wife and children received asylum in the Brandeis home in Dedham during the patriotic struggle to prevent that crime) remained true to his ethical standards.

The Supreme Court had counted many able, many profound lawyers in its changing membership. It had even counted justices who were deeply concerned about justice and liberty as well as legality — indeed, Oliver Wendell Holmes, Jr., was an associate justice when Brandeis was finally enrolled among the nine. But never before or since had a lawyer been appointed who was acclaimed as the Attorney for the People and because he so served the people.

In explaining the nomination to the Senate, Woodrow Wilson wrote:

"Many charges have been made against Mr. Brandeis; the report of your subcommittee has already made it plain to you and to the country at large how unfounded those charges were . . . I myself looked into them three years ago when I desired to make Mr. Brandeis a member of my Cabinet, and found that they proceeded for the most part from those who hated Mr. Brandeis because he had refused to be serviceable to them in the promotion of their own selfish interests and from those whom they had prejudiced and misled. The propaganda in this matter has been very extraordinary and very distressing to those who love fairness and value the dignity of the great professions . . ."

"I cannot speak too highly of his impartial, impersonal, orderly and constructive mind, his rare analytical powers, his deep human sympathy, his profound acquaintance with the historical roots of our institutions and insight into their spirit, or of the many evidences he has given of being imbued, to the very heart, with our American ideals of justice and equality of opportunity: of his knowledge of modern economic conditions and the way they bear upon the masses of the people, or of his genius in getting persons to unite in common and harmonious action and look with frank and kindly eyes into each other's minds, who had before been heated minds, who had before been heated antagonists."

"Holmes and Brandeis dissenting" soon became a phrase of our liberal heritage. The difference of temper in the two partners is signalized by Holmes' comment after a discussion of the issues of liberty raised by the California "criminal syndicalism" statute, on which he and Brandeis joined in a ringing dissent. "I'm afraid," Holmes said, "Brandeis has the crusading spirit. He talks like one of those upward-and-onward fellows." But how Holmes really felt about Brandeis, and how deep was the harmony of insight and aspiration of the two men are revealed by Justice Holmes' remarks in his foreword to the volume of essays published on the occasion of Louis Brandeis' seventy-fifth birthday. "He always has had the happy word that lifts up one's heart. It came from knowledge, experience and courage and the high way in which he always has taken life." . . . "Whenever he left my house [this was before Brandeis' appointment to the bench] I was likely to say to my wife, 'There goes a really good man.' I think that the world would now agree with me in adding what the years have proved 'and a really great judge'."

The Right to be Let Alone

Every justice of the Supreme Court is by the necessities of his task not only the expositor of the nation's fundamental law, but the re-maker of its import and direction. He is an *official* philosopher of American life; his decisions, because of their enduring practical force, have a social significance far beyond the deliverances even of presidents and cabinet members. As Brandeis knew, and as he was ever warning his brethren, it is the easiest and simplest thing in the world to erect prejudices into principles, and a vigilance against one's own unrecognized propensities is as imperative as a vigilance against others'. On one thing, however, he had come to a certainty beyond all doubt — that the enduring American task, nay the enduring human task, was to preserve to each man "the genius of his own independence."

So far as I can see, Mr. Brandeis' judgments, all his opinions regarding human nature and human relations, whether in business, in government or anywhere else among the institutions of the nation, were growths of this soil and corollaries of an interest partly philanthropic and humane. He continued a Zionist the more because of his irreducible democratic humanism, because he came to apply the conceptions of the Declaration of Independence, which were among the postulates of his faith, to all sorts of human associations and groupings of individuals, as well as to individuals,— to the little societies, the unprivileged and the miserable, as well as to the great and powerful.

He had told the United States Commission on Industrial Relations, in the course of testimony concerning industrial unrest which covers 150 pages of the Commission's report, "We must bear in mind all the time that however much we may desire material improvement and must desire it for the comfort of the individual, that the United States is a democracy, and that we must have, above all things, men. It is the development of manhood to which any industrial and social system should be directed. We Americans are committed not only to social justice in the sense of avoiding things which bring suffering and harm, like unjust distribution of wealth; but we are committed primarily to democracy. The social justice for which we are striving is an incident of our democracy, not the main end. It is rather the result of democracy — perhaps its finest expression — but its rests upon democracy, which implies the rule by the people. And therefore the end for which we must strive is the attainment of rule by the people, and that involves industrial democracy as well as political democracy."

Louis Brandeis reaffirmed this expression of his faith in many of his famous decisions. I cite, however, only the much-quoted sentences of one of the greatest of his dissents: "The makers of the Constitution undertook to secure conditions favorable to the pursuit of happiness. They recognized the significance of man's spiritual nature, of his feelings and of his intellect. They knew that only a part of the pain, pleasure and satisfactions of life are to be found in material things. They sought to protect Americans in their beliefs, their thoughts, their emotions and their sensations. They conferred, as against the Government, the right to be let alone — the most comprehensive of rights and the right most valued by civilized men."

And he affirmed for the Jews but no more and no less than for the Czechs or the Jugoslavs, the Poles or the Arabs, and all the other little and oppressed peoples of the world, the equal right to be let alone.

His realization of bigness as a curse sprang from this same root. "Size," he held, "brings monopoly instead of competition; size submerges the talents of millions of people, and the wealth of the nation is gauged by the capacity of great numbers and not by the few." Jefferson, it is well known, had the same feeling about bigness. Its philosophical expression is notable in William James, the philosopher of Brandeis' generation: "As for me," James wrote to a friend in 1897 "my bed is made. I am against bigness and greatness in all their forms, and with the invisible molecular moral forces that work from individual to individual, stealing in through the crannies of the world like so many soft rootlets, or like the capillary oozing of water, and yet rending the hardest monuments of man's pride, if you give them time. The bigger the unit you deal with, the hollower, the more brutal, the more mendacious is the life displayed. So I am against all big organizations as such, national ones first and foremost; against all big successes and big results; and in favor of the eternal forces of truth which always work in the individual and immediately unsuccessful way, under-dogs always, till history comes, after they are long dead, and puts them on the top."

Brandeis' sense of the possibilities of the under-dogs, of the possibilities in the insights, initiatives, and powers of the alternatives to the dominating organizations and their ways, underlay his deep and practical sympathy with the organization of liberty in cooperative societies both of consumers and producers, as Jewish Palestine so well knows. It governed his attitude toward the monopolistic limitation of the just initiative of the little man which he made clear in his condemnation of the National Industrial Recoverty Act, and in his approval of the Florida chain store tax. He regarded all such limitations as inimical alike to the genius of each man's individuality and to the general welfare.

In his dissent from the majority regarding the tax on chain stores, he wrote: "There is a widespread belief that the existing unemployment is the result, in large part, of the gross inequality in the distribution of wealth and income . . . individual initiative and effort are being paralyzed, creative power impaired and human happiness lessened; that the true prosperity of our past came not from big business, but through the courage, the energy and the resourcefulness of small men; that only by releasing from corporate control the faculties of the unknown many, only by reopening to them the opportunities for leadership, can confidence in our future be restored, and the existing misery overcome; and that only through participation by the many in the responsibilities and determination of business, can Americans secure the moral and intellectual development which is essential to the maintenance of liberty."

Brandeis and Holmes: Freedom Comes First

And, of course, what was basic in the political economy of American life was absolutely indispensable in the spiritual economy, of which the Bill of Rights is more especially the guardian. With Holmes he stood out as the Court's great champion of spiritual freedom, of the freedom of the press, of speech, of conscience and of association; with Holmes he insisted on equal liberty for faiths and opinions which he deeply rejected, as well as for those that he deeply approved. So he joined with Holmes in another great dissent which vindicated the eligibility to citizenship of persons so deeply convinced of the evil of war as to be unwilling to fight in one. Holmes regarded such a faith as fantastic "but," he wrote, and Brandeis underwrote it, "if there is any principle of the Constitution that more imperatively calls for attachment than any other, it is the principle of free thought—

not free thought for those who agree with us but freedom for the thought that we hate . . ." Brandeis knew, I think, more deeply, more ultimately than Holmes that the genius of all men's independence can only be strengthened by the exercise of that independence, and he regarded this genius as the essence of the American tradition.

"Those who won our independence by revolution," Brandeis wrote for himself and Holmes in that noble dissent against confirming the conviction of Anita Whitney for criminal syndicalism in California, "were not cowards. They did not fear political change. They did not exalt order at the cost of liberty. To courageous, self-reliant men, with confidence in the power of free and fearless reasoning applied through the processes of popular government, no danger flowing from speech can be deemed clear and present unless the incidence of the evil apprehended is so imminent that it may befall before there is opportunity for free discussion.

"If there be time to expose through discussion the falsehood and fallacies, to avert the evil by the process of education, the remedy to be applied is more speech, not enforced silence. Only an emergency can justify supression. Such must be the rule if authority is to be reconciled with freedom. Such, in my opinion is the command of the Constitution. It is therefore always open to Americans to challenge a law abridging free speech and assembly by showing that there was no emergency justifying it."

The American Root of Brandeis' Zionism

I have already indicated that Brandeis came to his ultimate conception of Zionism from that invincible humanism of his, from his fighting faith in freedom, his certainty beyond all doubt that the propositions of the Declaration of Independence are valid for all the families of mankind. Regarding Zionism too, he vindicated faith, as was his wont, by "inductive reasoning from the facts."

After his appointment to the Supreme Court Mr. Brandeis' writings consisted exclusively of his judicial decisions, the best of them being, as we have seen, his dissents. His friends and disciples have, however, assembled several collections of his utterances made before he gave up action on the field for judgment on the bench. Those consist of occasional pieces — lectures, speeches, arguments — each addressed to the analysis, elucidation or solution of some immediate and particular problem which confronted the author in his professional capacity.

All of them, occasional pieces and judicial decisions alike, are communications, fitted to time and place and circumstances, of their author's democratic faith. But so far as I know, in only one piece are that faith and its philosophy expressed as such without the limitations of a particular business-like need or special professional occasion.

"True Americanism"

This piece was a speech made on July 4th, 1915. The municipal authorities of Boston had invited Mr. Louis Brandeis, "the people's lawyer" to give the Fourth of July oration of that year. It was an exciting and anxious time. Europe was coming to the end of its first year of the Great War. The American nation, whose strict neutrality had been announced by President Wilson, was being invaded by propagandists for both sides, the Allies and the Central Powers. Demands so diverse and confusing were being made upon American citizens that it seemed desirable to the authorities to reaffirm what it means to be an American and what the true, the living import of Americanism was. Especially was this Fourth of July to be celebrated as an Americanization Day, an Americanization Day not only for newcomers but for natives. All needed to rediscover the ideals which are the soul of their country and the institutions and economy which are the necessary body of its democracy. Mr. Brandeis chose for his theme "True Americanism."[1]

I well remember the hot afternoon in Faneuil Hall on which he delivered the oration, the stratified audience — Beacon Hill and the Back Bay; the West and the North Ends; South Boston and East Boston, distributed duly and in good order according to cash, caste and sect; the stuffy smell of the hall, the gaunt figure and the Lincoln-like mask of the orator, his vibrant voice and the measured yet passionate delivery, affirming anew, amid the perplexities and tensions of an ever-nearer world-war to make the world safe for democracy, the American faith in the Jeffersonian principles; the faith in the democracy which rests upon each man's right to be himself, the right to be different, and which itself consists in the cooperative union of the differents. Our democratic establishment, the People's Attorney

[1] It appears in the collection *Business — A Profession,* first published in 1914 and since having passed through four editions. The 4th edition was published by Hale, Cushman and Flint, Inc., of Boston in 1933. The address is the concluding essay in the book.

pointed out, is an arrangement of devices by which every individual is a ruler in his own right, and exercises this right through his vote. Being a ruler, the equipment required for ruling is a necessity of life. This necessity of life includes those rights which our Constitution guarantees — the right to life, liberty and the pursuit of happiness. Life, in this connection, means living, not existing; liberty, freedom in things industrial as well as political; happiness includes, among other things, that satisfaction which can come only through the full development and utilization of one's faculties.

These determine the American standard of living. Its establishment and upkeep require continuous education and industrial liberty. Such liberty calls for the cooperation of workers "as in trades unions"; and for the control of "overweening industrial power . . . Control and cooperation are both essential to industrial liberty." Nor control and cooperation alone. The industrial establishment of the nation has the duty and obligation to insure democracy by securing to the American citizen "also some degree of financial independence."

The devices whereby the citizen might provide himself with financial independence were those always advocated by Brandeis — conspicuously by the organization of cooperatives as well as labor-unions.[2]

Men to whom the principles of the Declaration of Independence are the articles of their abiding faith, and who labor to implement them in the changing conditions of the changing times are as men reborn. They have been Americanized in their hearts and are the true Americans.

[2] "Farmers, workingmen and clerks" he wrote in another connection, "are learning to use their little capital and their savings to help one another instead of turning over their money to the great bankers for safe keeping, and to be themselves exploited."

> "And may we not expect that when the Co-operative Movement develops in America, merchants and manufacturers will learn from farmers and workingmen how to help themselves by helping one another, and thus join in attaining the New Freedom for all?
>
> "When merchants and manufacturers learn this lesson, money kings will lose subjects, and swollen fortunes will shrink; but industries will flourish, because the faculties of men will be liberated and developed."

And in one of his dissenting opinions he declared many years later:

> "Americans seeking escape from corporate domination have open to them under the Constitution another form of social and economic control. It is more in keeping with our traditions and aspirations. They may prefer the way of Co-operation, which leads directly to the freedom and equality of opportunity which the Fourteenth Amendment aims to secure."

But now Brandeis carried the logic of the Declaration a step beyond where the Founding Fathers had left it. He extended the implementation of the American faith to still another dimension of the modern scene.

Jefferson and his contemporaries had above all confronted political tyranny and social caste. They sought to guarantee the individuality of the individual in and through an agricultural economy. The connection between the democratic way of life and the variety and character of various cultural associations of individuals in the making of a national being and a general civilization was not a problem for them and they gave it no attention. But in 1915 it had become a problem and Brandeis met it with the realism, the logic and the insight with which he had met less general problems of protecting the forgotten American from predacious corporations, tariff-writers, insurance companies. He extended the concept of "true Americanism" from individuals, to associations of individuals, to religious sects, churches, communities, nationalities, cultures. During a decade America had been described as a "melting pot" and "Americanization" was conceived to consist in the procedures by which individuals abandoned their different individualities, including their spiritual and cultural inheritances, and conformed to the requirements of the ruling classes of America with the same submission as the people conform to requirements of the ruling classes of Europe. In 1910 in an interview published in the December *Jewish Advocate*, Mr. Brandeis had set forth a democratic version of this conventional view. He warned that "habits of living, of thought which tend to keep alive difference of origin or to classify men according to their religious beliefs are inconsistent with the American idea of brotherhood and are disloyal."

But, between that time and the date of the Fourth of July address, there had come to his attention inductive studies of the character and condition of American culture and an exposition of the cultural forces that gave the American mind its dynamic competency, its flexibility and its richness. It was shown that each religious sect, each cultural group, is a fellowship with its own group-individuality and that this individuality orchestrates itself into the content of American civilization and plays its part in nourishing the spirit of American democracy and enriching the national achievement. Culturally, too, the American spirit expressed the principle of *e pluribus unum*: it has an extraordinarily vital and flexible unity consisting in the teamwork of the different, and embodied in the mutual respect and tolerance and interpretation which has come to be known as Cultural Pluralism.[3]

Mr. Brandeis preferred to call that which is basic in this Cultural Pluralism "inclusive brotherhood." Inclusive brotherhood, he declared in his exposition of True Americanism, is the "one feature in our ideals and practices which is peculiarly American." It has involved "equality of nationalities as well as equality of individuals. It recognizes racial equality as an essential of full human liberty and true brotherhood, and that racial equality is the complement of democracy. America has, therefore, given like welcome to all the peoples of Europe." "America has believed that we must not only give to the immigrant the best that we have, but must preserve for America the good that is in the immigrant and develop in him the best of which he is capable. America has believed that in differentiation, not in uniformity, lies the path of progress. It acted on this belief; it has advanced human happiness, and it has prospered."

Brandeis as Zionist

At the time Mr. Brandeis was expounding True Americanism to a Fourth of July audience in Faneuil Hall in Boston, he had been almost a year chairman of the Provisional Executive Committee for General Zionist Affairs. This Committee had been formed to take over the responsibilities of the World Zionist Organization when the First World War made it impossible for the organization's officials to function. Persuaded that here was a responsibility which the logic of democracy brought home to him in immediate and specific terms, Mr. Brandeis reluctantly assumed the chairmanship of the Committee. His practical impact on the Zionist movement, and through it on both the Jewish and non-Jewish conception of the Jewish problem is one of the most momentous in the modern history of the Jews. If his democratic faith brought Louis Brandeis to Zionism, he, more than any single individual of our time, brought democracy as an ideal and a program into the internal life of the Jewish communities of the world, particularly of the *Shtadlan*-dominated ones of the United States. He took a voluntary brief for all the Jewish people as

[3] Cf. "Democracy *versus* the Melting Pot" (first published in *The Nation*, February 18 and 25, 1915) in *Culture and Democracy in the United States*, by H. M. Kallen, New York, 1924.

he had taken his brief for all the plain people of our American economy. Zionism was one more obligation of the people's attorney dedicated to the security of the genius of each man's independence. He gave himself to its tasks as he did to every task he undertook. He studied with unflinching pains and thoroughness the history, the psychology, the leadership, the social, political and economic structure and conflicts of the Jewish community. He made himself expert on every aspect of the being of Palestine, and he made his argument for Zionism simply a statement of the insight into which this extraordinary knowledge precipitated. His leadership brought new blood and new standards and a new spirit into the Zionist movement in America, transforming it from an incident of ghetto aspiration into a democratizing and liberating power. It challenged prestige and prerogative in established interests in the American Jewish community. It disputed authority, it gave point and direction to the communal unrest of American Jewry of east and central European origin and background. The old issues were raised afresh and redebated in the new setting created by the great civil war in Europe in which the Jewish people of eastern Europe were at once made the victims of both the belligerents. Laymen as well as rabbis addressed themselves to the fray, and "universal Judaism" and "the mission of Israel" were fulminated against Zionism from a hundred pulpits.

In the course of the controversy, which was an incident to far more practical issues, Brandeis took occasion to state in unmistakable terms his understanding of the view of the American Zionists regarding the Jewish problem and its solution. He demonstrated more forcefully than it had ever been demonstrated before the futility of trying to evade the problem by definition. "Councils of rabbis," he wrote, "and others have undertaken at times to prescribe by definition that only those shall be deemed Jews who professedly adhere to the Orthodox or Reformed faith. But in the connection in which we are considering the term, it is not in the power of any single body of Jews — or indeed of all Jews collectively to establish the effective definition. The meaning of the word Jewish in the term Jewish Problem must be accepted as coextensive with the disabilities which it is our problem to remove. It is the non-Jews who create the disabilities and in so doing give definition to the term Jew. These disabilities extend substantially to all of Jewish blood. They do not end with a renunciation of faith, however sincere. They do not end with the elimination, however complete, of external Jewish mannerisms. The disabilities do not end ordinarily until the Jewish blood has been so thoroughly diluted by repeated intermarriages as to result in practically obliterating the Jew." That also persons of Jewish blood recognize this situation as a constant factor in their setting and react to it thus is shown furthermore in the behavior of even the most de-Judaized Jew. It is a behavior that acknowledges the claim of the group, and willy-nilly takes an interest in its fortunes. The Jewish problem, consequently, is the problem first of securing for the members of this group, distributively and collectively, "the same rights and opportunities enjoyed by non-Jews," and second, of securing to the world "the full contribution which Jews can make if unhampered by artificial limitations."

Liberalism, through which, at the beginning of the last century, it was hoped both these ends should be realized, had failed. Anti-Semitism remained, "universal and endemic," and the Jewish Problem, with all the diversities between the conditions that determine its manifestation, remains one and the same. The failure of liberalism is coincident with the oppression of nationality: "enlightened countries grant to the individual equality before the law; but they fail to recognize the equality of whole peoples or nationalities. We seek to protect as individuals those constituting a minority, but we fail to realize that protection cannot be complete unless group equality also is recognized." The Zionist movement is dedicated to the consummation of this recognition for the Jews. It is a movement essentially "to give the Jew more, not less, freedom; it aims to enable the Jews to exercise the same right now exercised by practically every people in the world — to live at their option either in the land of their fathers or in some other country; a right which Irish, Greek, Bulgarian, Serbian, or Belgian may now exercise as fully as Germans or English." The struggle for this right, involving as it must and does the recovery of group self-respect and the revitalization of the tradition and idealism of the fathers, is the chief, perhaps the only bulwark against the demoralization which Jews have, since the French Revolution, been undergoing in America and Europe both, and which yields an excuse to the anti-Semite. "The sole bulwark against demoralization is to develop in each new generation of Jews in America the sense of *noblesse oblige*, a sense which can be best developed by actively participating in some way in furthering the ideals of the Jewish renaissance; and this can be done effectively only through furthering the Zionist movement."

Zionism, thus, is in Brandeis' view, the salvation of the Jew who elects to build his life elsewhere than in Zion, no less than of the Jew who chooses the destiny of a Judaean. And not merely this. Zionism is demanded as well in the interest of all mankind. The satisfaction of these interests is possible only through organization. "Organize," Brandeis urged, "in the first place so that the world may have proof of the extent and intensity of our desire for liberty. Organize in the second place so that our resources may become known and be made available. But in mobilizing our forces it will not be for war. The whole world longs for the solution of the Jewish Problem. We have but to lead the way, and we may be sure of ample cooperation from non-Jews. In order to lead the way we need not arms, but men; men with those qualities for which Jews should be peculiarly fitted by reason of their religion and life, men of courage, of high intelligence, of faith and public spirit, of indomitable will and ready-self-sacrifice; men who will both think and do; who will devote high abilities to shaping our course and overcoming the many obstacles which must from time to time arise. Organization, thorough and complete, can alone develop such men and the necessary support."[4]

Within three years the Zionist organization was transformed from a loose federation of societies into an integrated association of individuals; from a somewhat timid ghetto enterprise seeking largesse for Palestine and aghast before a budget of $15,000 to a clear-sighted democratic undertaking, aiming at $3,000,000 for the year's work in hand; the democratic Congress movement developed to challenge and to conquer the old oligarchic control; the powerful support of the American interest was brought to bear on the negotiations regarding Jewish claims in Palestine and assured the making of the Balfour Declaration. Attention was assured by the powers to the claims of the Jews of Europe in a peace program aiming at a democratic implementation of the "principle of nationality." And the Zionists were committed to a certain method and form of organization which should, so far as possible, assure the new development of Jewish Palestine as a democratic economy and culture. The commitment is known as "the Pittsburgh Program." It is a body of seven "resolutions bearing

[4] *Zionism and World Politics*, Ch. XI, pp. 136–139. The entire chapter should be read for an account of the impact of Brandeis on Jewish thought and life in the United States.

on Palestinian policy" adopted by the Zionist Organization of America at its convention in Pittsburgh in July 1918. Mr. Brandeis had the decisive voice in their final formulation.[5]

THE PITTSBURGH PROGRAM

In 1897, the Resolutions declared, the first Zionist Congress at Basle defined the object of Zionism to be "the establishment of a publicly recognized and legally secured homeland for the Jewish people in Palestine. The recent Declaration of Great Britain, France, Italy and others of the allied democratic states have established this public recognition of the Jewish national home as an international fact.

"Therefore we desire to affirm anew the principles which have guided the Zionist Movement since its inception, and which were the foundations laid down by our lawgivers and prophets for the ancient Jewish state, and were the inspiration of the living Jewish law embodied in the traditions of two thousand years of exile.

"1st. Political and civil equality irrespective of race, sex, or faith, for all the inhabitants of the land.

"2nd. To insure in the Jewish national home in Palestine equality of opportunity, we favor a policy which with due regard to existing rights shall tend to establish the ownership and control of the land and of all natural resources, and of all public utilities by the whole people.

"3rd. All land, owned or controlled by the whole people, should be leased on such conditions as will insure the fullest opportunity for development and continuity of possession.

"4th. The cooperative principle should be applied as far as feasible in the organization of all agricultural, industrial, commercial and financial undertakings.

"5th. The fiscal policy shall be framed so as to protect the people from the evils of land speculation and from every other form of financial oppression.

"6th. The system of free public instruction which is to be established should embrace all grades and departments of education.

[5] For a detailed account of their development and its consequences see *Zionism and World Politics*, Ch. XIX "Vita Nuova?"

"7th. The medium of public instruction shall be Hebrew, the national language of the Jewish people."

This program might be said to sum up and to crystalize Louis Brandeis' fundamental faith — that the inwardness of the social enterprise is to secure to each man, to each association of men "the genius of his own independence." In all his subsequent relations with Zionism, Zionists and Palestine; in his differences perhaps even more than in his agreements, he was guided by this faith. It may be read in the famous Zeeland Memorandum, and in the character, the organization and the methods of the Palestinian enterprises which received his interest and support. In due course, the Palestine Development Council, the Palestine Cooperative Company, later unified into the Palestine Economic Corporation and this again differentiated into the Central Bank of Cooperative Institutions in Palestine, the Palestine Mortgage and Credit Bank, and the like, were conceived and developed by Mr. Brandeis' friends and followers as instruments for turning the Pittsburgh Program as nearly as possible from a program into an achievement. The bulk of his fortune he has left as a trust for this end. Ever Louis Brandeis' aim was, in Palestine as in America, a free society of free men, enhancing the genius of one another's independence.

The Launching of the American Jewish Congress

The American Jewish Congress is the first democratic consequence, in the Jewish communities of the United States, of this undiscouraged striving after a free society of free men enhancing the genius of one another's independence. The Jewish Problem being "universal and endemic," being the problem of every individual Jew and every group of Jews, it could be met, Mr. Brandeis pointed out, only as these individuals and groups freely and openly came together to take counsel and reach decisions. Inasmuch as such a direct coming together was not practically possible, it had to be achieved through representatives directly elected and responsible to their electors. The project to create a body of such representatives came from a group of devoted Jewish liberals and workingmen; but it was the insight and leadership of Brandeis which turned the project from a wishful aspiration into a dynamic actuality against the passionate opposition of Jewish interests both of the right and the left — the same interests which persist in opposing the Congress effort to democratize the Jewish communities of the United States today. After much heated argument and redundant negotiation, elections were held by every Jewish community in the land and the chosen delegates assembled as the first session of the American Jewish Congress. The date was December 15, 1918.

In the course of the long discussion preceding the creation of the Congress Mr. Brandeis, in three public statements,[6] developed the implications of "True Americanism" for the pattern of Jewish communities if they were to be developing modes of our American way of life. He made it clear that one could not have it both ways: that one could not accept democracy as a citizen of the country and reject or frustrate democracy as a member of one of its Jewish communites. "Among a free people," he declared, "the body which makes a decision must necessarily be democratic, since among the free people there can be no self-constituted body of men possessing the power to decide what the action of the people shall be."

For a leadership can be responsible only insofar as it is democratically chosen, and is by reason of such choice answerable to its electors. Such a responsible leadership can be created only through the methods of democracy. It can lead only by means of the democratic methods of free and open discussion and open decisions openly arrived at. "Secrecy," said Mr. Brandeis, "leads necessarily to suspicion and misrepresentation of Jewish purposes, and deprives us of non-Jewish support. We seek action in the open so that there will be no misunderstanding, either among our own people or among our fellow-citizens, as to our aims and methods. We need to avoid any real or seeming secrecy of action and of aim which might cause mistrust and which might breed prejudice. The needs which the Jewish people seek are so simple, and their difficulties are so well known, that no one has yet been able to set an adequate reason for holding a Jewish conference in secret."

Alone through an American Jewish Congress can these needs be served and these difficulties overcome responsibly, openly and effectively. "The Congress is indispensable if the end sought is to be attained." Every Jew, by employing democratic methods and participating directly in the processes whereby are reached decisions which

[6] Jewish Unity and the Congress, 1915; Jewish Rights and the Congress, 1916; A Call to the Educated Jew, 1916.

concern his position and destiny, can share in organizing on a nation-wide scale a united front against anti-Semitism, and in defense of the democratic way of life on which his freedom and security depend. Self-discipline, self-defence through democratic organization — this is the instrument of freedom for the Jew as Jew as well as for the Jew as man.

Such organization is the modern, as contrasted with the medieval, *shtadlanic* way of aiming at security and freedom. It is the only way appropriate to any Jew who is also a free citizen of a free country. And those Jews who enjoy the privilege of education and the spiritual advantages of the liberal arts and sciences have a special responsibility for the maintenance and the defense of the democratic principle alike in the Jewish communities and in the non-Jewish world. *Noblesse oblige!*

In due course the immediate tasks for which the Jews of America had united — some most unwillingly — in the Congress, were accomplished. The peace treaties which officially terminated the First World War became a part of the law of nations, and the Congress, according to agreement, was disbanded. But the situation which had caused the formation of the Congress was not disbanded. Everywhere in the Eastern Hemisphere it was aggravated, and the tasks which the Congress had set itself became each year more urgent than before. The forces in the Jewish communities of the United States which had conceived the Congress hence called it together again. But only the representatives of the plain people came. In its second phase the Congress took the form of a confederation of Jewish religious societies, brotherhoods, communities and fraternal orders. To the problems of the Jewish position abroad, its members now found added new problems at home. The Congress movement began to take form as a major step, a final step, in the Americanization of the internal structure of the communities composing American Jewry. As events moved toward the Second World War, the Jew became the surrogate and symbol of the democratic way of life upon which the Nazi sadistocrats concentrated their destructive hatred and brutality. Of all peoples, the Jews were singled out by the deadly foes of democracy for special identification with the principles and program of democracy. And everywhere in the world, under their impulsion, traditional anti-Semitism took on a variety of new forms in new intensities.

Not since 1648 has the Jewish crisis been so profound and the Jewish need so bitter. In its anxiety and despair, the Jewish mind thereupon fled for refuge to all sorts of nostrums and *isms*, to all sorts of locations and occupations. The rich turned even to Fascism; the masses hungered for the bare chance to earn their bread in freedom and eat it in peace. Babel arose in Israel; a tumbling tower of talk, of saviors, and salvations. One excited person after another raised his voice and constituted himself the Messiah of a special plea. Yiddish captains of journalistic industry were heard shouting in the name of organized labor. Powerful financial magnates and the attorneys of their retinue were heard shouting in the name of philanthropy and religion; those undertook to "unify" philanthropy; to draw the fate of all Jewish institutions, as Jewish, into their own hands by controlling their sources of income. Some of the disinherited young, facing a future of unemployment and destitution, were heard shouting in the name of Communism. "Liberals" were heard urging a flight into assimilation. Rabbis were heard crying a return to the synagogue. Each only intensified the anarchy, the confusion born of fear and fed on anxiety. And so it still is. Because of the multitude of its saviours and the warfare between them, the Jewish cause is being defeated by default. Because no orderly method of free discussion and agreement, when set up, is loyally adhered to, no common decisions are reached. No common action is taken. While through it all, the plain people of the Jewish communities cry for peace and unity, for the unity of counsel and unity of decision of which, as Mr. Brandeis declared more than a quarter of a century ago, alone a democratic Jewish Congress can be the true instrument . . .[7]

Louis Brandeis had gone to the Supreme Court not long after his first statement regarding the Congress movement, and it is a matter of record with what intensity, with what scrupulous concentration, he gave his energies to discharging the duties of his high office. Yet he filled such leisure as he had with an unflagging interest in many causes and movements — of which the democratic Jewish Congress continued to be a significant one — and was to the last generous of his time and counsel, as I have reason to know. His faith in democracy remained ageless and invincible. He was sure beyond all doubt that the surest vindication that any Jew can achieve for himself as man, as citizen, as worker, is his vindication of the democratic principle of his equal right with all men as Jew.

[7] Now, in 1943 the pressure of another war and the impact of the Jewish tragedy have at last brought into being an American Jewish Conference to deal with post-war Jewish problems through a united Jewish instrumentality.

THE PEOPLE'S JUDGE

So, during practically a quarter of a century while the People's Lawyer was serving as the People's Judge, he gave of himself and of his goods freely, without reservation and without afterthought, to the attainment of this ideal — in Palestine as in America. As a Justice of the Supreme Court of the United States, for the most part alone with Holmes, he stood up against both friends and foes on behalf of that equal liberty of different people wherein he knew the integrity of the national life to reside. I have heard labor leaders vigorously denounce him and financiers grudgingly approve him. But all he was ever concerned about was to render unto each his right. If you knew him at all, you knew that he would render it.

From those of us who, since the formation in 1914 of the Provisional Executive Committee for General Zionist Affairs, have been accustomed to think of Mr. Brandeis as "The Chief," his dying, weary and full of years as he was, takes away, with a hurt I cannot describe, the central pillar of the edifice of our work. Even if we saw him very little, merely to know that he existed, that he was there, that he could be called upon for counsel, gave a feeling of security, a sense of firm ground for the feet. He brought home to us what rarely comes home: that always, as Emerson said, "the present hour is the decisive hour and every day is doomsday." He imparted to us the courage of decision. Yet, it was of the ultimate inwardness of his simple religion of courage and freedom that no man may be indispensable to another, that each must stand on his own feet and make his own fate, if he is to vindicate the genius of his own independence and not cause wounds in the independence of his fellows.

The cooperation which Louis Brandeis believed in and practiced was the cooperation wherewith men help each other to be freer and more independent than ever. The phrase *noblesse oblige* was often on his lips, and he spoke it with no other than this unprecendented revolutionary meaning. This is what Albert Einstein had in mind when he said, on the occasion of the Chief's seventy-fifth birthday: "The development of humanity rests less in the brains of inventors than in the consciences of men like Brandeis."

The Jewish people in this, their tragically decisive hour, on this, their literal doomsday, have, if they are to survive and not perish, an ineluctable need to ponder the faith, to serve the vision and to emulate the courage of Louis Brandeis.

1943.

Stephen S. Wise — In Remembrance

THE prescribed period is now passed, when according to ancient Judaist custom, the dead are not publicly spoken of nor their memory invoked. I do not know the origins of this custom, nor what, in today's fear and hopes, supports it. It may be that a fantasy older than history requires the completion of a lunar cycle before a spirit comes at last to rest. But whatever be the ancient springs and present force of this custom, the practices that follow, of formal rememberings, formal praisings, which are presumed to honor and to reverence the dead, seem to me of the many tragic and pitiful undertakings of our human enterprise, among the most tragic and most pitiful. For the dead are out of reach of honor or reverence from the living. Everywhere in the world, alike the spontaneities and the conventions of mourning bear witness that death is the end, death is ineffable, that it cannot be undone. No dogma nor any rite restores the dead person to living presence among the living. No hatred nor any violence can touch him, nor yet any love or kindness reach him. Equally nothing to him are life's tragedies and life's ecstasies. No, it is we, the living, who benefit in the eulogy of our dead which custom everywhere prescribes. To remember and to appraise those whose battle is ended is somehow to bring in the rememberers a heightened courage, a deepened vision: it is to add a new endurance to their tragic sense of life.

And so I must be glad to join with you this night in remembering Stephen Wise. But not in remembering him with any detail of recollection. Save as a symbol of the living person, no detail can be of the least importance. Details are infinite: a man lives hour upon hour, day upon day for seventy-five years; his times bring him into contact with the miscellany of the entire earth. He touches the sensibilities of every continent, and of the islands of the seas; all sorts and conditions of men encounter him, react to him, and from their experiences form an image of him. And each is a vision of a different perspective from

Address delivered May 17, 1949, at the Rev. Dr. Stephen S. Wise Memorial Exercises held at The Jewish Club, New York City.

a different need of judgment, of that manifold whole presence, of that vital flame who was Stephen Wise. What, now, can any one say of him that is not necessarily a fragment and a fragment of a fragment? Then, as the days pass and the years pass, these fragments of vividness crumble, living memories thin away into ghostly remembrances, until there is nothing left of the man alive but faint images fading into the general dimness of the undifferentiated past, time-bleached manuscripts and letters, official documents, all a multitude of black marks on blackening paper, nothing more. Life exacts from the most loving and devoted of one's own family, from one's most loyal comrades and truest friends, labors and struggles in which there is no place for recollection, save only as it may add skill to the labor and wisdom to the struggle. Thus, everywhere in the world the meaning of the dead is that which they signify for the future of the living. This significance resides in no personal trait or image. It is expressed by no figure of the poetic imagination, or of the scientific. It dwells in the shared causes in whose services the dead died and in the shared spirit which is the ongoing life of such causes.

So must it be with Stephen Wise. Those of you who attended the funeral ceremony in Carnegie Hall may recall that, as against the few thousands who were assembled in the Hall, tens of thousands stood in the downpour on the streets outside, men and women of every rank and station, from all parts of the land. A friend who came too late and was prevented from entering the Hall heard from a stranger who was similarly stopped that he had just flown in from Florida to attend the funeral. They stood together with the crowds on the rain-soaked street until the funeral cortege had passed.

Leaving the Hall, when the mourning rites were over, I passed through those crowds. They were a cross section of the nation, not Jews only, nor Reform Jews only, but Americans of every race and clime. I saw Negroes, Hindus, Chinamen, faces and features suggesting the miscellany of mankind. And I thought, these multitudes standing together silently in the rain are the symbol, perhaps the truest symbol, of the role and meaning of Stephen Wise. Jew he was, an unflagging leader in labors for his violated people, but his role was not primarily Jewish alone nor his service peculiarly Jewish. They were American, and Jewish inasmuch as they were American. Stephen Wise, as you have heard, was a child of immigrants, himself an immigrant. He belonged to a generation of pioneer immigrants by whose labors our land became a growth in power, by whose struggles it continued a growth in freedom. It is to find this freedom that they had left their old homes for the new. I cannot but think that this freedom is the key to the faith and works of Stephen Wise.

In the dedication to freedom, the innumerable contradictory qualities of the man, which irritated his friends and by which his foes justified themselves, were reconciled: the vanities always dissolving in a basic humility; the prophetic judgment tempered to a charity that forgave, in fellow-workers, cowardices and disloyalties I myself have never been able to forgive; the arbitrariness dissolved in a good-will by which the man who was on occasion peer and companion of the great ones of his times, was not less the equal friendly companion of the little people who looked to him for light and leading. He could not endure hierarchy, he flouted social distance. Having a fighting faith in freedom, he was able to join in some mode of common action sects and parties so different from one another, that union seemed a delusion; men and women so diverse in skill and vision that their harmony seemed a paradox. Thus, Stephen Wise, the founder and rabbi of the Free Synagogue, head of a Judaist sect practically without a theology, with no concern for the prescriptions of the *Shulchan Arukh* or other items of Judaist customs and tradition, lived and labored also the beloved and trusted leader of the most orthodox of Jews, as well as of most Reform Jews; Stephen Wise, the most radical of the reformers, was among the most devoted of the builders of the Zion which Reform had rejected; Stephen Wise, most imperious of leaders, was the always rechosen president of an American Jewish Congress whose democratic doctrine and discipline harnessed and drove their leaders by their intransigencies, reduced them, on occasion, even to impotence. In the figure of this man, the diversities of American Israel did come to a certain unity, their seemingly irreduceable conflicts were compromised once and again to a pattern of cooperation. Only a very great patience, a very great courage, could undertake or accept the inconsistencies of compromise on which cooperation depends, and only a deep conviction of the mystique of freedom could sustain the patience and the courage. This mystique is the spirit in the body of America. It incarnates in institutions the American faith in the equal liberty of all human beings; in the equal worth and dignity of the men and women, each different from the others, that together make up the people of the earth, among whom the Jewish people are an equal one.

It is this ideal, which liberated Stephen Wise from the works and ways of the ghetto, that he brought to the children of the ghetto, to set them free. The expression, Free Synagogue, signalizes it. The pattern of Zionist thought and action in America signalizes it. Because of it, that process of abandonment of the Jewish heritage and aversion from the Hebraic spirit which is called Reform and assimilation was reversed. Instead of diluting the Jewish in the non-Jewish and the anti-Jewish, every community of Jews in the communion of America began to take in and to assimilate the different as nourishment of the Jewish being. What a distance between the years when as a matter of religious conscience the chiefs of Reform excommunicated Stephen Wise or me for thinking as we did about Zion and the Jewish people, and these days of a Central Conference of American Rabbis, few of whose members are non-Zionist and none are anti-Zionist! Of recent years there has occurred a repristination of that first flight from and aggression against the organic diversity of the Jewish being which is known as Reform. Forced by what I can not but judge to be a deep-lying mood of insecurity, the spokesmen of this new version of the old Reform are voices of a religious society all of whose public faith and works consist in exhibiting their own Americanism in the form of assaults upon the American being of the great majority of their Jewish fellow Americans from whom they have cut themselves off. The American people, no less than its Jewish members, are fully aware of the fears and insecurities which move this tiny sect to their un-American protestations. They know that relief from such emotions comes only as the men and women of America care to implement in their ways and works the American Idea, that the American people is a One consisting in the uncoerced teamplay of the Many in the common effort to secure to all together, their diverse yet equal rights to earning their bread in freedom and living their lives in peace. Stephen Wise made his own characteristic contribution to implementing this American Idea. If it centered in the Jewish communion into which he was born, he also carried it into the affairs of his city, into the affairs of his nation, into the affairs of the world. An inveterate pacifist, he cared enough about peace to be ready to fight for it and to recognize the two World Wars as wars in defense of peace. But he also knew that peace is indivisible, and that its strength is the organization of the unequal in equal liberty. So his labors on behalf of Israel were labors sustained by a vision of global fellowship; his invincible opposition to Nazism and all its work was an opposition illumined by his faith in equal liberty and equal security for all men everywhere. If he sometimes extravagantly identified himself as a Jew, "I have been a Jew three thousand years," it was because he recognized in the intolerable sufferings of the Jew the most poignant of all symbols of every victim of tyranny and persecution, struggling after freedom and safety.

For his faith in freedom, he himself suffered greatly and endured greatly. He was always a brave man, with a gaiety of spirit, and a spontaneous courage that often seemed quite other than Plato's wisdom concerning dangers. But in these last years Stephen's courage and gaiety became as noble and moving as anything I know. Throughout these years he lived sick with the sickness which killed him, enduring its pains and poisons, and the treatment they required, so far as might be, and carrying on as if they were not; doing, day in and day out, the work of two men. That he could thus live on was of a piece not only with his vital lift, but even more with the generosity and the power of forgiveness that were a part of it. His generosity was uncommon at best, and rare indeed in members of the cloth. He gave his possessions as unstintedly as he gave of himself, to persons and to causes alike. So, again, though his foes talk up his capacity for absorbing praise and his susceptibility to flattery, those who knew him at work from day to day can say also, and more tellingly, how he disregarded insult upon insult, even the unpardonable, and worked in the ranks with the insultor when the cause required it. Or how he would loyally accept the decision he disapproved and illustrate in action a teamwork some of his associates would not contribute.

These traits, far more than his unique eloquence are what made Stephen Wise the powerful champion of causes that he was, and kept him in the place of leadership his eloquence might have brought him to. There are many kinds of personal power, many modes of leadership. Some impose themselves, others are chosen. Yet it is not what a man is in himself that makes him a leader. It is the event that multitudes of other men find in him the concretion of their common purposes and the symbol of the meaning of their own lives. For the Jewish communities of our country, these purposes are automatically their own development as voluntary societies of democracy, with the methods and the forms of democracy implementing, creating, and contributing to the national life, an American Jewish culture. For the Zionist enterprise they are the American intent embodied in the Pittsburgh Program, as the ground-plan of the just political economy in Israel. For the nation, they are the extension of civil rights on equal terms to all Americans, the integral separation of church and state, as the basis of our democratic economy of spiritual even more than material abundance. For the world they are the same aspirations, defined in the Charter of the United Nations Organization and its Assembly's Declaration of Universal Human Rights. To Stephen Wise's heart these many causes were one cause and he served them with an indivisible devotion which won him a reciprocal devotion from the great miscellany who recognized in him the leader. Toward the very end of his days, the night we were celebrating his seventy-fifth birthday, he challenged a great authoritarian power in religion on its claims regarding the separation of church and state and its demands upon the conscience and education of mankind. He was then a man dying, but he was the most living man upon that platform. He died, living. And this is what set Stephen Wise apart from most of us, who but live dying. He never stopped. He only was stopped. In his awareness, to the last instant before he went under knife, the enduring ideals and the social instruments through which ideals are realized remained the vital moments of his attention.

Let, then, their life continue in *our* attention. The way to remember our dead, especially those who have been leaders and become legends, is, never to lay down the work, ever to keep alive in our lives the causes that had lived in their living, and to advance their spread and strength.

Albert Einstein as a Jewish Intellectual

ON THE fourteenth of March, the free and civilized portions of the world took note of the sixtieth birthday of Albert Einstein. On this day there was a moment of thanksgiving and gratulation in every place where truth is reverenced and science is free, on every hearth where the fires of liberty still burn and men keep the faith of human brotherhood and human freedom. To the Jewish communities of the world this birthday would at all times be an event of high moment. How much the more, when a spirit as noble, as brave and as great as ever was born into the house of Israel enters upon the seventh decade of its span at a time of bloody injustice and cruel betrayal, when the people most need to be rededicated to faith in the freedom and fellowship of men, and to be confirmed in the courage to devote themselves to reestablishing this freedom and fellowship and to defending them *in* their lives no less than *with* their lives.

All the years of Albert Einstein's manhood have been such a dedication and such a devotion. Of all the traits that on a sixtieth birthday might be honored in this most distinguished of scientists and humanists, — this bravest of libertarians and simplest of Jews — these seem to me the most significant, the most meaningful; and in responding to the invitation of the president of the Zionist Organization of America to join in the tribute of the organization to Albert Einstein, it is that I therefore elect to signalize.

Heine's Flight from Judaism

Das Judentum ist ein Unglueck. The expression is Heinrich Heine's. He spoke it, from his heart, about one hundred years ago. A Jewish intellectual, eager to live as a free man in the republic of letters and to exchange his visions and his works in a free trade with the intellectuals of the world, Heine found his being a Jew a wall and a chain, shutting him out and holding him down, and he took the steps that he fancied would free him from that prison house. Heine's mood and

Reprinted from *New Palestine*, March 1939.

Heine's attitude were a symbol and a prophecy of the greater number of the Jewish intellectuals of the nineteenth and twentieth centuries.

The flight from *Judentum* took many forms. In religion, it took the form of personal conversion to the faith of the majority, or of the transformation of historic orthodoxy into the various cults of reform. In general culture, it presented itself as the dualism of the *maskil*, who would practice Judaism at home but follow the ways of the world abroad. In the social sciences, it developed in theories and doctrines designed to minimize, if not nullify, all that identifies the Jew as Jew, and to redefine him in terms merely of his activities in the economy of a society or in its politics, or in its education and culture. Whatever the field, the effort was to dissolve away, or at least to reduce to triviality or irrelevancy the differentiae wherein the Jewish essence was presumably defined, and so to assimilate the Jew into the happier majority that he might be included in their happiness. The qualities of the majority were by these Jews consciously or unconsciously treated as human and desirable; the qualities of the Jew as undesirable and somehow not human. The intellectuals' flight from Judaism thus served to justify the non-Jew's misprision of the Judaism from which those Jews were in flight — and which, short of suicide, they could not escape.

Plight of Jew

As a Jew, a man was eternally a member of an eternal minority hemmed in by disabilities. As a Jew he never counted as an individual, he never was responsible alone in himself, and for himself alone; he always carried a double responsibility; it was a responsibility unjust, imposed; but a responsibility inescapable. As a Jew he was subject to persecution and danger physical and spiritual; as a Jew he had to submit to being the theme of innumerable ancient lies restated in a variety of modern inventions, against which the truth he offered seemed powerless. Being a Jew cut him off from the free exercise of his talents and the full use of his powers. Being a Jew shut him out from the station and recognition that his merit deserved. To achieve the status of his equals he had to be better than his betters. What, then was there for him to do? What could he do, if he wanted to get on in a world unjust to Jews, but cut off all associations and contacts that called this handicap to public attention? What could he do but repress in himself all the qualities of heart and mind, all the ways and works of the daily life, which bound him to his Jewish setting? So far as he could, the Jewish intellectual would dissolve all difference and merge his identity in the majority, to the point where he could pass, anonymous and unlabelled, purely and only a writer among writers, a doctor among doctors, a professor among professors.

Of course while nobody was aware of his Jewish origins and background, he himself was. He could hardly help feeling that he was practicing deception and pretending to be other than he actually was. He could hardly escape the anxious behavior that goes with this state of inner conflict and insecurity. He could hardly escape the neuroses which his position generated, nor fail to manifest the stigmata of maladjustment which such neuroses breed.

Position of Intellectual

Thus, the de-judaized intellectual of Jewish origin in the non-Jewish world presents the characteristic tensions of personality and adjustment which the conflict with himself and his flight from his inescapable social inheritance breeds. In the academic environment, these are exaggerated and aggravated. There the pretense of scientific impartiality and intellectual detachment is all too often a screen for a seething of passion and prejudice mostly concentrated on little things and little ways.

Until Hitler clarified the fact that the flight from Judaism was a flight nowhere, Jewish scientists and men of letters, holding academic posts, in the main moved and lived and had their being in a sort of abstracted world, by definition not peopled by Jews and Englishmen and Frenchmen and Italians, or by Judaists and Catholics and Methodists and Baptists, and Moslems and Brahmans and Episcopalians, but by universalized "human beings," pure intellects dealing with universal intellectual problems, in a manner as unhuman and impersonal as a machine packing chewing gum or a press printing labels. In the United States, Hitler shattered this illusion sufficiently to lead many Jewish intellectuals and academicians for the first time in their lives to associate together as Jews in order to deal with issues common to them as Jews.

Albert Einstein's Gift

Now, one of the great gifts of Albert Einstein, to his fellow-intellectuals of Jewish origin as well as to all men, is the demonstration by the continuous example of his life and labor, how healthy for the person and for the work of a Jew are self-respect, open acknowledgement and open defense of the positive values of his Jewish inheritance; and how unhealthy and futile is the flight from Judaism.

For in his own field, Einstein is the superlative master whom none can deny that believe in truth and follow the method of science and not the method of Germany. But he, from his beginnings, has made the most of his Jewish connection and Jewish relationships. He has accepted them as an opportunity and an obligation, and he has taken them as simply and as naturally as he takes his breathing or his working at his appointed scientific tasks. He has never been in flight from Judaism. He has never treated *Judentum* as an *Unglueck*. He has accepted the burden and responsibility of his "accident of birth" as readily as he has accepted the liberties and privileges of his scientific position. He has said *Yes* to his Hebraic inheritance. And because he has said *Yes* he has been able to go about among his peers a free man and a whole man, undivided in his spirit, unshaken in his ways, doing his work untramelled by any of those traits born of anxiety which mark the Jewish intellect in the academic scene. By affirming his integrity as a Jew he has vindicated the integrity of the Jew as a man and a scientist, and has made his life a light and a leading for all Jews to inner freedom and outer respect. Of the great Jews of his generation, none has lifted the torch of self-respect so high for the Jew; in none has the courage born of inner freedom burnt so brightly. And in this and through this, none has been a more potent vindication of self-respect and freedom for all mankind.

There are many other things that men of science, men of art, men of religion and men loving truth and justice might, for his sixtieth birthday, signalize in Albert Einstein's life and labors. To me this one thing stands out, most fertile, most beautiful.

Ben Rosen and the Jewish School

WHEN Ben Rosen died he had just completed a series of four articles which the *National Jewish Monthly* published under the general title *Preface to a Program of Jewish Education*. These articles were in a sense an extension of the remarks he had made at a reception which the Board of Governors of the American Association gave in his honor at the beginning of his service as Executive Director of the Association. The interval between the two statements is the period of this service, and the second statement reflects the experience Ben had gained in the course of the discharge of his duties, the judgments he had formed and the conclusions he had reached. Underlying all this was, of course, a certain basic philosophy of society and a conception of the place of Jewry in American life. Ultimately, this philosophy amounted to his fighting faith, the assumptions on which he grounded and shaped everything he said and did, at least in the period of this service.

But the philosophy was only implicit, if I am not mistaken, in his entire career and in his way of life, but became explicit toward the last. The Jewish school had been Ben Rosen's vocation. One got the feeling that he had been called to it as truly as Samuel had been called to prophecy. As a youth, a pupil of Samson Benderly's in his revolutionary *cheder* in Baltimore, the quality of Ben's spiritual interests and the direction of his growth were in no small degree functions of his continuing relationship with that pioneer in Jewish education for American Jews. Ben was among the first of that small group of disciples who fitted themselves for service in the Jewish schools not only by means of Jewish studies, but with a general education in an American university and a special education in a teacher's college. If the American Jewish teacher of today is another person than yesterday's *melamed* of Europe's ghettos, the transformation is a consequence of the new idea of the *melamed* which Benderly championed, and of the arduous labor to incarnate this idea in their own lives and works undertaken by the little group of young disciples who became his support in his Bureau of Jewish Education in New York City. If the Jewish school is changing from a room in a tenement or a house in a slum into an architecturally functional, well-managed, well-kept educational structure, it is due to the way these young disciples brought their American ideas of proper housing to bear upon Jewish establishments. The ongoing process of the revision and reorganization of content, of the alteration of improvement of method, of the reorganization of teacher-pupil and parent-teacher relationships which marks Jewish schooling everywhere in the United States today had its initiation in the efforts of this youthful company, among whom Ben Rosen stood out. The total event, whether its agonists knew it or not, constituted an Americanization of the Jewish education of Jews.

Now the process of Americanization is by no means as simple or obvious as it has been made to appear. For the different communities that make up the American people, with their different periods of settlement, their different ethnic affiliations, different religions and social heritages, their different dialects, diets and other culture-patterns, Americanization generated different aspirations and different obligations at different times. Wherever any community settled — except on the frontier — each had for its neighbor some other community that had been on the spot earlier and established itself with its folkways, mores and prestige-values. The "green" newcomers being new and different, could not be admitted to parity with their longer established neighbors. Like freshmen at the college, they had to be penalized for their newness and difference. Even after they had become naturalized citizens, fully Americans under the law, and equally entitled to its protection, they were not regarded as socially complete Americans. Their Americanization had to consist in social identification. In most matters — especially in matters of speech, dress, diet and diversions — the newcomer sought this identification. He accepted the neighbor's judgment that to be different from the neighbor was to be inferior to the neighbor, and he automatically strove to overcome his inferiority by laboring as hard as he knew how to abolish his difference. The only community establishment where this effort met any inner check was the religious establishment. There, especially if his cult was of the ecclesiastical fundamentalist variety, he met resistance. Most churches retained the language sacred to worship as well as its ritual. In practically all other dimensions of life Americanization took the general form of "keeping up with the Joneses," of a struggle, by the new neighbor, to make himself good as his betters by making himself the same with his betters.

But this "the betters" could not allow. Such an identification would denude them of their superiority and deprive them of their prestige. Their social attitude toward the aspiring and emulative newcomer was simply that of southern "whites" toward native negroes but directed upon other modes of difference than pigmentation. "The betters" of any neighborhood or region just could not bring themselves to permit that the effective meaning of Americanization should be identification; they required that it should mean subjection and submission. They required that it should consist in such conformation of the inferior to the wishes and ways of the superior as would not only keep this relationship intact but would strengthen and perpetuate it on the farm, in the factory, in business, in finance, in the school and the sports, in art and letters and "society." The Ku Klux Klan, the National Manufacturers' Association and the Daughters of the American Revolution, each according to its own interest and in its own way, came to be regarded as the champions and spokesmen of this gospel of Americanization. The theory and practice which give it form and force had the effect of both pushing the pioneering newcomer back into his ethno-cultural group and causing him so to hate it as to render him an aggressor against the characteristic ways and against himself as suffering the penalties of these ways. He and many of his generation became centrifugal forces in his community, men and women in flight from their parents, from one another and from themselves because they felt innocently burdened and unjustly hobbled by the thoughts and things which bound them together in one ethno-cultural group. The denials and rejections which these preached gave rise to a counteraffirmation of what was denied: other groups formed that undertook to practice a conscious and intense centripetality.

The whole community was shaken by their conflicts. The modes of life and thought which the antagonisms engendered were both complex and varied. Some individuals cut themselves off from all association with members of their ethno-cultural group. If they failed to form other associations, they became mavericks, persons uprooted and on the loose, at a loss within and insecure without. At the bottom of the social pyramid they tended to develop into tramps or delinquents; on its upper ranges, they tended to manifest the mobile personality traits and ethical and esthetic iconoclasms which led to their being described as "marginal" types. Others retained their ethno-cultural ligatures, but labored to whittle away from the patterns of family and community, into which their persons were woven, all their differentiating characteristics, sometimes stripping everything away but the ethnic or denominational label. Still others sought anchorage and security in purposefully isolating themselves in their ethno-cultural heritage, and purposefully excommunicating everything that differed from it, devising new and unprecedented instruments of insulation even against every cultural osmosis from other communities. Others, per contra, desired to preserve and to nourish the unaltered identity of their ethno-cultural heritage by means of such osmosis; and drew for it underpinning and buttress from the works and ways of the neighbor. Many, again, recognized that alteration cannot be prevented, and undertook simply to keep down its scope and tempo; they worked to conserve the heritage by making the smallest and slowest adaptations and adjustment they believed its survival to require. The general situation elicited still other responses, but none so consequential as those mentioned. The agonists of all, however, contended that their several methods, and theirs alone would free their group from the penalties of being different. Each was moved to accuse those who proposed principles and programs other than theirs of keeping the entire ethno-cultural community subject to those penalties and of rendering them harsher. Each, of course, felt it needful to give to the doctrine and discipline by which it hoped to save itself such a form that it might be easily and surely passed on to the generations to come. Each automatically added to the already existing instruments of indoctrination and propaganda new ones of its own, from vernacular journals to schools, from schools to *landsmanschaften*, friendly societies, "youth organizations."

The development has been generic. It may be observed in every ethno-cultural community — the Negro, the Indian, the Chinese, the Japanese, the Hindu and the Syrian, as well as those that owned the faiths and works of the different countries of Europe for their first cultural portion.

Now, Jewish communities were involved in a great many more differences than non-Jewish communities. They were not only distinguished from their Christian neighbors as Jews; they were also distinguished from each other according to the European lands whence they had trekked to seek the opportunities and freedoms of America. As immigrants from Germany or Poland or Rumania or any other European land, they tended to settle in the neighborhood of other fellow-countrymen; as Jews they were involved simultaneously in the invidious distinctions, the conflicts and the rivalries between the various Jewish enclaves, and in the interdependence which their common status of Jews in a world which held them to be outlaws of its faith imposed on them everywhere. For Jews, hence, "keeping up with the Joneses" was a more complicated and arduous enterprise than for their immediate non-Jewish neighbors. It called for a transvaluation of their German, Polish or other European culture-derivation, as well as of their Jewish social heritage. The processes of "Americanization" consequently needed to be more self-conscious, imperative, speedier and intenser in Jewish than in other communities. And inasmuch as the school has been an establishment of the Jewish community since centuries before the beginning of the Christian era, the process in the school is as representative as it can be anywhere.

Now, before the democratic revolution, the Jewish educational establishment possessed an age-old homogeneity and consistency. Because Jewish communities were ghettoes, geographically, socially and culturally isolated from the neighbors' thoughts and ways, *beth hasefer*, *beth hamidrash*, *beth hakneseth*, *talmud torah*, *yeshivah*, however housed and however conducted, maintained an astoundingly unchanged curriculum of doctrine and discipline, much the same in every land where Jews were domiciled. The *Haskalah* does not appear to have had much influence on the essentials of Jewish education, nor did the appraisals and intentions of Ahad Ha'am very much affect the programs and policies of Jewish schools. It is only when and as the walls of the ghettoes were themselves breached, and the community's survival, to say nothing of its growth, ceased to be a function of its isolation and seclusion that curriculum altered intent and content. The section of existing Judaism by various cults of reform, the expansion and transformation of *Hibbat Zion* into Herzlian Zionism with its emphasis on the secular uses of the sacred tongue, the multiplication of concepts and programs of diaspora nationalism with the strengthening and perpetuation of the ghetto's Yiddish culture as one mode of it, all either modified the traditional curriculum of the school or established rival schools with competitive curriculums.

Because of the school requirement which European states set for their subjects or citizens the consequences to the continuity of the tradition of the Jewish schools were not so very alterative. In the United States, however, particularly after the turn of the century, the impact, on private schools of all sorts, of the required enrolment of all children in free tax-supported public school systems brought revolutionary results. How revolutionary, for content, method, the training and proficiency of teachers and administrators, may be judged by comparing Catholic parochial schools in the United States with the same schools in the Province of Quebec, Canada, or in the South American countries, or in any European country where Roman Catholicism is the state-supported religion — Franco Spain would be the most consecrated and devout instance.

And the steady transformation of the Jewish educational establishment of tradition may be considered a sufficient parallel. Into the companies of traditional *cheder* and *talmud torahs* there were projected the diversified Sunday schools of the newer denominations of Judaism, the clubs and youth organizations of the Zionists and other organizations of interests such as the people's schools of the the Yiddishists factions. All such schools and clubs were singular to the new societies which devised them and supported them. That which they taught, the mediums and methods of their teachings, were the doctrines and disciplines relevant to themselves, devised to ensure their own continuance through the generations. They were free enterprise in education, and their values were functions of the competitive differentials of the specifications of Jewish culture they sought to maintain in the nation's educational scene. Even where denominational interests were in a position to emulate the parochial school of the Roman Catholics, the public school system contained and reshaped the Judaistic educational undertakings. At the very least it injected secular subject matter in the curriculum; it projected, in the personality of the teacher, a measure of the personality of the *melamed*, and in the school room a measure of the *cheder* as a place for children to study in. So the public school was inevitably a base for the odious comparisons of the proverb. Where all-day schools were out of question — and they were, and remain, possibilities only to a very limited degree — attendance at public school sharply cut the hours of Jewish schooling, and imposed the problem of selecting from the traditional curriculum what should be most essential and most dynamic and be effectively communicated in the much abbreviated period of instruction of the next generation. Willy nilly, the pressure of the public school pointed up the advantages to the transmission of the Jewish heritage that might accrue from a cooperative union of the diverse, competitive educational enterprises. And it was such a union which the Jewish communities of New York City, that had combined into the famous *Kehillah*, more or less consciously sought to establish when they set up their Bureau of Jewish Education and brought in Samson Benderly to be its head.

The story of this undertaking, of its diversification and extensions and transpositions of its influence on the educational enterprise of Jewish communities elsewhere is familiar and needs no elaboration here. At the end of a generation, leadership in the theory and practice of American Jewish education is still largely the leadership of the dedicated young men whom Benderly had gathered around him during those beginnings. Ben Rosen had worked by the illumination of this philosophy in Boston; it was his light and leading during his twenty-two years of service as director of the Associated Talmud Torahs of Philadelphia. It underlay, generally, his efforts at organization and coordination, at improving the system's personnel, its textbooks and its methods. But function as this new Jewish education was of the American way in education, it tended, as content and as intent, to remain retrospective and isolate; an instrument for transmitting and keeping in memory and habit some selected conceptions and records of the Jewish past, it aimed hardly at all adjusting the Jew as Jew to the conditions of the present and creating for his Hebraic spirit a vital and abundant future.* Moreover, however completely any interest, sect or denominations Americanized its educational arm, it could hardly help undertaking to keep its school work segregated from that of others different from it in doctrine and discipline.

It was particularly this state of things that the men and women who formed the American Association for Jewish Education — so many of them former colleagues and associates of Samson Benderly — hoped to improve upon. When they came together for the first time in Atlantic City, Hitler had been scourging and poisoning the West for six years; political events were moving toward collapse into World War II; European anti-Semitism was having its doctrinal and practical extensions in the United States; in the Jewish communities there was a blind and deep anxiety expressed by all sorts of effort at "defense," "public relations" and the like, but as yet no insight into the responsibilities of education for enlightening the mind and arming the heart of the Jewish child if it was to grow up and live bravely and healthily as Jew, in a world whose every institution penalized the Jew for his Jewish difference. These responsibilities were pointed out at this

* See, *Jewish Education*, XI, 2, 1939: "The Education of Jews in our Time."

meeting; they were, it was urged, the prime task of Jewish education in our time.

With the experience of more than a quarter of a century in the reform of the Jewish school, Ben Rosen, in the short time that followed, brought to bear this reappraisal on the educational enterprise of the American Jewish Community. Held back as he was by personal habit and occupational responsibility, he reflected deeply upon the record; he analyzed principles and practices and discussed their nature and their consequences with friends and colleagues; he explored alternative issues both of idea and of action. The convictions he arrived at led to his resigning the prestige and security of his Philadelphia organization and to his taking on the hazard, the strenuosities and the undefined status that went with the tasks of building the ideals of the American Association for Jewish Education in the educational establishments of the American Jewish communities. In his *Preface* he put these convictions into words, stressing the fact, that in what concerned education, all Jewish sects, parties, denominations must have, in so far as they are all *Jews*, certain common objectives. "Regardless," he wrote, — I am afraid far too optimistically and unanalytically — "of the special emphasis or specific interpretation which divergent groups in Jewish life place upon the aims of Jewish education, there are certain common objectives to which they all subscribe:

1. To build up in the child, youth, and adult a clear and positive feeling of belongingness to the Jewish group and to prepare him to live in a Jewish environment. He must learn how to live intelligently and worthily those aspects of his life which are Jewish, so that these become for him sources of significance, self-worth, personal dignity and inner security — and not elements of confusion, shame, conflict and distraction. This he can achieve best through an intelligent understanding of present day Jewish living and the relevance of the past to the present.
2. To develop in the Jewish child, youth, and adult a desire to participate intelligently and actively as a Jew, in his home, in his synagogue and his community. Not only is he to be made aware of his responsibilities as a Jew, he must be willing to share in these responsibilities. Through meaningful participation he will gain in his appreciation of the heritage of his background, its cultural values, its contribution to the enrichment of his own personality, to his group and to the world generally.
3. To prepare the Jewish child, youth, and adult to live in his American environment. Democracy implies the right to be different. But the distinctiveness of the Jew must be made meaningful to him, so that

he understands the place and value of cultural minorities in human progress. A happy and normal adjustment to this non-Jewish environment will enable him to draw upon his inner strength, to withstand and to dispel the hurtful effects of anti-Semitism on his personality.

4. To perpetuate Jewish life and culture. Education is the sole positive basis upon which the community can preserve Jewish group life, its institutions and ideals, by transmitting its heritage to the growing generation.
5. To strengthen the loyalties to American democracy, which are largely built upon the classic ethical tradition of Judaism. A Jew becomes a better citizen who has been educated to understand the rights, privileges and responsibilities implicit in the democratic way of life.

The reasons are many why Ben could carry the American idea in Jewish education no farther. I could wish that he had had the time to think through, and to point up the responsibilities of the Jewish school for the education of Jews who are not or do not wish to be Judaists, and the significance of the Hebraic spirit and Jewish way as a culture as well as a cultus. I could wish that he had recognized more fully the dynamic actualities of Jewish differences within the whole Jewish community and their implication for the Jewish school. His tasks of organizing and coordinating did not leave him the opportunity to see that he was not giving the weight it requires to the fact that the right to be different obtains not only as Jew differs from non-Jew, but equally as Jew differs from Jew. As Ben set down his objectives, he imparted a factitious unanimity to the enclaves within the Jewish community, one that does not in fact exist, and perhaps would be dangerous to the community's vital forces if it did exist. One more objective for Jewish education — to my view the paramount objective — must be that each Jewish enclave shall have scientific insight, sympathetic understanding of all the others differing from it, and shall have the desire and the will to orchestrate its different thoughts and ways into a free cooperative union of the differents. Jewish education needs a "Springfield Plan" inward to the Jewish community.

However, Ben was a pathfinder and forerunner. It remains for the survivors to turn the path he blazed into a system of open roads.

1946.

Book III: The Jewish Education of the American Jew

To Educate Jews in Our Time

THE Jews of the world are living through a crisis more bitter, more tragic than any which they have been called upon to suffer since 1648. Many and heavy are the responsibilities which the time has laid upon the fortunate Jewish communities of the United States; responsibilities to provide relief and supply refuge; responsibilities of salvage, shelter and new beginnings, wherever these are possible. The bitter cry of innocent martyrs rising from the soils of European despotisms can scarcely be quieted with even the most generous dedication of men and means.

But the means cannot be assembled, the men can be neither aroused nor consecrated, without education. The problem of education precedes, accompanies and survives all other problems. These can be successfully solved only as the problem of education is successfully solved. In education the entire community of Israel in America face their most serious problem.

Education is the most serious problem among Jews because, at no time since the Chmelnicki pogroms, has Heine's tortured summary, *das Judentum ist ein Unglueck*, been tearing the hearts of Jews everywhere as it tears them today. The post-war generations not only have seen the generous idealism of democracy defeated and in retreat on all fronts in Europe and Asia; even here in the United States they are finding their normal desires and aspirations as human beings, their hopes for a job, a career, a family, doubly blocked; once for their youth, in common with all youth; and again for their Jewish names, their Jewish parentage, their Jewish being. Their forefathers, facing such a check, had for consolation and support their deep faith that the suffering of Israel is implied by the mission of Israel, chosen by God to bear witness to His unity and law. You of course, and all others who are Zionists, possess a more secular substitute for that inward faith: the vision of a happy and just homeland to be established in Palestine, the efforts toward its consummation, provide a moral and spiritual dike against the tides of ruin that beat against the integrity of the Jewish being. But to the

Address delivered at conference to organize the American Association for Jewish Education, May 7, 1939, at Atlantic City, N. J.

multitudes of young Jews neither Judaism nor Zionism serves as a strength or a shield. Born into the machine age, creatures of its scientific *Zeitgeist*, determined by its mood, attitudes and valuations, they draw but scant comfort from the ancestral faiths, whether religious or secular. Indeed, they doubt, they challenge, they reject the faiths. In the colleges those who hold to them are an unesteemed minority — "greasy grinds" on the fringes of the academic community, members of Avukah, members of Hillel. The acknowledged "elite" are the "brothers" and "sisters" of the fraternities and sororities that compose the social ghettoes of the academic scene. There the children of prosperous Jewish parents who are not admitted to the societies of the Gentiles imitate the ways of these Greek-letter gentiles and live the lives of amateur Gentiles. Like their elders, they are in flight from their Jewish inheritance, and thus in flight from themselves, into a make-believe world where self-suppression and self-deception take the place of reality.

Do not commit the sin of blaming them for this. The phenomenon is universal and endemic. Its causes reach into the homes of the most self-respecting and self-conscious Jews. One of your most thoughtful and effective leaders told me this afternoon how, in spite of the admirable training he has given his own children, they also manifest the attitudes of doubt and fear and the disposition to flight from the *Unglueck* which they cannot help feeling to be inwardness of their Jewish inheritance. Exposed on the one side to the contagions of suppression and evasion spreading from the "elite;" suffering on the other from the repeated impacts of non-Jewish responses to the word "Jew" — responses which show them that its connotations for the non-Jew, its emotional, moral, intellectual connotations, are not happy ones: the non-Jew does not feel exactly praised or honored if he is called "Jew" — these young Jews automatically seek to withdraw as far as may be from this painful and belittling connection. Week in, week out, since 1933, young Jews and young Jewesses come to see me, hurt, bewildered, angry, not knowing what to think or what to do. Wherever they turn, they are blocked. However adequate their qualifications, the medical schools, the schools of engineering, the law schools, the schools of education have no place for them; the economic establishments, great or little, have no jobs for them; the institutions of higher learning discourage them and shut them out. They labor under a double handicap. The first they share with all youth regardless of ancestry or creed. It is the unemployment common to the time and scene. The second inheres in their being Jews. This, largely without being conscious of it, they resent and hate, and seek in every way possible to throw off. As the record of our Jewish synagogues and temples and schools and community centers shows, the number of young who make use of them does not increase; relatively, it diminishes. In seeking employment, they do everything they can to rid themselves of every association carried in the word *Jew;* they see it as causing an arbitrary and needless abrogation of their right to work; as an impediment, through no fault of their own, to their earning an ordinary living. Jewish youth are emotionally, and when and as they can, practically, in flight from Judaism and Jewishness. They give signs of an anti-Semitism peculiar to themselves; a hatred of that in themselves which handicaps them, so that they reject it with hearts and heads, even though they cannot in fact separate themselves from it, or it from themselves. It conveys to them nothing positive, nothing to which they can give a brave, self-reliant *Yea;* no spiritual inwardness whence they may draw strength and courage.

What is hatred and denial among these young, is fear and concealment among their parents. The latter endeavor to conduct themselves as if no problems and no obligations exist. Having given their pittance to the charities, they demand to be let alone, not to be bothered. Deeply afraid of anti-Semitism, they urge that American citizens who are Jews avoid anything and everything that would cause them to be noticed as Jews. They want such citizens to profess the principles of democracy, but to avoid the practice. They want the Jew to withdraw from affairs, to abandon his obligations as citizen, as artist, as scholar or doctor or lawyer, to retire into a ghetto of the emotions, and there silently stew in his fears until the rapine of anti-Semitism shall pass by.

So, young and old hope, each by their separate ways, to escape the hurt of anti-Semitism, and to win sympathetic and helpful consideration from their non-Jewish fellow citizens who believe in democracy sufficiently to wish to practice it also toward Jews. The record shows that their methods doom their hopes to defeat; that, like the scratching of an itch, the remedy aggravates precisely the condition it was intended to improve. Freedom for Jews has not come and cannot come from hatred toward Jewishness by Jews; or from the suppression and concealment of Jewishness by Jews. Freedom rests upon candid self-acquiescence and self-respect, generous, open, unashamed and brave. The democratic peoples will be concerned over equal liberty for the Jews, individually and collectively, only as Jews are concerned about this liberty for themselves. Why, sincere democrats ask, should any one care to protect for the Jew what he does not prize for himself?

But the repressions of the old and the negations of the young have still other consequences. The fear, the anxiety, to which their attitudes are due, are not observed. The attitudes are observed; and when observed, they work as inhibitions upon the democratic good will and the feeling for fair play of the non-Jew. The Jews' negation of Jewish values becomes a component of the Gentiles' denial of any value in the Jew. Old and dormant feelings of prejudice, transmitted to each generation in infancy, are reawakened. Well-financed Nazi and Fascist propaganda play upon them and feed them. The propaganda provides them with a complete philosophy of anti-Semitism, fabricated in Germany by new-made professors of this art of poisoning, and covering every department of human endeavor — religion, politics, economics, "race"-relations, art, and science.

Such is the situation which sets the task for the educational work of every American Jewish community.

The work is, to bring to the growing generations of Jews that knowledge of their people and themselves, as they are, as they were, and as they hope to be, which will enable the young to go out into a culture continually poisoned by anti-Semitic lies, in a spirit self-acquiescent and self-respecting, determined and hopeful, taking up their lives as Jews and as Americans with a serene courage, without illusion. The work is, to bring to the older generation clear understanding that the safe ways are the open ways, that protective coloration or concealment is self-humiliation, that fear-born silence is self-degradation without self-preservation. The work is, to vindicate the value of the Jewish spirit in that free teamplay of diverse cultures which constitutes civilization. The work is, to enhance the *cultural pluralism* in which the democracy of the spirit consists: never to teach Jewish things except in their dynamic connection with things not Jewish; ever to show how each nourishes and strengthens the others, so that the virtues of any live in the solidarity of all.

For it is education that must be the chief agent of immunization against the feelings of unworthiness, of injustice and of irremediable hurt brought into being and sustained by contemporary anti-Semitism. Only education can a little replace accident and luck in enabling the young to envision their place as Jews realistically; to know the burden of being a Jew as a pioneering of the spirit; to accept it, and accepting, to transform it from a burden into a glory. This is the prime task for the education of Jews in our time. It cannot be accomplished by a mere re-hashing of the past, by a revamping of ceremonial survivals, or by other tricks of the modern pedagogue. It requires a new insight and a different mood than those which have prevailed among Jewish educators. For it calls for such a conversion of a past, dead but unburied, as will transform it into a *living* force; as will make "Jew," in the ears of the Jewish boy or girl, over from a tragic label or a synagogal association or a dietary regimen, into a configuration of ideas, emotions, attitudes and values which will bring aspects of their Jewish inheritance to bear instantly and nobly, but not consciously, on their present situation. Such an objective calls for another sort of curriculum, and another organization of it, than the prevailing one, with other emphases and perspectives. In such a new curriculum the present would have to take precedence over the past; contemporary and modern heroes, personalities like David Lubin and Louis Brandeis, Albert Einstein or Ben Cardozo, who embody the excellences that are required of Jewish Americans, of American Jews, would have to take precedence over the heroes of tradition. For in the conduct of life, actual example is the indispensable teacher: the living model which can be emulated outranks the verbal image, the logical precept. The lives of such models assimilate organically values called non-Jewish to values called Jewish; they exhibit the excellences of American and Jew as an indivisible orchestration into a single vital whole. They provide a natural pattern for such orchestration in all community structures and functions, and in every personal aim. They are the avatars of that integrity, lacking which no life can accept itself, no mind be truly free.

Do you remember the verse in the thirteenth chapter of the Book of Job — to me the noblest and deepest book in the Bible — which the official versions render, *Though he slay me will I trust in him?* The Hebrew is:

הֵן־יִקְטְלֵנִי לֹא אֲיַחֵל אַךְ־דְּרָכַי אֶל־פָּנָיו אוֹכִיחַ

and the correct translation is:

Behold He will slay me; I have no hope
Nevertheless will I maintain my way before Him.

Elsewhere there is another verse:

Mine integrity hold I fast and I will not let it go
My heart shall not reproach me so long as I live.

The bitter Heinesque sentiment: *das Judentum ist ein Unglueck* with the flight of Jews from their Jewish inheritance which it animates, has alienated the generations of Jews from that integrity whose equal right it is the will of the democratic way of life to guarantee. It has made of Jews their own worst spiritual enemies. It has led them to bring up their children with nothing positively Jewish to take pride in, to fight for. Hence it leaves them spiritually on the loose and ethically at a loss, fleeing from that in themselves which they cannot escape, now to the right, now to the left, now in an ever-recurring circle. If Jewish education is to serve the Jewish spirit, it must find a way to change the spiritual looseness into spiritual integration, the ethical lostness into moral assurance, the flight into an advance in the front ranks of the hosts of democracy.

So much for the tasks of education within the Jewish communities. But education has a duty also respecting the communities not Jewish. As the members of the communities mingle in the common tasks of the daily life, so their education must mingle. Jewish schoolmen must bring to their non-Jewish fellows accurate knowledge of the Jews, their ways and their works. Alone the truth, ascertained and tested by the principles and with the methods of science, can overcome and finally replace the lies and libels of the anti-Semite as well in the heart of the Jews made afraid by them openly and freely to live as Jews, as in the heart of the non-Jew made afraid by them to live with the Jew. For the non-Jew's mood and disposition toward the Jew has its hidden reverberations in the Jewish spirit, which, like every other spirit, comes to value itself as its neighbors value it. Thus a proper spiritual hygiene of a free society is required to transform the negative stimulation now inherent in the word "Jew" into a positive one, and to develop and make permanent in happier terms both the unconscious and conscious connotations of the word. The first responsibility for such a hygiene falls on education. Without it, the uses of anti-Semitism as a screen for the attack on democracy by such charlatans as Coughlin or psychopaths as Mosley cannot be effectively exposed. Without it the conventional Jewish education of Jewish children — as so many of you here are painfully aware — fails of the purpose it intends. The children need to know more than Jewish history and Jewish holidays and all that. They need to know their dynamic contexts in the wider economies of community, state, nation, mankind. They need to know the nature of the anti-Semite and of his attack. They need to be provided with the cultural and intellectual weapons, not of defense merely, but of attack, since on the plane of the spirit, as on the battlefield, the best defense is attack. Did Job submit supinely, as his friends advised, to the assault of even insuperable Omnipotence? No, he resisted, he made his counter-charges, and held to his integrity the more firmly the harder he fought against its foes, natural and supernatural.

Failing this Joban spirit, things happen to mind and heart such as have been happening to the Jews of Germany. There are signs of it here among us Americans. Too often and too numerously, the Jewish young are thrown into a concern with mere animal survival instead of the conservation of values. Too often the tendency to flee is superseded by a tendency to surrender. Such a trend has not been uncommon in the history of persecuted Jewry, but it has never been so widespread and so hasty as today. Before the World War, and in every earlier generation, the will to integrity has been stronger than the will to mere survival. Often it seems as if the present generation not only retains nothing Jewish to strive for, but that it has lived so soft that it has lost the wisdom of its fathers regarding victory and defeat. The generations of Maimonides and of Spinoza knew in their hearts that death in battle is not the same as defeat. They knew in their hearts that so long as they held fast to their integrity, they might be killed but they could not be conquered; that then death was only martyrdom, not defeat; and that the ideal which was their life was victorious by this death. They knew in their hearts that only submission could be defeat, that only acquiescence in the false judgments and valuations of the enemy, only consenting to live without integrity under the degradation and enslavement of the enemy's sadist will, could be defeat. This inward knowledge the present generation of Jews lack; and unless education knows how to bring it to them, education fails.

I repeat, the children of Israel must know how to live as Jews strongly, bravely, in serenity without illusion. Who shall teach them this? Who can impart to them the Joban courage and the Joban integrity? Where shall be found the dynamic leadership which can use the traditional materials of the schools and yet not fall subject to it? Who can make the achievement of the past livingly relevant to the crisis of the present? Where is there to be found a twentieth century Maimonides? Perhaps the times which need him so will bring him forth. But the times, like God, are apt to help only those who help themselves. The schools can merely transmit conventions unless there is a repristination of the spirit which gives conventions life. They can do nothing for the children unless there is a new spirit in the parents of the children. The education of youth cannot be accomplished without the education of the adult. They must go together. Indeed, the claim that the adult should be awakened and informed is perhaps the greater claim. For the elders determine the atmosphere and set the tone for youth. At present they dwell in darkness, hurt, searching and seeking blindly, asking for light and meaning, and receiving for answer a babel of tongues and counsels. Their greatest need is for a philosophy of life which shall so restate the democratic vision that it will show them clearly and distinctly the Jew's place in the social aggregate as of right and not on sufferance, and the Jew's service to the aggregate as based on equal liberty and not on compulsion. The philosophy of Jewish life which our needs call for must be at the same time a philosophy of all life. Its foundation must be the basic insight on which democracy rests: the insight that difference, that individuality, is primary; that cultures and faiths, like genera and species, are by nature many and not one; that in the effort of many individualities, singular and collective, each different from the others, to live together with the others, a division of labor ensues, an orchestration of mankind takes form wherein each does his part, and by doing his part enriches the part of everybody else; that it is for the Jew so to do his part as Jew, and so to enrich the part of everybody else.

To give Jewish individuality a positive content within the practical frame of reference of science and industry, to establish it in the perspective of this democratic philosophy of life, thus restoring his Jewish inheritance to the Jew and bringing back the Jew to a living Jewish inheritance, is the task of Jewish education. Synagogue and temple are not succeeding at this task; the community center is evading it; the current educational enterprise is inadequate to it. Today, this meeting, by creating the American Association for Jewish Education, initiates a new struggle on a new and more dubious front, a struggle the outcome of which none can tell in advance. The important thing is, never to abandon the struggle, never to accept defeat. Defeat is created by its acceptance, but while there is fight there is hope. The American Association for Jewish Education necessarily begins its career as a battle; though all education is a battle and never was and never can be anything else, the education of the Jew as Jew is more so than any other. To educate him into his peculiar integrity is to live in battle, to fight it with joy in the fight itself; to accept it as end as well as means. For the sought consequences of education, as of most excellences of life, remain in the nature of things contingent beyond control, as all educators know to their cost. Only the action and its spirit can be real *now*, can be as brave and wise *now* as we will to make them. May the Association achieve the courage and the wisdom as I am sure it has the will!

Jewish Education and the Future of the American Jewish Community

THERE is no need to labor the point that other things being equal the future of any community anywhere in the world depends on its educational instruments. How we live, how we think, what we think, what we want and how we try to get it are not things we are born with; they are things we learn. Each of us is born an animal and may grow up to be anything his elders like. They shape him into a person similar to themselves by exposing him during the first six or seven years of his life to the control and conditions of a social atmosphere and institution which give shape and meaning to his ways of feeling, thinking and doing. No matter what happens to an individual afterwards, unless he undergoes a catastrophic re-conditioning, the modes in which he is set in his early years fix the quality and direction of his being for the rest of his life. Changes do take place, but they have to be as drastic as war or terrible as disease to alter that initial bias and direction. Consequently, what America or any other part of the world is going to mean after the war is being determined largely by the kind of directional set established in children at home, on the streets, in schools. We call such a set, with its attitudes, symbols and material conditions, "culture." The emphasis upon the home is primary, its role should not be underestimated. The emphasis upon the street is important and should not be overlooked. But insofar as home and street define feelings and attitudes and establish habits to which accrues an intellectual content — a way of believing and pattern of thinking upon which to ground and by which to rationalize action — these accrue through the school.

In democratic countries the great center of reference and context of all education is the public school. This is especially the case in our own country. Whatever a Jewish or any other kind of community do about their *special* cultural disciplines has to be done in some sort of dynamic relationship to the general public school system. Thus, it may sometimes be necessary for the Jewish school to correct the deficiencies

Address delivered at the Conference on Jewish Education, American Association for Jewish Education, East Central States Region, Cleveland, November 28, 1943.

in democracy of the public school. Intellectual and spiritual interpretation of America may depend upon what the public school lacks and the Jewish school supplies. Hence, what we teach and how we teach it become matters of prime importance not only for the Jewish community which is a part of the greater American community, but for the whole nation.

In the making of the nation, we cannot overestimate the influence of education as embodying a vision of life and its logic. This vision is the frame of reference of the "future." Usually when we say "future" we mean some image of something absent, an image which is fixed and unchanged. But the real future, the future which occurs, has no fixed character. The image Thomas Jefferson had of America is not the America which appears today. But insofar as Jefferson's contemporaries and their descendants share the image, the image has influenced the direction of change. Changing itself, it has been, and continues to be, a force in the change of everything else.

Hence, "future" is something that is happening *now*. In the degree that the past lives and grows and is transformed by the process of living, and also in the degree that the present carries the past as a dead burden, the past affects the future. If it is a *living* past, it is a part of your personality, particularly if your personality is itself alive and strong. The past is then a growing concern, not a burden carried on the back of your psyche and character. It is flesh of your flesh and bone of your bone and spirit of your spirit.

Now, the Jewish tradition is a bookish tradition. The Jewish student is a son of the People of the Book and his learning tends rather to loading him with knowledge than habituating him to the uses of knowledge in the art of living. Therefore, it is important for us to bear in mind that one of the chief obstacles to success in Jewish education *is* education. There is teaching and there is learning, and most of the time the chief obstruction to learning is teaching. Just as no one can eat for you, so no one can learn for you — you must do it for yourself. Teaching is something that someone not yourself does to you. The attitude and behavior of the teacher may be and all too often is the chief inhibition in learning. I am afraid that the record of too many Jews in acquiring Jewish learning is that they began by resenting the subject matter because they were moved by the teacher's attitude, to dislike the teacher. The teacher usually taught as if teaching was doing to the pupil what the pupil, if he is to learn, must do for himself. This is to assimilate his subject, like his food, into his personal being and to expend it in every phase in his feeling and doing.

What is the bearing of the subject or content that a child or adult is required to learn on its self-hood and personality? You must answer this question before you can frame a realistic and mature philosophy of Jewish education or of any education. Most of us think of Jewish education mostly as indoctrination in the verbal past, partly as discipline in ceremonial action and ritual. We expect the child to learn documents and perhaps dietary habits and rabbinical responsa that have no particular relevance to the existence and survival of the child where and how it now lives; nor to the conditions to which its life must adjust or which it must adjust to its personal ways. This problem of relevancy has not been adequately considered in planning Jewish education. We are not educating Jews, children or adults, in terms of this indispensable relevancy. We think more of repeating and conserving the past than of making a vital future by means of the past.

The future, we must never forget, is being made now. It is being made by the conditions of a great civil and religious war in which two ways of believing about human beings and human relations are joined in a struggle that both cannot survive. We call one democracy, we call the other totalitarianism. With totalitarianism goes authoritarianism. It means a certain body of doctrine, a revelation, and a way of life which follows from that body of doctrine, held to be infallible. Anyone who differs from that is classified as a heretic or infidel and as deserving either to be outlawed from the community by the believers or to be exterminated by the believers. Thus the Nazis divide mankind into two races — the Nordic race and the Human race. They hold the Human race to be by nature and God's will but a slave and a tool which God created to serve the Nordic race. To be human is to be of a different kind than the Nordic and the Nazis wage war against the Human race and enslave it because it is different. They insist that the different has no right whatever to live, to grow, to be free or to find happiness. They penalize the different for being different.

This sort of belief is not new. It is as old as civilization itself. In all ages certain societies have waged war upon others because they had the power and the arms and claimed for their power a theological ground, and for their authority a divine source. Asserting a mandate from God, they shut out and cut off, they coerced, enslaved, or destroyed all those who did not agree with them. Wherever you turn in this world, to Europe, Asia, Africa, South America and elsewhere, you find the authoritarian, you find the recurrent effort to destroy or enslave that which is different. The difference may be anything — faith, thought or way of life; sex, race, color, religion, occupation, language, culture, what you will. But being different, it is refused equal status in the society of the privileged and chosen, who declare themselves the keepers of the infallible revelation, and the favorites of the deity.

Democracy is the opposite of all this. It received its first statement as a fighting faith in America and the most effective efforts to implement it were first made here. The American ideal of democracy is the equality of the different. We have a national religion — not Christianity or Judaism or Mohammedanism or Buddhism, or Mormonism or Vedantism or Confucianism — a wider religion which embraces them all, which affirms for all the different sects in the world the equal right to live and flourish in a community whose unity assembles their differences freely and without penalty. This is the import of *equal* in the Declaration of Independence, saying "All men are created equal." *Equal* here does not mean *the same* — *equal* does mean that none shall be penalized for being what he is; that all, as they are, have an identical title to "life, liberty and the pursuit of happiness." To secure this equality of the different "governments are instituted among men." This means that the function of institutions is service, not rule, save as rule is a method of service. There are ecclesiastic, economic and many other, as well as political, governments. This country is a nation of various governments all organized to function so that the people associated together by their means, live better, more freely, jointly and severally than if each lived alone. Free government is the cooperative undertaking of different people on terms of equal partnership, deriving its just power from the consent of the governed; it proceeds by drawing power from the grass-roots and delegating it to the political and other agencies of whose activities government consists. Regularly it returns to its source, in the people: always it is responsible to its source.

When we talk about the Four Freedoms, what we really mean is not, not to be hungry or afraid — a full belly and a safe place are not the inwardness of Freedom. Your inward freedom is to be able by your own strength to control your own life on your own terms. It is, never to be the slave which every man and woman is made into in totalitarian countries. No matter how safe and well fed they might be, they never have been either strong or masters of their own lives. They live like cattle on dairy farms, who receive everything but own nothing. Their very lives are not their own. The dairy cow is reduced to a milk-producing machine which exists for the dairy man, not for itself. Or take a prisoner in jail. There a man is most free from want and fear. All his needs are ostensibly satisfied, but do you ever hear of a prisoner, in his right mind, who wants to stay in jail? When we speak of freedom from want, we don't mean freedom from want, but freedom by our own efforts to get what we want — the equal liberty of action which is the first and last term of the American idea of liberty, and which comes closest to its ideal in the freedoms of thought and inquiry and expression and conscience.

Those are the essential freedoms. First and last it is those we are fighting for. In those freedoms the Jewish people have a paramount stake, because the Jews as a people have more than any other community been penalized for being different, especially in those respects. The penalty has been primarily a theological penalty, imposed with the attainment of political power by the Christian establishment. It began with the exclusion of Jews from citizenship in the Roman Empire. This exclusion was based on the position assigned to Jews in the Christian scheme of salvation. The theologians said that the Jews had been chosen by God for a special purpose from the whole human race, which God had cursed when Adam and Eve were expelled from the Garden of Eden for eating of the fruit of the tree of knowledge of good and evil. This sin of Adam's, described as "original sin," the theologians considered hereditary. Because of it, they said, the world is the evil place it is. The only way that the children of Adam could escape the consequences of their first parents' sin is that someone else should be punished for it. This some one else is the Christ, the son of God who offered to expiate Adam's sin for Adam's children. So, God sent his only begotten son to take the burden of Adam's sin upon himself, to suffer a shameful death upon the cross. He sent him as a Jew to walk on earth, to die and to live again. And anyone who accepts the redemption and atonement of that death can be saved from death himself. But the Jews rejected the redemption; Jesus had come unto his own and his own received him not. Therefore, say the theologians, God rejected the Jews. He doomed the Jews to wander, out-cast from the family of mankind, until the second coming of the Lord in glory. In the course of time the theological fiction regarding the Jews became established in the legal, social and economic order of the Christian world. Until at last the Democratic Revolution, signalized by our Declaration of Independence, challenged and denied that order of privilege and servility, and affirmed that all people, however they were different from each other, had the right to live with each other on equal terms. In every western land then, the Jews became a symbol of the advance and spread of this democratic ideal. Wherever you find a genuine extension of the democratic way of life, the Jew is free once more to contribute to the enrichment of that life with his own Jewish works and ways; he may, without penalty, live his own life in his own way and make his contribution in his Jewish terms. That is why, when the enemy of democracy attacks democracy, the symbolic focus of that attack is the Jew. Thus, in Nazi Germany, in Fascist Italy, in Falangist Spain, the Jew is the chosen symbol of the freedom they hate.

The contagion of their authoritarian use of that symbol has spread everywhere. You need only to think of the survey in Fortune magazine; in answer to the question, "Do you believe that there are any groups conspiring to take power in the United States?" 21% said Jews were. Think of Boston, of Cambridge, where gangs of adolescent youths and girls have been infesting the Jewish sections of the city, stopping other children and asking "Are you a Jew?" If those they stop say "yes," they are beaten up.

Obviously, any education that Jews may plan for the future development of their inner strength as grown-ups or for the protection of their children must take into consideration this way of thinking about Jews and these facts. They are anti-Semitism. They are the context of Jewish community life. The context has been deepening in the past and will continue to deepen in the next ten years all over the world. Community differences, rivalries and conflicting relationships have been intensified. Evidence is found in England, in Rumania, in France, in Poland — wherever you turn. The Nazi contagion spreads. And it shows a mounting volume here in the land of the free. We have the problem of spiritually arming ourselves and our children against it. Remember that at first children know nothing of anti-Semitism. But it is anti-Semitism that endows the word Jew with a practical meaning for them — it, the experience of anti-Semitism, and not the instruction they get in Jewish schools; not the ideas they acquire in Sunday schools etc., of the differences of Jewish sects, parties and special interests in Jewish communities who denounce, each the other, as causes or occasions of anti-Semitism. The fact is that to the anti-Semite, the difference doesn't exist. Anti-Semitism imposes a unity upon Jews whether they like it or not. The necessity of defense against the practice and theory of anti-Semitism which will be in flood after the war, imposes community; it compels the conflicting Jewish sects and parties to work together. Since only by working together may each be better defended than if he worked alone.

This fact should guide Jewish education. It is especially important for the development of the personality of the Jewish child. The Jewish child grows up to a double responsibility. It has to recognize that Jews are members of one another; that each Jew carries a responsibility not only as an individual but as a member of a group called Jews. This double burden has implications for education. It is the frame of reference for the conditions of the child's life. Finding itself being penalized for being a Jew, the child naturally asks, "Why?" You reply, 'It is God's will; accept and suffer." Or you say, "ignore it; only nasty non-Jews inflict handicaps and suffering." Or you say, "Certain other Jews cause it. To be a Jew, don't be like those others." And thus you set up a disposition toward aggression of Jews against Jews, Jewish anti-Semitism, which is a flight first from people like oneself, then from oneself. There are many forms of this flight. The child may say, "I am a human being; not a Jew." It isn't aware that it must be *some kind* of human being. And that *what* kind is decided for it at birth. A baby is only the potentiality of a human being. It is not born human. It is educated into humanity by the unconscious contagion and conscious discipline of the family scene, with its emotional tone, its inherited attitudes and symbols; by the religious society into which families are associated; by the community in which they live and move and struggle for their being, and by the school which is the community's vehicle of conscious social transmission — in a word, by the folkways and mores which constitute culture. These educate, and education is humanization. For the early years it is always singular, concrete, local. It is never abstract or general. The family scene, its emotional climate, its symbols and ideas and attitudes provide the content and give the direction of the growth of infant into child, child into youth and youth into adult. In a family of Jews, all that attaches to the word "Jew," be it joyous or painful, vitalizing and releasing or inhibitive and a cause of despair, enters into the dynamic core of the growing psyche of that family's children. Later suppression can neither eliminate it nor abolish its hurt; later overemphasis cannot ease the pang of it and bring the Jew not at ease with his Jewish being the ease and emotional health he seeks.

This is why certain aspects of Zionist propaganda are to be deprecated. These consist in urging that Jews who are not in Palestine are in exile, that they are strangers and sojourners where they are, and that

Palestine alone is their home. This kind of propaganda serves only to repeat and to justify the anti-Semite. It involves an unconscious denial of the first principle of democracy, which is that all human beings, whoever they are and wherever they are, are equal in right to life, liberty and the pursuit of happiness. It is simply not true that we American Jews are not at home but in exile in our country. Being at home or being in exile is not a geographical location but a human relation. Jews may be in exile in Palestine as surely as anywhere else in the world if their existence in Palestine is shut into a ghetto, and cut off from freedom and growth. People are at home with each other wherever they live together, each with his neighbor, in such way that their togetherness strengthens and eases and frees for healthy growth the separate character of each. We do not need Palestine because we are in exile. Being at home and not in exile, we still need Palestine. It is as democrats believing in democracy that we need the Jewish Commonwealth in Palestine — because its existence, its growth and freedom would right an ancient wrong; because they would achieve for all Jews — those who really are not in exile and those who really are — that equalization of status for their group which all nationalities claim and struggle for and must achieve; because the Commonwealth's existence would advance mankind toward equal liberty. This, and not exile is what the Jewish schools of the American Jewish community need above all to teach their pupils concerning the Zionist endeavor.

Moreover, that endeavor is but one of the many undertakings of the community, and it is neither single nor simple. The Zionist movement consists of many sects and parties that are all agreed as to their end and in conflict, in some instances bitterly and irreconcilably in conflict, as to their means. But through their very conflicts and antagonisms they are members of one another, united with a unity which should be an orchestration of their differences and makes and keeps them all Zionists together.

The same observation applies to the Ashkenazim, the Sephardim, the Hassidim, the Mizrachites, the Agudath Israelites, the Conservatives, the Reformites, the Reconstructionists, and the other Judaists, white and black, who together constitute the congregations of American Judaism. It applies to the fraternal orders, the Congresses, the Committees, the Federations, the Welfare Councils, and other associations in which the Jews of American Jewish communities come together and through which they seek to defend the community's being and to advance its interests, as a part of the American scene. In their conflicts no less than in their cooperation they are members of one another — and to the anti-Semite identical with one another, living for the same ends by the same means. Each, according to its traits and activities makes its own contribution to the character and spirit of the American Jewish community. Each is suffused and modified by its relation with the others, and the community as a whole is an orchestration of their differences of tone and timbre. This orchestration is what the culture of the community consists in. It is a present, living, growing event, and the past — the total content of the curricula of our schools — can have value and meaning only as it is itself taken up and digested in the living present.

Obviously, if Jewish education is to be a relevant education, if it is to serve its function as the transmitter of the characteristic social inheritance of the Jew and the sustainer of the Jewish community, it must concern itself with the totality of the present, and with the past as a *living* past, a changing propulsive component of the present with its opportunities, its dangers, and its challenge to insight and courage, particularly to courage. It will communicate to the Jewish child the extension and intension of the meaning of the word "Jew." To be born into the Jewish inheritance, to grow up identified as a Jew in this Christian world is to be born into a future of outer hardship and inner conflict from which it is natural to seek escape, even when escape is self-defeating and renders the hardship and conflict all the greater. The education of such an one must be an education that will enable him to live bravely and affirmatively, to accept the realities in good cheer without illusion; to stand up and not yield, vindicating the integrity of his Jewish being according to the democratic rule of equal liberty for all men, proclaiming that liberty to all the land and all the inhabitants thereof.

Can the Jewish school, be it Sunday school, *cheder* or *talmud torah*, or what have you, do this, with its limitations of time, scene, equipment, personnel and outlook, against the contagions of the home, the pressures and solicitations of the non-Jewish environment? It cannot. Jewish parents delegate to it an insuperable task, when they lay upon it the entire burden of Jewish education. In this matter it is even more needful, if they are in earnest, that they educate themselves as well as procure education for their children. Far more than the young whose future they shape, they need this knowledge and these attitudes, this sense of history as the living past. They need to employ it in the daily life at home. They need to communicate it, they need to share it with the larger community which environs the Jewish community, of which the Jewish community is a part.

The easiest and surest vehicles of such communication and participation are as a rule aesthetic and cultural. They range from the specialties of the kitchen to the singularities of song and speech, of religious holiday and secular festival. These should be developed to express today's positive meaning of the word "Jew" for the Jew from within, and to share with the non-Jewish neighbor from without. Jewish education, if it is to assure a healthy future for the Jewish community, must address itself to the task of communicating to all the members of the community, grown-ups as well as children, the doctrine and discipline of the Jewish way of life which will keep it an abundant reservoir of manhood and womanhood whose traits the city, the state, the nation can continuously draw into their own more comprehensive vitality and strength. For in our democratic society this vitality, this strength, consists in the union of its multiplicity and variety, in the orchestration of the different. The power and promise of the city's or the nation's being do not consist in the suppression or the abolition of the different among its components. The power and promise of the nation's being consist in the release and teamplay of the differences among its components. Jews have the difference designated by the word "Jew" to contribute to this teamplay. It cannot be contributed as merely a remembered past, however proud. A past only remembered and not taken up and consumed in the present is like undigested food, a burden, a poison, not a nourishment, which those whom it weighs upon perforce endeavor to spew out and forget. Jewish education, if it would serve the Jewish community, has the task of making the past a living past, not a parasite upon the present, but the sustaining nourishment of the present, relevant to the tasks, the problems and the dangers of the changes and chances of the entire community endeavoring to realize the ideals of the American way.

Religious Education in Democratic Society

UNTIL recent years, the trends of democratic sentiment in democratic society have been steadily less and less favorable to the privileged status which custom and tradition allow to "religious" organizations, "religious" interests and "religious" personnel. This status is a survival from the so-called "age of faith," an age in which one particular ecclesiastical establishment was powerful enough to maintain an exclusive monopoly of doctrine and discipline, to crush competitive religious societies, and to suppress or destroy religious alternatives as heresies. When this monopoly was first ordained it was a new thing in the world. The republics and kingdoms of antiquity did not know the practice. In them the gods and their service were either an affair for each family, each occupational group or each political government; the state religion was one among others, with its special functions, and the idea of a struggle between religious and secular interests for supremacy was not easily thinkable. The Christian churches took form and grew up in the emotional climate of this pluralism of cultus. Indeed, they were themselves pluralistic, and their fertile early history was characterized by marked differentiations of doctrine and discipline about which gathered many sects. These sectarian differentiations were reduced to uniformity not by the desire and intention of their communicants but by the command of the secular imperial power, which rewarded the unity it enforced with a privileged status ordered by fiat. From Constantine to Justinian, emperors multiplied the privilege of clergy until, when there were no more Roman emperors in Rome, clerical prerogative had become identical with the exclusive control of what was left of the intellectual enterprise of the western world, and of not a little of its property and power. Imperial favor had been granted always in the certainty, on the part of the Christian successor to divine Augustus, that the church would remain an instrument and agency of the state and the head of the state be always the Pontifex Maximus of

Reprinted from *Jewish Education*, Vol. 13, No. 1, 1941.

the Church. Justinian had described himself, without challenge or denial, "vicar of God," "supreme master of beliefs."

Events falsified the certainty and for a time reversed the relations between Church and State. Some eight hundred years after Justinian, Pope Benedict VIII's Bull, *Unam Sanctam* claimed for the Papacy, as against all other powers, the imperial especially, complete obedience in all things. But this Bull's totalitarian claims were put forth when the wherewithal to make them good was lacking, if it ever existed. It initiated an era of steady recession of ecclesiastical power, without, however, any abatement of ecclesiastical claims. In various parts of Europe, in France, and conspicuously in German-speaking countries and in England, the ancient subordination of church to state was restored; the chief of the state was acknowledged as the head of the church, and the religious establishment was made once more an instrument of policy, foreign and domestic.

Nor did this condition remain stable. In protestant countries, in spite of initial suppression and persecution, religious societies multiplied. Each set up its own doxy with its own ritual and its own way of life. Each made the same claim as its alternatives and rivals to possessing the one true infallible revelation of the will of God to man, and the sole vehicle of his grace and salvation. At first the state demanded conformity of doctrine and discipline to those of the state church. It censored, it persecuted, it killed. But ultimately it abandoned both its claim and its effort. Religious societies grew and multiplied. Their number and variety, and the number and variety of their doctrines and disciplines, became too great to be coerced, or to coerce one another. As Monsignor John Ryan recognizes, there is safety in numbers: "Constitutions," the Monsignor writes in his book, *The Church and the State*, "can be changed, and non-Catholic sects may decline to such a point that the political proscription of them may become feasible and expedient." Non-conformist sects had increased to such a point that political proscription of them had become unfeasible and inexpedient. The Christian communions had found their way back to the pre-Nicene freedom of differentiation in doctrine, in discipline and in association.

The fact that there had come into existence many religious societies, neither sanctioned by the State nor bound to it, and that the State had to deal with each of them on equal terms, was formulated as the principle of the separation of church and state. On this principle, the state is seen as a political association which adheres to no religion but extends the equal protection of its laws to all, ultimately including those which, like Judaism, Mohammedanism or Buddhism, tradition had excluded because infidel and misbelieving.

As the idea of the separation of the church from the state spread and was made effectual, its principle was transferred to other than religious societies. Business undertakings, professional associations, colleges of scholars or craftsmen, trades and artisans' unions, racial groups, women, — each organization of interest begged, labored and fought for a similar liberation from coercion and a similar equality of status before the law. The world over, but most thoroughly and successfully here in the United States, the direction of social change was *from* an order fundamentally of fixity, status, caste and authority, *to* an order fundamentally of social mobility, contract, free association and civil, religious and intellectual liberty. Mankind had begun a movement toward democracy as a rule of association and a way of life.

Democracy may be said to obtain in any society where the power of the state rests on the consent of the governed, and is separate not only from the doctrine and discipline of each and every religious communion, but also of every other organization of interest, economic, racial, cultural, or intellectual, yet assures to all the equal protection of the laws. Democratic society is a society based on the equal right of different people freely to live and to grow according to their differences. It is a whole which supports no special interest of those composing it, but maintains the equal liberty of all such interests to achieve whatever power and influence they are capable of, not through privilege, not through invidious advantage, but on their merits. It assures them opportunity to try, in fair competition, without fear or favor, to do the same job better than their competitors. To be thus mobile, democratic society must be open society. All of its associations, including the state, must tend to be voluntary associations which its individual members enter into and dissolve freely, on equal terms. Democratic society is composed by the free association of different interests on the foundation of this equality in right. Upon this foundation it conducts its economy as free enterprise, its science as free inquiry and free thought, its religion as free conscience, its arts as free expression and communication. The culture of such a society is necessarily a pluralistic culture, a confederation and self-orchestration of these variables and differentiations into a stream of living ever freer and more abundant. Democratic government is the arm with which democratic society provides itself to keep the bed of this stream open and secure, to safeguard the equal right of different individuals and associations of individuals. Its task is dual, at once that of a roadbuilder and a traffic cop. And it is even more to assure fair play, to check unfair competition, to cut off invidious advantage and to prevent the trespass of interests upon one another, than to construct and maintain the open roadways of equal opportunity for all.

II

Now, it has long been a commonplace that the continuity of a way of life depends upon how it is passed on through the generations. The tools and techniques of transmission, the personality of the transmitter, are in fact all that there is to education, whether direct or indirect. Aristotle noted very long ago that "that which contributes most to the permanence of constitutions is the adaptation of education to the form of government."

It is such an adaptation of schooling which, in the course of the last hundred years, democratic society has succeeded in bringing to pass, not easily, not freely, but by dint of harsh and bitter struggle against the powerful resistance of all sorts of vested interests, ghostly and material. Nor is the struggle by any means over. The free, public democratic education as exemplified in the American educational establishment, continues, as in the days of its first victory, to perform its tasks under something like a condition of siege. It is beleaguered by all sorts of pressure groups, the advance guards of all sorts of special interests, each with a special plea for special privilege for its own especial doctrine and discipline. And in the forefront of these, the most clamant, the most insistent, are the interests of sectarian religion. Where others are more or less aware that they argue on sufferance, the religionists demand, as of right. They assert, in the words of the director of the Weekday and Vacation Church School and Community Relations for the International Council of Religious Education, Mr. Dyer Blair, that religion must be "a part of the basic curriculum of the public school." And short of this consummation, they require that one or another of the facilities of the public school shall be put at their disposal, so that they may "reach the unreached" and "church the unchurched" until the whole enterprise of democratic education is once more subsumed under the doctrines and disciplines of the churches. In one way or another these claims are sounded on all levels of the educational establishment: in the great private colleges like Harvard or Yale or Brown, that once had been seminaries for the indoctrination of clergymen and now purport to be organizations for the pursuit of truth; and in the great land-grant universities like Michigan or Wisconsin or California that make less pretense of "the higher learning" and search and seek in field and laboratory after useful knowledge.

The reasons given for these claims are various and not always candid. Their upper limit is the pretension of the Roman Catholic hierarchy that it has inherited a mandate from God to teach the deposit of faith, supernatural and infallible, which God has entrusted to his vicar on earth and to his ecclesiastical subordinates, and to them alone. According to this claim, the church's mission to teach extends to all people, Catholic and non-Catholic alike; and according to Pope Pius XI, in the Encyclical *Divini Illius Magistri* "there is no power on earth that may lawfully oppose her or stand in her way." Thus education is God's charge to the Catholic Church and only to the Catholic Church, and the control of educational undertakings, both public and private, and of every branch of learning so far as religion and morality are concerned, are claimed as the church's inalienable and exclusive right. The canon law forbids the teaching of anything to Roman Catholic children contrary to Roman Catholicism, and makes attendance at non-Catholic schools conditional on special permission from Pope or Bishop.[1]

The lower limit of churchmen's claim to prerogatives in education is the proposition, affirmed even among the most liberal Protestants, that in some peculiar and organic way, "religious" education is character education, whereas non-religious education is not and cannot be. What kind of character, is not said, but assumed; and one may safely add that it must at least be a character conformed to the pattern and interest of the sect molding the character, and disciplining it to special church loyalties, sentiments and practices by means of instruction in the Bible, and in the dogmas and the rituals of the sect. Instruction in non-religious subjects such as arithmetic, history, chemistry, music or housekeeping somehow cannot be character education and falls outside the field of morals. Morality is peculiarly bound to religion and religion peculiarly identified with a special and specific doctrine and discipline.

[1] Where their rule cannot be enforced they temporize, as is the case in the United States. "Realizing that segregation was impossible," writes President Shuster of Hunter College in an article on "The Conflicts Among Catholics," published in *The American Scholar*, "wide-awake leaders started a movement to foster religious instruction in the public schools."

Thence it follows that character must be weak and morality lacking where children have not been molded, body and mind, to this doctrine and this discipline.

The pretensions of the clergy to a superior ability to shape character and maintain morality constitutes the least common denominator of their claim of special privilege for the doctrines, the doings, the property and the professional personnel of the sects. It is an ancient claim which has its root in the fact that the Emperor Justinian, having rid his churchmen of the competition of the secular schools by closing them, gave education to be the exclusive monopoly of the clergy. During a thousand years, so long as there was any schooling, it was schooling in religion, with the clergy as teachers and church dogma as the ultimate limit of what might be safely said and taught concerning the life, the labors, and the destiny of man.

Thus the claim of the more or less exclusive intimacy of religion with morals possesses the authority of age, and is generally accepted without scrutiny. Yet wherever the scrutiny is made, the claim seems to rest on very debatable evidence. For example. Recently Columbia's foremost psychologist, Prof. Edward G. Thorndike, made a study of the American way of life in American cities. He reported that in cities where the general goodness of life is high, church membership is low; that in cities where church membership is high, the average in good reading, home ownership, continuance in school is low, while illiteracy and child labor are high. "Unless the better communities under-report their church membership," said Dr. Thorndike, "or the worse communities over-report theirs, we must suspect that the churches are clubs of estimable people and maintainers of traditional rites and ceremonies rather than powerful forces for human betterment."[2] These findings of Thorndike's confirm earlier and current findings of educators, psychologists and penologists, psychiatrists and criminologists regarding the claimed influence of religious instruction on delinquency and crime. Thus, that leader of the Essentialists in educational theory and practice, Prof. William C. Bagley, writes:

> The states and sections of our country where religious 'fundamentalism' shows the fewest signs of 'collapse' are the states and sections which have the heaviest ratios of the most serious crime (homicide) and which in proportion to their population, have produced the greatest number of criminals. And among the states that have the lowest ratios of serious crime

[2] E. L. Thorndike: *Your City*, New York: Harcourt Brace.

> and apparently produce the fewest criminals in proportion to their population are certain states in which a more liberal spirit unquestionably prevails.[3]

"Most criminals," writes Prof. Carl Murchison, "belong to some church and frankly admit the fact. The big majority attend church services every Sunday morning in the Maryland Pen . . . 14.3 per cent are frankly agnostic. The criminal is religious, the vast majority belonging to some established religious denomination."[4]

In *The Individual Delinquent*, Dr. Healy declares:

> It is quite evident that formal religious training has not prevented delinquency in many of our cases, when other strong personal or environmental conditions were not, as such, squarely met. Participation in religious education and religious communion has been quite general among our offenders, but of course the answer given by pastors of all congregations is that these have had the word, but not caught the spirit. Occasionally in certain unstable types there is a tendency to religious emotionalism and anti-social conduct at the same time. It is curious that in not over a dozen cases have we heard expressions of formed irreligious opinions . . . certain it is that, through not taking into account these other backgrounds of delinquency, such religious experience as most of our offenders have had has not proved thus sustaining. Many a parish would be bettered if the fundamental sources of misconduct were studied, enumerated and treated in a scientific spirit.[5]

William Healy and Augusta Bronner studied 1636 deliquents before the Chicago Juvenile Court in 1910, and found that 90 per cent of them were of religious background (56 per cent of the total being Roman Catholic) and less than one-tenth of one per cent definitely of no religion.[6]

III

On the record, does it not seem as if the claim of the sects to a special prerogative in the education of youth is based upon two special pleas: one, that "religious" education exercises a peculiarly salutary influence upon morals; the other, that churchmen once upon a time did have a practical monopoly of schools and schooling and the Cath-

[3] W. C. Bagley: *Education, Crime and Social Progress*, New York, 1931, p. 43.

[4] *Criminal Intelligence*, Worcester, 1926, p. 144.

[5] Boston, 1924, pp. 151–2.

[6] *Delinquents and Criminals*, New York, 1926.

olics among them continue to claim this monopoly, while the Protestants ask merely for a privileged relation of their various doctrines and disciplines to the general educational establishments.

Neither plea is a reason, both are rationalizations of a special interest. If everywhere in democratic society the clergy have been deprived of their monopoly over education and public education has been largely separated from religious education, it is not because of any antagonism of the people to religion, but because of the opposition of the clergy to the equalization of educational opportunity for all the people. By and large, the American public school system was established and enabled to grow and to serve, through the efforts of plain people, of workingsmen's organizations and of intellectuals or philanthropists like Horace Mann, whose fundamental faith was in the democratic ideal and the democratic way of life. By and large, what has been achieved, has been achieved against the obstructionist tactics and unremitting resistance of the sectarian interest.

That this interest should be in conflict with that of free, public education was natural enough. It sought a fundamentally different goal by a fundamentally different method. The goal of the free public school of democratic society has to be the support and strengthening of the common faith in the democratic way of life and thought by the development of habits of thinking and doing which, in Aristotle's phrase, should contribute most to the permanence of the democratic constitution. It accepts the instincts and impulses with which children are born for what they are; it provides them with enchanneling action on the environment that disciplines them into habits by the methods of free inquiry rather than authoritarian rehearsal; and it opens up new ways for the continual growth and reconstruction of personal traits and social relations. As John Dewey says, the primary business of the school, in democratic society, is to train all the children in cooperative and mutually helpful living.

But regardless of how unanimous may be the verbal agreement of churchmen with this notion of education, it is contrary to their actual interest. The primary business of sectarian instruction is naturally enough the growth and prosperity of the sectarian organization. Each needs devout communicants who will believe beyond any question that their special sectarian discipline and doctrine and theirs alone can save the human soul. Their method requires the minimizing of observation, reflection, and choice of alternatives and the maximizing of indoctrination, repetition memoriter, and exhortation. Their goal requires that minds should be molded into automatic acquiescence in dogmas regarding all sorts of matters, from the Immaculate Conception to birth control. It is true, of course, as Mr. Dyer Blair points out, that in many of the weekday church schools programs have been enriched, methods have been changed in the direction of the democratic way. That is, efforts have been and are being made to meet the competition of the free public school and to do the same job, if not better, at least as well. But as truly religious observers note, when such efforts are successful, they tend to bankrupt their primary business. The content of instruction becomes secularized; the denominational interest is deprived of its privileged position among the other interests that compose the diversified theme. The method of instruction introduces that fair consideration of alternatives which opens the way from conformity to dissent and differentiation. Interest shifts from *a* religion to religion, and religion becomes a personal attitude, instead of an infallible creed. Character, then, is detached from any special doctrine and discipline, and becomes a habit of doing and thinking which may be developed as response to any material with which the environment challenges personality. There ceases to be a privileged material: arithmetic, English, history, art-work, social studies, botany or chemistry become no less shapers of character than denominational doctrines and disciplines. Those become secularized and are assimilated to their proper place in the social studies. This, if I am not mistaken, is why lifelong students of religious education, devout Christian experts in its techniques and goals, like George Coe and Harrison Elliott, are sceptical of both its pretensions and results. In his book, *Can Religious Education be Christian*, Harrison Elliott declares that "a fundamentalist procedure and true education are not compatible."

Nevertheless, "the fundamentalist procedure" must be insisted on, if the claim of any denomination to a privileged position is to be enforced. Such pundits of Catholicism as Mr. Mortimer A. Adler[7]

[7] Concerning this manifestation at the Conference of Science, Philosophy and Religion in New York City last September, the *Christian Century* said:

> "It is doubtful if a more indecent spectacle has ever been staged in the long tradition of American culture and scholarship than that which the members of this conference had to sit through. The spirit of tolerance . . . has rarely been subjected to a test quite so exacting. Mr. Adler was answered by Professor Sidney Hook, of New York University, and others, who unfortunately, and perhaps forgivably, replied in kind.
>
> ". . . Mr. Adler's proposal that we return to the thirteenth century philosophy and theology of Thomas Aquinas, which is the official doctrine

thunder in the index, with epithets and gestures, the commonplace old charge of the clerical against the modern world — that it has fallen into materialism, irreligion, sin and war because fundamentalist doctrine and discipline have been displaced by the conceptions of science, the methods of democratic education and non-invidious subject matter. The free public schools, the charge is, are ultimately responsible for the state of the world. Because of them, churches are empty, the religious schools are poorly attended, the churchmen are poorly supported, and the earth is given over into the hands of the wicked. When the historic and sociological record is called up, when the data studied by Drs. Shaw and Myers and Bagley and Healy and Bronner and so many others are cited, the excuse is given that the types studied by these experts did not really and truly learn religion. But if this excuse has anything to it, then exactly those persons least exposed to the doctrines and disciplines of the denominations, being the least criminal or delinquent, are the most religious. What is called "religious" education, it might be noted, had been in control of the training of western mankind during a thousand years, what is called secular education less than a hundred. If there were any such connection as is claimed between character and some special doctrine and discipline, all clerics would by this time have been shaped into paragons of their morality. As John Stuart Mill[8] noted in 1859, when the Churches still

of the Roman Catholic Church, inevitably conjures up the bugaboo of authoritarianism and priestly control of knowledge and education. Ecclesiastical fascism is no more palatable to modern scholarship which has tasted the sweets of intellectual freedom than is political fascism. Mr. Hutchins himself is distinctly tinctured with this same scholasticism, but he writes and speaks with a degree of reserve . . . which suggests that he is better satisfied with his diagnosis than with his prescription.

". . . But the introduction of the category of revelation backed by a scholastic theology which makes revelation a form of knowledge and the official church its custodian, simply scares a modern scholar into a state of intellectual vertigo.

"And he has good reason to be scared. The hard-won freedom of intelligence to inquire into every field of reality, including that area where certain 'truths' are held to be sacrosanct because they were once delivered from above — this freedom the modern man will not easily surrender. It is unfortunate that, in one university at least, where the teachers and students have made a fair start toward emancipation from the parochialism of science, the primary issue should have been momentarily obscured by the introduction of irrelevant issues such as Mr. Adler has raised."

[8] *On Liberty*, p. 75.

had control of such education of the people as England provided: "not one Christian in a thousand guides or tests his individual conduct by reference to the laws of that morality. . . . Its doctrines in their integrity are serviceable to pelt adversaries with . . . they have no hold on ordinary believers. . . ." In point of fact, men have long learned from experience that it is as vain to require that a beautician must be beautiful, or that a physician must enjoy good health, as that "religious" education should result in good character. The causes do not reside in that domain of social life.

IV

It should be clear now why I have described the arguments on behalf of what the McLaughlin statute calls "religious observance and education," at the expense of the time of the children and the teachers of the public schools, as rationalizations. The churches are suffering from technological unemployment, and they naturally and properly are desirous to get their jobs back and of multiplying them. Unfortunately, they seek this end, not on their merits, but on the basis of privilege established by special legislation, often requiring modifications of constitutional provisions regarding the entire separation of the church from the state. As is well known, efforts at modification range from proposals to provide free text-books "for all parochial schools of whatever denomination," or laws providing bus service for children enrolled in parochial schools to the current amendment of the education law of the State of New York, which ordains that the public schools "release time" to the denominations for "religious observance and education."

Although the friends of democratic education are at present agitated about this particular item of sectarian privilege, it is, as we have seen, but the latest loss to free, public education in the course of the generations-long war which the ecclesiastical interests are waging against it. This is why, the event, which by itself alone cannot do much damage, has aroused so much fear for the freedom and integrity of the public schools among those whose common faith is democracy as a principle of association and a rule of life. The record gives them reason to distrust the vested interests of the sects. They fear that this privilege is but initiatory and may open the door to the ultimate one. Already in one place or another, the release of time has been followed by a requirement of service, the requirement of service by demands for space and personnel. There were symptoms as early as 1936 when the Catholic National Confraternity of Christian Doctrine met for four days in New York City and the press reported that one outcome of the meeting would be that the City Board of Education would be asked to make an important change in its policy to give the children a free hour each week for required religious study in their own churches — and, of course, with all that is implied by the word *required* — taking attendance, keeping records as a regular part of the pupils' school grades and counting the records in arranging promotions. In other communities the range of already existing encroachments is even wider. Perhaps it is not without a certain irony that the entire undertaking got its first practical start in 1913 in Gary, Indiana, where the superintendent of schools, taking a leaf of efficiency out of industry as there conducted, initiated a continuous use of the school plant so that the industrialist taxpayers might get out of them a maximum of service at a minimum cost. The Gary System, as it came to be called, involved releases of children from the plant for any purpose whatsoever — instruction in music, reading at the library, a visit to a playground or movie. And, of course, church was not excluded. The churchmen were quick to seize the opportunity, and to employ their claims to superior moral influence in order to acquire a monopoly of this released time. They crowded out the competition, not on merit, but by privilege. It is too much to expect that other special interests will not seek to profit by their example, and use their precedent to overcome or subordinate to their own purposes the clerical advantage of position. Such setups as those headed by M. K. Hart or the fascist priest Charles Coughlin, a chamber of commerce, an industrial combination like the power trust, a political party, and ultimately, even the trades-unions to whom the public schools owe so much of their existence and development, may be expected sooner or later to make demands like those of the churches. Some already have, though not yet so openly. In the circumstances, the democratic groups which have opposed denominational nibbling at the public school structure can hardly be reproached for feeling that sectarian successes have darkened the prospect for what Harrison Elliott calls "true education," and for the school life of teacher and pupil.

V

Up to this point, you will have noticed, I have made no mention of the Jews. There had been no occasion. Up to this point, they had played no part, as an aggregation of religious and cultural communities, in the controversy here reviewed. Always the cult of a minority — much of the time a handicapped and persecuted minority — amid Christian majorities, Judaistic doctrine and discipline had been throughout the *soi-disant* dispersion of the Jews a thing apart, separate from the state and permitted by it and the church to exist on sufferance and not as of right. If Judaism was to survive at all, it had to survive on its inner vitality; if it was to grow, it had to grow on its own power. When democratic society opened to Judaism equal liberty and the equal protection of the laws of democratic government, Jewish response to this freedom and this security was first of all a multiplication of sects, with many adding themselves to the pre-emancipation few. The meaning of "Judaism" became, in the course of the last hundred years almost as diversified and on occasion as contradictory as the meaning of "Christianism," but Judaism retained, even more than Christianism, a living continuity of experience and context. With all other religions, Judaism is undergoing the challenge, the permeation, and the transformation of the secular influence flowing from science, from industry, from the democratic way of life. Its educational establishments, its day schools and Sabbath schools are also confronted with the competition of the great democratic system of free public instruction. Its rabbis and synagogues and temples are also in a state of technological unemployment. A scant minority of the Jewish children of the American Jewish communities seek or receive the education in matters Jewish which all can have, and if they only knew it, cannot do without.

During two generations now, Jewish citizens, laymen and professionals alike, who are concerned for the survival and growth of the Jewish way of life on democratic terms and in the context of our wider democracy, have been wrestling with this competitive problem. It is the problem which led to the organization of the American Association for Jewish Education. It is the problem which has exercised the rabbinical colleges, the teachers' seminaries, the various local and regional education committees, not to mention other less directly concerned groups.

Now, so far as I know, the effort to solve this problem has never employed claims regarding impact on morals or character, though on the record they might plausibly have been made. It has never led to any demands on the public schools, whether for time or anything else. It has persevered within the bounds of a loyal adherence to the rule of absolute separation of church and state. Although the need of the young of Israel for a fundamental Jewish education has a tragic import, personal and social, happily absent from the lives of their Christian friends and comrades, no attempt was ever made to meet this need, to "reach the unreached" save outside the limits set by the public schools engaged in training the children of democracy for democratic citizenship. The Jewish educational effort was limited to exploration and experiment within the communion of Israel itself. It was clear to the devoted company of laymen, clergymen and teachers that Judaism must win and hold the allegiance of the growing youth of Jewry on its own merits as a way of life and thought, on merits proved in an open field of competing alternatives, religious as well as secular. They saw that Judaism could hold this allegiance on no other ground. Believing in democracy, they saw the faiths and culture of the Jews living and growing, if they *were* to live and grow, as one communion of mankind among many others, each different from the others and each strengthening and being strengthened by living with the others. Like their non-Jewish neighbors, they learned much from secular competitors concerning matter and method, replacing whenever they could indoctrination by inquiry; rote and exhortation by activities and projects; trying always to make Jewish education at least as significant, as vital and as liberating as that in the progressive public school and supplementary to that of the school. It may be true that they have not much to show for their pains, but the important thing is that they were pains taken with no trespass of the bounds separating church and state and without demand for privilege of any kind.

In New York, when the McLaughlin Bill was first being agitated, the Jewish Board of Ministers there, the Jewish Teachers Association and the Jewish Education Association joined with the Public Education Association, the Progressive Education Association, the Society for Ethical Culture, the Civil Liberties Union and others to oppose the Bill's passage. When it became clear that some such bill would pass, they offered as an alternative an adaptation of the original form of the old Gary Plan. This now figures in the record as the *Dismissed Time Plan.* It calls for one or more shorter school days, the complete dismissal of all pupils without *requiring* attendance anywhere and a concentration upon making "religious" education able successfully to compete on its own merits and with its own strength, against its general, cultural, vocational and other competitors. It calls for keeping the public school and the synagogal or church school independent of one another in all ways, from the making of records to the planning of curricula, thus to maintain a strict loyalty to the principle of the separation of Church and State. Meanwhile, where the "released time" plan had become law, as in New York, the responsible authorities for Jewish education propose the maximum of interfaith cooperation compatible with the safeguarding of the democratic rule regarding the separation of church and state. Such a proposal calls for an unfailing alertness on behalf of the democratic way even more than of the sectarian doctrine and discipline. It calls for that courage which Plato describes as wisdom concerning dangers, a courage as rare and difficult as it is indispensable to a minority so precariously placed as are the Jews. Happily, the responsible leaders of the Jewish education movement, as I have come to know them, do not lack this courage.

Critical Problems in Jewish Education

LISTENING to discussions of the contents, methods and purposes of Jewish education, I sense about them, every so often, a certain self-isolation. There is a disposition, very wide-spread among us, to treat the education of Jews in Jewishness as an independent variable, without much regard for the social and cultural setting that Jews must live in as Jews. The disposition is traditional, its springs are ancient. Our status in the pre-democratic western world as a people shut out and held apart has given it an accent and meaning which our admission to the equal liberties of the democratic way of life alters only slowly and not consistently. How long is it that the education of Jews as Jews has ceased to be the education of generations imprisoned in a ghetto? Ghetto education had, of course, the virtues of its defects. Practically everywhere in the world where Jews lived, the content, the methods and the purposes of their education were the same. Jewish education was endowed with an extraordinary unity and consistency. Nor did anybody pay much attention to the fact that the price for these putative excellences was, to live cut off and shut out from the full, diversified, fruitful communication with non-Jewish communities such as we enjoy, not unprecariously, here in our own country.

Some of the consequences of this enforced isolation are with us this day. Concentrated on both the specific and the general problems of the education of Jews in American Jewish communities, we are hardly aware of the fact that we have come together to discuss them on Washington's Birthday, and that this holds something symbolic, something spiritually significant. That we should be able to assemble for this purpose on the birthday of the "Father of our Country," has an almost religious meaning for us. As the military leader of the War for Independence, and as a guide in the post-war construction of the nation, Washington helped to define and implement the American Idea, of which our generation are beneficiaries, privileged beyond our fellow Jews anywhere in the world, to live our lives in freedom

Reprinted from *Jewish Education,* Vol. 19, No. 3, 1948.

and earn our bread in peace. That we are able to meet here this evening, for this purpose, follows from the event that the American Idea could be, and was, made the plan of organization of the American nation and the formation of the American way of life.

Nowhere else in the world, not in Canada, not in Australia, nor in New Zealand, nor in Sweden, nor in Switzerland,— I mention only the freest countries — do Jews enjoy the full equality of status which is their right under the Constitution of the United States. The Constitution implements the American Idea, and the intent of this Idea is a departure from the past record of human relations so complete, so profound, that it is still revolutionary, that it has not yet become the practical, the fighting faith of all Americans throughout the land.

Fundamentally, the American Idea is very simple. And in its simplicity it contradicts and opposes the ways of men with one another that prevail throughout the world. It is the idea that people who are different from each other can live together with each other, can work together and play together, in such a way that each is freer and happier and more abundantly himself than he could be if he had to go it alone.

In their ghettos, the Jews of the world were compelled to go it alone, and the effects of that imposed segregation are still apparent. It repressed the neighborliness that is spontaneous in all of us. It kept Jews and non-Jews from ever becoming neighbors. The Christian world held religious belief to be *sine qua non* for political right. It required State religions, and the organic identification of Church and State. It erected a wall between neighbors of one religion and neighbors of another religion, a wall which the folkways and mores still support. But the American Idea breached the wall. It instituted separation of Church and State as organic to the national being. Thus it opened the way to free communication between peoples of different faiths, to the development of the spirit of neighborliness and good will between the different. In countries where this separation does not yet obtain, religious minorities are penalized for their difference; neither Jewish education, nor any other unsanctioned by the State Church, can have equality of status under the law, or any fundamental security. You need only look at Spain and Russia.

Once the principle that faith and worship must be free, that no religious belief is entitled to greater privilege than any other, has become incorporated into a people's basic thoughts and ways, other liberties enter into the structure of the national being. One such, fundamental to the American Idea, is free and equal access to education. According to the American Idea, the survival and growth of a democratic people depends on the range, the diversity and the adequacy of the education of its individual citizens. Equality of educational opportunity is one of the articles of the religion of democracy, the American religion. It affirms that education makes real the equality ordained by law. Hence, in the more than century and a half since the adoption of our Bill of Rights, the American people have established and maintained the greatest system of free public education in the entire world. We are paying more for education than all of Europe and most of Asia put together. And all the nation's children, without regard to creed, race, sex, occupation or social status, are presumed equally privileged to attend the tax-supported free public schools from kindergarten to university.

Given the honor which the Jewish community traditionally pays to learning, if not to wisdom, given the age-old dependence upon education for the transmission of the Torah, it is natural that the young of the Jewish community should flock to the public schools, and that the task of the truant officer should be light among them. In most communities of this country, as you well know, schooling is not merely permitted, it is required. And Jewish children fulfill this requirement with distinction. To meet it, however, means to reduce the number of waking hours available for other purposes in guiding the growth of the children. It means curtailing the time available for their special interests as Jews. It means as a rule that their education or instruction in the cultural inheritance of the Jewish people must come after they had already spent at least five hours in the public school. It means that what they learn in a Hebrew day school or a Sunday school, they learn in the context of what they have been taught in the public school. It means that their attending a Jewish school, which can not but be voluntary, must be secured as against many other competitive interests. Among those will be not only the children's need of play in the open air; there will be also their parents' desire to give them special training in music or dancing or one or another of the arts. There will also be the feeling of many parents to overcome that such Jewish education as is available provides little beyond a certain training in the faulty repetition of Hebrew prayers and the like, and that the study of other subjects would be far more relevant to living as a good neighbor among other Americans.

Under such competitive conditions, the modification of the theory and practice of education which Jews brought with them from the ghettos of Europe was a foregone conclusion. Nor was the conclusion foregone for Jews alone. The much more numerous, powerful and less flexible Catholic establishments also underwent reforms, with the consequence that American parochial schools, conducted in the context of the Nation's free tax-supported schools, have become among the best in the Catholic world. Lacking this competitive context, Catholic schools might all have stayed on the level of those of Spain or Southern Italy, or one or another of the countries of South America; Jewish schools might all have stayed on the level of *talmud torahs* in Galicia or other parts of darkest Europe. In Jewish education, certainly, this non-Jewish competition has been a benefaction. The new theory and practice of education developed through the initiative of Samson Benderley and carried forward today by the group of dedicated men and women whom we have come to call "professionals," are emulative responses to this competition. Our "professionals" *are* members of a profession and not merely *melamdim* because they received training in American teachers' colleges, because they are aware of the problems and concern themselves with their solution as men scientifically trained, who know that education, to be truly fruitful, must be based on science and practiced as an art. Willy nilly, they labor to bring the content and the methods of the Jewish school within the larger goal and up to the competitive standard set by the best public school.

Their task is further complicated by the fact that with liberty has come secularization in all the dimensions of Jewish life. Recall that the earliest of American Jewish communities stayed almost exclusively religious communities, that the education they provided was entirely "religious" education. But, as in the free world of America, the personal habits and group customs of the ghetto wore down, as communication with non-Jewish cultures and activities opened up, diversified, multiplied, new interests were added to the old or displaced them; new institutions, new communal enterprises were set up; first Yiddish, then English, were made emulative of Hebrew as the vehicle of literary expression; religious leaders challenged the established orthodoxy and branched off into new sects with new liturgies, new ideals in new tongues. The meaning of the word "Jew" which, at the beginning of the nineteenth century had been reasonably singular and unambiguous, diversified. Its definitions multiplied into a series of different and often mutually antagonistic formulations. You can run a gamut. Put at one end a notable Jew but not religious, like, say, the late

Mr. Justice Brandeis. Set beside him some person who describes himself as a Judaist; that is, as believing in such and such religious dogmas which he identifies as Judaism, but as participating in no other way in the being of the total community of Israel — any rabbi of the American Council for Judaism, Inc. could be such a person. Then, at the extreme opposite end set some carrier of the total complex of European orthodoxy, say some chassidic *baal-mofes* like the *Lubavitcher Rebbe*. Between these two extremes you could then line out a series of persons, societies, fraternal orders, synagogues, temples, philanthropies, newspapers (Yiddish, English, Hebrew), and what have you. Some of the series would call themselves orthodox, some progressive, some conservative, some reconstructionist, some Zionist, some Bundist, some Yiddishist, some free. Each, in all likelihood, could be subdivided into right and left and center factions. All would be definable by what they specifically thought and believed and did about the entire Jewish heritage and its bearing on the identification of Jew as Jew.

If this does not mean that the singular, certain, exclusive conception of what is a Jew dead and gone, what does it mean? If it does not mean that belief in a Judaism is no longer indispensable to being a Jew, what does it mean? If it does not mean that students of the Jewish being must distinguish between Judaists who are not Jews and Jews who are not Judaist, what does it mean? Obviously the two terms are no longer identical, any more than Swiss, German or French or Italian are identical. Obviously, the word "Jew" is a more comprehensive term than the word "Judaist," sometimes including the meanings of the latter, but with its meanings never included by the latter. Each and every one of the different meanings of both words becomes the focus of a set of personal and group attitudes, of ways of thinking and feeling and knowing, which together constitute the vital intention of "Jew" for the particular person or the particular group. Each then tends to compete with the others for approval, allegiance and support. Each tends to accuse the others of being the cause of the misfortunes of the Jewish people. It is always the other fellow's Judaism that is disaster, not one's own.

Now what are the implications of this situation for the education of Jews as Jews?

When we say "Jewish education" we employ, for the most part, an abstraction. The actualities for which the expression stands are the various educational instruments of the various societies, sects and communions, each with its separate doctrine and discipline, interest and goal; each different from the others and sometimes bitterly at war with the others. To what consensus can you bring the cult of the Lubavitcher with its expectation of the miraculous redemption of Israel through a God-sent Messiah, and the cult of the American Council for Judaism, Inc. for some of whom the Messiah seemed already manifest in Houston, Texas? Now add, to the irreconcilables who together apply the term "Jew" to themselves within the total Jewish community, the anti-Semite who gives the word still another meaning from outside the Jewish community. The latter's meaning retains an identity, a consistency which has remained practically unmodified since it was first fixed by the Christian dogma of salvation. It is perhaps the most potent of the forces which have generated the multiplication, and the flight from one another, of the Jewish groups and sects; and ironically, it nullifies all the differences it has brought about. To the anti-Semite, that Jews are different from each other and at war with one another is a matter of indifference. They are all, together, singly and simply, Jew.

Now, except for prayers to the Lord to defend Israel from his enemies, Jewish education has ignored the nature, the activities and the consequences of anti-Semitism; it has paid no attention to its influence on personality or its effect on group-behavior. The generations of Jewish youth, coming our of the *chedarim*, the *talmud torahs* or the Sunday schools, come out with factional or sectarian conceptions of "Jew," spiritually unequipped to face the modern version of the traditional aggressions against the Jewish being; and, on the whole and in the long run, if not alienated, indifferent to the survival and development of the Jewish group. Early aware that Jewishness is a burden, that "the yoke of the law" imposes many other bonds besides those of the *mitzvohs*, they will seek, consciously and unconsciously, to rid themselves of their burden. The more diverse, manifold and richer their intercommunication with the cultures of the surrounding society, the more likely they are to feel their Jewish heritage not as opportunity but as obstruction, and to seek to reduce it to a minimum if not to eliminate altogether from their lives. This is why "liberation" has tended to become synonymous with assimilation, and the Jewish history of our times the history of a general flight from the Jewish being. That currently the flight is checked and a return is under way marks no fundamental inward change. It is a consequence, rather, of the added pressures and the resulting anxieties and fears due to an anti-Semitism heightened from a chronic to an acute aggressiveness.

This is the situation in which those of us concerned over the relation of Jewish education to Jewish survival confront today. It sets Jewish educators two fundamental problems.

The first is, to recognize what logicians would call the "extension" of the term Jew, and to see clearly that nobody can have a genuine, a complete, Jewish education who has learned only the point of view, the dogmas, the attitudes and the preferences of one sole sect or group or faction. To be complete, education in the Jewish being must embrace studying, knowing, understanding sympathetically and judging objectively not one set of values affirmed by one sect or part, but all the values of all the sects and all the parties and their interaction. It calls for recognition that the wholeness of Israel consists in this interaction of its different communities and communions; consists in the free trade of ideas between men such that the mutual aggressions of orthodox and reform, conservative and reconstructionist, Zionist and Bundist, Yiddishist and Hebraist, free thinker and *Lubavitcher chasid* can come to a consensus of understanding and cooperation. To be complete, Jewish education must so communicate the culture and history of the Jewish people to Jewish youth that they will be able to live and to work in a world unfriendly to Jews, spiritually whole, with heart and mind armed against all anti-Semitic oppression. This armor of the spirit cannot be the same that enabled our fathers and our fathers' fathers to endure. It cannot be the same because neither the climate of opinion, the culture, the knowledge nor the state of the industrial arts are the same as those of the ancestral world. The modern world is awake, as that of our forefathers was not, to the implications of America's Democratic Idea for the role of the Jewish community in the common enterprise of democracy. The modern world acknowledges the equal right of the Jewish community as a union of many diversities, to live out fully its own inner life; by so living to bring into active realization all the qualities of the Jewish culture-complex — the arts of the kitchen as well as the arts of synagogue and theatre; the lore and letters of the lay world as well as those of the religious establishments. America's Democratic Idea requires that the Jew shall know the full extension of the word Jew, shall affirm and defend the values it points to, together with his own right to llve and to sustain these values and to contribute them to the common life of the nation on equal terms with his non-Jewish neighbor.

To meet this requirement is to achieve the psychological rearmament which the younger generation so badly needs. To provide this rearmament is the second of the fundamental problems confronting Jewish education.

Now the educational establishment can solve neither of the two problems without developing a very different kind of teacher from the sort conventional to Jewish schools. It is significant, for example, that teachers in such schools are still prevailingly males. Obviously the Jewish education of youth should provide an attractive career for Jewish women, and every inducement should be offered them to seek the knowledge and skills that the career of a teacher modernly requires. Such knowledge and skills, indeed, should be a *sine quo non* for all teachers in Jewish schools who make teaching a life work. And provision is needed not only for the right training of a new generation, but for the continuous access of the old to the ever increasing new knowledge of the science and art of education.

Nor can the problems be solved without a fundamental rethinking of the curriculums of Jewish schools. It is these schools that can most swiftly and readily lay the foundation of common understanding between Jews of different Jewish loyalties. Their curriculum should, in effect, be an application of the principles of the Springfield Plan to the formation of Jewish mentality. Once this is undertaken, the community grows into a communion of the different and the local Bureau of Jewish Education becomes the sure vehicle of group cooperation. It is this cooperation of the different on equal terms which is the working principle of the American Association for Jewish Education. The Association's effort is centered on replacing segregation and isolation by free communication between the different educational interests, by common action, by consensus as to standards, and by a shared economy. Every new Bureau, every community-wide committee on education, represents a positive step forward in the direction of the spiritual service which the Jewish school must perform for every Jewish child and should perform for every Jewish adult. It is, however, I must also regretfully add, a step taken rather more in the course of blind adjustment to the exigencies of time and place, than a step taken in the fulfillment of an educational program based on a thoroughgoing analysis of the problems presented by the struggle of the American Jewish community to live, to grow and to make its own Jewish contribution to the life and culture of the nation.

While we continue to deal with the problems of the daily life as they arise, it is these fundamental problems that we need to think through. If we do think them through to a basic plan and program, then it ought to be possible so to educate the next generation in due course, that its members will be able to accept themselves freely as Jews, without fear, without suppression, without apologies, without flight; will be able to face anti-Semitism as a continuing condition of their existence and to repel the attack of the anti-Semite with courage and without illusion. On the whole and in the long run, Jewish education has ignored both the nature and the meanings of this universal and endemic condition of Jewish existence. In this, the school has been unfair to the child, and the parent, who is largely responsible for the neglect of so central a social fact, has been unfair to the school. To overcome the unfairness, the education of the elders must go on concurrently with the education of youth. Adult education and the education of children are two branches from the same root of healing. Jewish parents, even more than Jewish children, need to learn democratic self-respect. And the way of their learning must be the way of scientific objectivity, sustained by sympathetic understanding, which alone can attain successfully the standards set by the American public school. The curriculums which the Jewish school provides, alike for young and for old, the methods it employs, the settings in which it employs them, must be such that, instead of struggling to get the majority of the children to the Jewish school, it should be a problem to keep them from it.

Jewish Education for American Jews

NOT so long ago the newspapers of the country carried on their front pages a piece of news so extraordinary as to be startling. It emanated from the Senate of the United States, and it was entitled "A Declaration of Conscience." The author of this declaration is a great lady, the Junior Senator from Maine, and among the signers were Senator Tobey of New Hampshire, Senator Aiken of Vermont, Senator Ives of New York, Senator Hendrickson of New Jersey, Senator Thye of Minnesota, and Senator Morse of Oregon. All are members of the minority party in the government of our country, figures in its parliamentary opposition.

The leadership of their party did not share their conscience. Their declaration spoke, not for the entire opposition but for what, in the idiom of British political division, might be called the loyal opposition. Their intent was to repudiate a certain attitude of heart and mind that had grown to ominous proportions in the nation's legislative chambers, and was being projected among the people of the states. Their Declaration of Conscience signalized this attitude by an image. They figure it as "the four horsemen of calumny — fear, ignorance, bigotry and smear." Holders of elective office by the suffrages of the peoples of their respective states, they refused to accept the benefits of a party victory which their party might seek to win through invoking fear, ignorance, bigotry and smear.

Of those "Four Horsemen," the mightiest is fear. There are today deep springs of fear, not in the nation's way of life, but in the manner and methods by which our people are sometimes led, and more commonly misled, to believe that our American way of life is in immediate danger from a Fifth Column within, and from an immensely powerful aggressor scheming for a global empire of doctrine and discipline without. From the day that the hot war of Nazi and Japanese assault upon the world's free society was replaced by the cold war of Communist aggression, men have been aware of an explosive division in the principles and policies of man's earthly enterprise. The abuse of

Address delivered at Hebrew Teachers College, Boston, June 11, 1950.

it has brought an enormous literature, that ranges in quality from editorial flatulencies of the yellow press, to the solid, reliable analyses of statesmen and sociologists. It has reshaped a great deal of thinking about the nation's schools; so that teachers are required to take oaths not exacted from other public servants and so that the president of Harvard University has published a book which he calls "Education in a Divided World." Unhappily, not much of the expression concerning the divided world has dealt with the need of accurate information, scientifically valid, regarding either our own being and powers, or regarding the aggressor's. Most of it has played on fear, and has therefore nourished the ignorance which feeds fear, and the bigotry which fear breeds, and the smear which is spread by demagogues who invoke fear for their own unsavory purposes.

Visitors from abroad sense the mood of fear which pervades the nation, and they see us as a giant so frightened that he forgets his own strength, and no longer truly believes in himself or in the springs of his power. These springs have been a fighting faith in freedom for all men. Throughout our history, from the War for Independence to the War for the Four Freedoms, this faith has been the source of the nation's energies, the shaper of its institutions, and the singularity of its way of life. It underlies the attitude toward existence which is the opposite of fear. It underlies courage; it enables the initiatives of inquiry which education enchannels; it leads to the understanding which nullifies ignorance, to the toleration which liquidates bigotry, and to the just rule of law which renders smear futile. As fear is the wellspring of ignorance, bigotry and smear, so freedom is the matrix of a courage of which understanding, tolerance and justice are the living attributes.

Custom conceives of courage as a sort of animal hardihood, a vital blind thrust or aggression such as impels the moth to the flame or a dog after the motorcar or a drunken man to look for a fight. We are used to conceive courage as an instinctive going into danger without fear, spontaneous, impulsive, and counting not the cost. Courage so conceived is not, however, human virtue but animal drive; it is not an expression of freedom but of bondage; and biologically it is far more treacherous to survival. Its moral level is not other than the level of fear. Courage as a virtue of mankind is neither the antithesis nor the absence of fear. Rather it presupposes fear and consists in its transformation by an insight into what the dangers are which arouse it, and by the mobilization of all available knowledge and skill into the competency to meet and overcome these dangers. Courage is no blind thrust against a fearful object. Courage is the redirection of the energies of fear in a plan of action shaped by an understanding of the conditions of victory. It requires, in addition to what Plato called wisdom concerning dangers, knowledge of one's own powers, confidence in them, and the readiness and skill to hazard the future on their use without guarantees. It consists in the decision to take what the military call calculated risks, to bet one's life on an event whose outcome cannot be a sure thing. The decision is an act of faith, freely made, born hence of a prior conviction which cannot be other than the fighting faith in freedom.*

Since the fourth century of the Christian era the Jewish people have stood in far, far greater need than the peoples of India, of courage so understood. For during this entire era Jews everywhere in the Western world have had to live their lives and do their work face to face with a dogma about their status and role in the destiny of man which carries a permanent threat to their lives and liberties. It shuts them out from the fellowship of mankind, concedes them no rights that any Christian is obliged to respect, and requires that they shall be wanderers on the face of the earth, with every man's hand righteously raised against them. This dogma defining "Jew," this meaning

* Something of the sort is what Jawaharlal Nehru saw in the decision that liberated India, and that last fall he commended to Americans. Speaking in Chicago, he said: "May I tell you of one lesson which helped us tremendously in India in the early days of our struggle? In those days we were weak and we had a powerful empire governing us. The great question was: 'How can we oppose it?' If anybody raised his head it was struck down. Then Gandhi came and told us not to be afraid. It is a very simple thing to say, but there was something in his voice, in his eyes, and in the way he said these things that had a powerful effect. *It is an extraordinary thing how that sense of fear vanished from the Indian people, because they realized what could happen to them.* They could be jailed. They might be shot at and perhaps killed. Their property might be confiscated. After all, one could survive all these things except death. But why be afraid if it came one's way? It sounds naive, but it worked that way and there was a magical change in India. The British Government of the day didn't quite know what to do about it. *The moment a people are not afraid of the state, the state with all its armies and navies cannot put them down. They can kill them but they cannot put them down. That fact is worth repeating and worth remembering.* Now I am surprised at powerful states having a sense of apprehension and fear when we, a weak and unarmed people with no strength behind us, could rid ourselves of fear and face an empire. If we can get rid of this fear, I think it is quite possible we can get rid of this war complex which fills the minds of so many people." (Italics supplied)

given the word "Jew" by the Christian account of history as the form of a drama of sin and salvation is, as you well know, the root of all anti-Semitisms. Although its acerbities have been somewhat mollified since the rise and spread of democracy as a way of life, and science as a way of knowledge, anti-Semitism is a chronic condition of Jewish existence everywhere in Christian society. It has imparted to that existence a continuing mood of fear. It has rendered membership in the Jewish community an anxious burden on the existence of the individual Jew, making him afraid and ashamed and creating in him a feeling of frustration which he is apt to relieve in forms of hostility to his Jewish being. This has been the case with Jews most notably since the democratic revolution did open the gates of the ghetto to the individual Jew and did, in principle at least, admit him to participation on equal terms in the diverse enterprises of the democratic culture. The intent of the Democratic Idea involved also the right of Jews to be freely and completely Jews without fear and without penalty; to be, as Jews, equal in status and rights with every non-Jew, Christian and other. But to many Jews democracy signified rather the opportunity to throw off the fearsome burden of being Jews, to escape the Jewish being and to seek altogether other affiliations and loyalties. In them the first fruits of freedom were flight from the conditions of fear. Their flight took many forms and went by many names; among them "conversion" (such as Heine's), "assimilation," "reform," and "nationalism." The first three were events in the countries of the Jew's habitation: and they consisted and still consist of a progressive thinning of the total pattern of Jewish communion to a ghostly *shema*. The last has consisted in the exaltation of fear into a gospel; it opposed to *galuth* restoration in Zion, and Democracy signified, and continues to signify, to its intransigent partisans, the right freely to withdraw from the unsafe lands where the anti-Semite ever threatens and to recover the ineffable predestinate security of a purely Jewish state in Palestine.

Thus, certain aspects of life in Jewish communities, particularly in the communities of our own country, have been singularly centrifugal. The traditional core of the communal being with doctrines and disciplines centered in the Bible, the Talmud and the *Shulchan Arukh* has undergone continuous fission, giving off sects, societies, parties and principles in accelerating profusion; with all in flight from the originating center and repellent to one another. The sustaining energy of this mutuality of repulsion is the fear nourished by a general climate of opinion of which anti-Semitism is a lasting constituent. It makes Jews aggressively afraid of Jews. It leads one group or sect or organization of interest to point the finger at some other as the source and seat of this or that evil which the anti-Semite invents to charge all Jews with. There are those in the communities of Jews in our country who are so afraid of being identified with other Jews whose faith they do not share, that no price is too great to nullify the identification, even the price of spiritual degradation and communal extinction. American Jews, thus, stand in a double jeopardy from fear. There is the jeopardy which they share with all Americans of our day and hour. And there is the jeopardy which fear of the Jewish being imposes. All Jewish groups in our country live in the need, as Jews, of the reconversion of their Jewish fear into a courage nourished by mutual understanding, mutual toleration, and a fighting faith in equal liberty. They live in the need of an orchestration of their differences into a cooperative union resting on the recognition by each of the right of each to live and to grow, and consisting in the free, strengthening communication of each with all on equal terms in a shared strategy of survival and expansion.

Twice in recent history have Jews signally manifested such a faith, expressed in such a courage. Twice has the conversion of fear into wisdom concerning dangers, reenforced by knowledge of their own powers, and embodied in the confident readiness to bet their lives on a doubtful future, come to heroic proportions in the bitter tale of Jewry's bondage and Jewry's passion. The first time was the Battle of the Warsaw Ghetto, for which I know no current parallel in the history of mankind *in extremis*. The second time was the establishment of the State of Israel. Each time the men and women whose choices launched the event were betting not only their own lives, but the lives of multitudes of their fellows, on an action whose successful outcome could in no way be guaranteed in advance. They were taking a calculated risk. They affirmed values for which they were prepared to fight and die, and fully aware that they might undergo all the bloody pangs of battle, and nevertheless suffer extinction at the last. The fighters of the Warsaw Ghetto almost to a man did suffer extinction. The people of Israel have won a precarious victory. The State of Israel has established itself in the company of sovereign states which make up the United Nations. But the requirements have become all the greater for that wisdom concerning dangers which is nourished by a fighting faith in freedom and a mastery of the skills and knowledge which project faith into works.

This requirement of courage becomes all the greater for Jews everywhere, as the cold war in a world divided turns on the heat. The reason should be evident enough. The significant role of the Jewish people in the civilization of the Christian West has been that of the essential Protestant. It has been to affirm and maintain, against the cruel intolerances of overwhelmingly superior force, the integrity of their separate conscience, the inalienable right to their own freedom of faith and worship. It has been, until the democratic revolution started the development of free societies and brought them relief, to stand up against the totalitarianisms of the spirit which sacerdotal religions seek to impose, and to endure the martyrdom of that resistance. But free society as a whole now confronts again the ominous menace of totalitarian power. To the black totalitarianism of the religious imperialists, to the brown totalitarianism of the Nazi racists who were conquered but neither silenced nor destroyed when Hitler was disposed of, there is now added the red totalitarianism of the Russian communists whose assault upon the freedom of men at home and abroad is made with a ruthless bestiality for which mankind's history provides hardly any parallels.

Each and everyone of these totalitarianisms is anti-Semitic. They undertake to persecute, to torture, to destroy the Jew as Jew, insofar as he holds fast to his integrity, and will not yield his Jewish difference. Each and everyone of these totalitarianisms has won over to its allegiance Jews afraid, and envious of the evil forçe they feared. Each and every one of these totalitarianisms has turned Jews against Jews, breeding in them the double anti-Semitism of the Jew turned in hatred on himself. But to offset these, the pitiful fear-impelled self-deceivers, the common man in every Jewish community, confronting the hates of an insuperable foe, has stood up, and did not yield, knowing in his heart, as the martyrs of the Warsaw Ghetto knew, that not to yield, even to perish by not yielding, is victory.

This insight, this spirit, has its ancestry in the spirit and insight of the prophets of Israel. Recall how Ahad Ha'am set prophet over against priest and prophetic freedom of conscience and urge to righteousness against priestly strictness of ceremony and demand for ritual rightness. Amos and Micah, Hosea and Isaiah and Jeremiah were also carriers of the tradition of protest, in God's name vindicators of the integrity of the private conscience. It is their precedent that the Jewish communities everywhere must needs follow, and especially the Jewish communities of our own free land. For here, as nowhere else in the world today — alas, also not in today's State of Israel — integrity of conscience is the law of the land, and integral to the nation's way of life. Here the law enables Jews of all sorts and conditions, of all persuasions and interests to live together with one another and with their non-Jewish neighbors freely and on equal terms. It is true that in many places law is not yet conduct, nor precept practice. But it is no less true that the democratic ideal demands an equal liberty for the different which the American people throughout the nation's history have worked and fought to lift from faith to fact. That all human beings are different from one another in countlessly different ways; — different as white and black and yellow and red; different as male and female; different as pagans and Christians and Judaists and Buddhists, and Brahmanists and Mohammedans and atheists and polytheists; different as farmers and fishermen, as miners and factory workers, as sailors and fliers and engineers, as doctors and lawyers and teachers, as clerks and accountants, as Texans and Bostonians or Frenchmen, or Poles or Koreans; and that they are equal as different; that the survival and growth of each depends upon its free trade in thoughts and things with all; — this is the democratic faith, the going and goal of the American way.

What does, what can, this faith mean for the survival of the Jewish community in America, for its development of its inner resources and its achievement of characteristically Jewish values to exchange with its non-Jewish peers in the free enterprise of the spirit which America aspires to be? Obviously, survival, development, achievement draw organically upon the security and spread of this democratic faith. Obviously, this faith is the religion of religions, wherein all others unite on equal terms, the union of them which guarantees to each an equal liberty and forbids to all special privilege or favor.

This faith is the common faith of all Americans, whatever their religion. It has its characteristic Bible. Among its books are some of the books of the Jewish Bible, especially the scrolls of the Prophets. But those upon which our time must needs lay its greatest stress are our Declaration of Independence, our Constitution — more particularly the Bill of Rights and the subsequent Amendments — and the Universal Declaration of Human Rights adopted by the Assembly of the United Nations Organization. There are many others, such as

Washington's Farewell Address, Jefferson's First Inaugural, his Bill of Religious Liberty for Virginia, his letter on the celebration of the fiftieth anniversary of the Declaration of Independence; Madison's Memorandum and Remonstrance, the Monroe Doctrine, Lincoln's Gettysburg Address and Second Inaugural, Woodrow Wilson's Fourteen Points, Franklin Roosevelt's Four Freedoms — but the basic ones are the first three. They utter the essentials of the religion of democracy — the ideal of equal liberty for all the families of mankind, and of the organization of this liberty through free association on equal terms in their religions, their governments, their economies and their cultures. The struggle to bring this ideal to event might be called the heart of American history, from the days that the people accepted the Constitution only on condition that it be amended with a Bill of Rights, to the present struggle over the equalization of all Americans before the laws, and in the folkways and the mores of the land; struggle with the Dixiecrats for the Americanization of the South; the struggle with sacerdotal power to protect the separation of church and state; the struggle to give to all Americans equal opportunity to work, to have a dwelling-place, to secure an education — the struggle for what Franklin Roosevelt summarized as the Four Freedoms.

The divisions in the Congress of the United States are a conflict over these freedoms. The senatorial Declaration of Conscience is a declaration in the interest of these freedoms. Recent decisions of the Supreme Court are decisions reaffirming these freedoms. Of course there is no final attainment nor any guaranteed conclusion. There are simply the ongoing struggles with their cumulative gains. But those are vital centers of the nation's being and the making of its history.

In the world which is not America, the world which is endeavoring after international democracy as the United Nations Organization, where the State of Israel is now an equal member, the struggle to establish these freedoms as the law of nations happens at this time to be focused in the United Nations Commission on Human Rights, whose presiding officer is Eleanor Roosevelt. There, the fourteen men and two women in charge of implementing the Universal Declaration of Human Rights, are required to deal with interests and attitudes that yield no evidence of any honest intention to give the Universal Declaration the effect of universal law. The Russians would exclude everything that might interfere with their sovereign right to impose their will on others, or that would allow others an equal privilege. The British would preserve the traditional practices of colonialism. The delegates of our own country would not admit private groups to petition for the redress of grievances. Both our government and the British refuse to consider the propositions regarding economic and social rights. Because our Senate could not be brought to accept a covenant on such rights, and for similar reasons, associations made up of men and women of good will dedicated to establishing the equality in right of all human beings as effective international law, oppose any and every covenant at this time. They prefer to employ the Universal Declaration as an instrument of global education that might ultimately lift it from intention to performance.

Now declarations such as this, such as our Declaration of Independence, are postulates for the development in equal liberty of all sorts and conditions of human societies, traditionally unequal in status and opportunity because they were small, weak, or otherwise different from the possessors of prestige and power. Without such declarations, the penalties on difference stay unchallenged, and the systems of prejudice which purport to justify them continue unexposed for the false pretensions they are. Short of preponderant power, the declarations are the lone available insurance of like rights for the unlike before the law. To the world's Jewish communities they are of paramount importance. This is why such a voluntary society as the World Jewish Congress urges unflaggingly that all the propositions of the Universal Declaration be the terms of the international covenant. This is why it is needful as well that they should likewise be employed as the rules of organization for Jewish communities everywhere, and particularly for the Jewish communities of the United States, and of the State of Israel. To achieve this here would be to accomplish the democratization, to complete, if you please, the Americanization of the American Jewish community. It would make actual the teamplay of the different, opposed and conflicting sectarian, political, cultural and educational organizations of interests that together make up the community's economy. It would achieve their orchestration, not merely that each might gain in strength and character through its cooperative association with the others, but even more, that the fullest potency of the Jewish being might be freed for the nourishment, growth and common defense of the free society of free men at home and abroad.

Both belief in such a teamplay, to such ends, and the attainment of the knowledge and the know-how to launch, to sustain and to keep enhancing it depend directly on education. The Jewish being is a way of life and thought. Its power to survive and mature is nothing if it is not the wisdom and the skills in which the upkeep of such a way — as of any way — consists. And the Jews are not born with such power. Nor are any other people. It is an acquired power, and each generation has to acquire it for itself. The process of acquiring is education. Education is the fundamental mode of communication between age and youth. Age teaches, youth learns. Teaching, when it is successful, is a transmissal of a community's social heritage. Learning, when it is satisfactory, is a taking possession of that inheritance, an assimilation and digestion of it, putting it to new uses in liberating the powers and perfecting the singularity of the new life. Jewish education, thus, would be most effective when the generations of Jews can each receive from their elders the Jewish social heritage, vary it, enrich it, expand it, and pass it on, not as a self-sufficient and self-sufficing tradition of faith and works, but as a freely interacting member of the cultures of the nation and of the world. There has been an isolationism in the Jewish education of the past which is as illusory as it is suicidal. No culture, no religion can feed on itself and grow by what it feeds on. That which we call Jewish certainly did not. Even the walls of the ghetto, which shut us in, did not shut the works and ways of non-Jews out. Even had we wanted to, we were not free to live to ourselves alone. In recent years there have been those who have wished to compensate for the liquidation of the physical ghetto by erecting a new ghetto of the spirit. It is a suicidal wish. Jewish education today must take full cognizance of the global perspectives of Jewish existence.

This is today's condition for the survival of Jews as Jews. Jews are not born. Jewish values, or the values of any other culture-group, are not a biological inheritance. They are not carried by the genes. They are carried by the institutions of the Jewish community, and the institution which is singled out especially to be their carrier is its schools. Education makes Jews, as it makes every other culture-group. It defines and communicates the beliefs, the values and the works which mankind call Jewish. It appraises and gives direction to the meanings which this or that segment of the community chooses from the aggregated multitude of doctrines and disciplines, always diverse and diversifying, and ever more frequently passing from affinity to mutual repulsion, which are called Jewish. First and last, education embodies both the means and ends of Jewish survival, and is the only institution able to incarnate in Jewish form the vital courage which the times require.

Does it not follow that, if Jewish education is truly to achieve Jewish survival, it may not give primacy, in the total manifold of Jewish culture and ideals, to the records of the dead past, to ancient languages and letters, without relevancy or import for the urgent needs and repeating crises of Jewish life today? Particularly for the Jews of the American community Jewish education must concern itself first, with the actual Jewish community where Jewish children are growing up and where their parents live and labor and struggle in the give-and-take with the thousand other communities which together make up the state, the nation, reach out to Israel and to all the residual world. Insofar as the past is important, whether as faith or works or both, it is important as a *living* past, with a dynamic relevancy for all its diversities of tongue and belief and culture of the human freedoms with whose prosperous survival the destiny of the Jewish community is ineluctably bound up. Moreover, the method of Jewish education for American Jews must be consistent with its matter. The old authoritarian modes of indocrination and catechism and repetition have, on the record, failed the task of Jewish survival. Their impact has been to repel the generations from the Jewish heritage, neither to hold nor to draw them to it. For the originals and the great talents among them, the alternatives to this heritage were automatically more meaningful and more attractive. What could not be openly learned was bootlegged. What had to be openly learned was secretly appraised as unworthy and rejected. The Jewish school failed to give the Jewish heritage an equal opportunity in the competitive field of the cultures, and it failed because of the segregation of the Jewish theme from the world-themes, and because the method of authority would accept no orchestration with the world-themes. The Americanization of Jewish education needs to assimilate far more rapidly than at its present pace all that is achieved in the scientifically verified arts of teaching, the scientifically understood processes of learning, with their techniques of free inquiry, impartial examination of alternatives, constant reconstruction of the wisdom of old books by the experiences of new life.

This has still another consequence for the education of the American Jew. We know, of course, that the vital process in education is the process of learning, and that teaching, even at its best, can be only an accessory to learning; that teaching is of little avail where the will to learn is not aroused and the pupil's attention persistently turns away from whatever is to be learned. Interest, as John Dewey long ago told us, is the precondition of effort; and relevancy to personal urges, to personal needs and hopes and fears is the occasion of interest. The Jewish theme, the Jewish school, competing in the American scene as they must with so many other items of relevance — the public schools, the playgrounds, with their abundance of possible satisfaction — do not seem able of themselves alone to arouse, to hold and to absorb the learner's interest. For this reason the teacher of the American Jew becomes a figure of paramount importance in the assurance of Jewish survival. He must have the personal qualities and the professional skills which can add to Jewish themes the differential attractiveness that leads to choosing them against other alternatives, developing the choice into interest, and interest into habits of expanding study. The teacher of the American Jew must be as different from a *melamed* or rabbi as a leader in free society is from a priest or a policeman. He must be equipped with the arts of democratic leadership not only for the classroom, but for the clubroom and the camp and the playing field; for group-relations of all sorts, whether they be called inter-cultural or inter-faith or inter-anything. He must have, in addition to his pedagogical know-how and special Jewish knowledge an awareness of the arts and sciences which make up their dynamic context, and an insight of what their relations mean. He must cultivate continuously a human, not merely a pedagogic, understanding of how personality develops from childhood to maturity, and he needs a great tolerance and sympathy for the recalcitrances and exacerbations that go with the process. One of his major requirements, perhaps, is adequate insight into the ways and works of the school world where his own school is a competitive unit. Without such insight he is not able to accept and meet the constant challenge which the non-Jewish school, public or private, presents the Jewish school; he is not able to strengthen his school so that it may be chosen and cherished.

In sum, the Jewish education of the American Jew will succeed or fail as the Americanization of the training and equipment of his teachers succeeds or fails. This has long been realized by our fellow-citizens who are concerned with Jewish education as the agency of Jewish survival in, and Jewish service to, American democracy. It has led them to form the American Association for Jewish Education and to seek to bring the men, the methods and the matter of Jewish education to the high functional excellence which the science of education enables, and which is necessary to the existence and progress of a democratic Jewish community. The role of the teacher, let me repeat, is critical. The great world in which Jewish children perforce live and move and have their being cannot be Jewish. Its values and allure present an unfailing pull on their interest and effort, and the children can neither be cut off nor shut away from them. On the contrary, they are better studied, understood, absorbed, and digested in the Jewish being, to nourish and strengthen it. But whether any Jew can thus assimilate the environing cultures to the Jewish center depends mostly on what the Jewish school has done for him or to him. It early fixes his attitude toward Jewish works and ways, conditions his choices between competing values, sets his reactions to anti-Semitism alike when chronic or acute. Today's American Jewish community must ask of its schools that they shall endeavor to replace the centrifugal impulsions which carry youth ever farther away from community by centripetal ones that may take them closer in; and that they shall do this not by devices of isolation from alternative interests, but by arts of free communication with alternative interests. Such achievements by way of such arts must needs be grounded in a deeply-informed conviction of the true meanings of liberty, and in a steady habituation in its discipline. The forms of this discipline would of course be established through the various institutions that make up the Jewish community, from synagogue and temple and center, to committee and congress and fraternal society. The school would need to draw from these and bring back to them a religious devotion to the full realization of equal liberty in every dimension of the national life, initiating this devotion in the Jewish being and carrying it thence to the entire people, to all the world.

To conclude then, the Jewish education of the American Jew must liberate his powers as Jew for self-knowledge, self-respect and self-help: It must nourish the courage which is wisdom concerning dangers. It must communicate a fighting faith in that equal liberty for different people which is the foundation of reason and the root of tolerance, and which is the one non-Jewish assurance of Jewish survival.

Such is the goal and such the task of Jewish education for American Jews.

Jewish Teaching and Learning in the American Scene

THE theme for this evening is "Jewish Education in the American Scene." We have been using the word "Jewish" and the word "Education" a great deal. I am not sure that any of us have done more than take those words for granted. What do they mean?

Meaning of "Education"

So far as it concerns professional educators, the word "education" starts up in them a set of reactions, habitual, automatic and rarely reflective. It arouses in them strong feeling. This is usually an affirmative feeling turning upon the stake they have as men and women in the social enterprise which is called education. But they can hardly help thinking of education far more as it affects them than as it affects their victims called pupils. Yet the true, important meaning of education doesn't reside in what the teacher does when teaching. It resides in what the pupil does when learning.

The prime, the sole, function of a teacher in teaching is to facilitate learning. Yet most teaching remains conspicuous for the ways in which it fails to discharge this function.

There is a reason for this. The reason has little to do with the lack or the possession of training by teachers. It does have a great deal to do with the social demands which are made of schools, and of the teacher's art or operation. I use that word "operation" so that you may make your own associations: "Let me tell you about my operation" — I mean, my education.

The operation involves the fact that parents, officials of government, priests, rabbis, bankers, college professors, all people on the social stratum of authority held either by inheritance or by achievement, expect that the younger generation, as it grows up and grows old, shall be trained to support the survival and the strengthening of

From address delivered at the Joint Conference on Jewish Education in Atlantic City, May 28, 1949.

that authority. The training, hence, is a training in conformation. It is called discipline. "Discipline," you recognize, derives from a Latin root, which means, a whip. To discipline anybody is to cause him pain, and a discipline is a painful operation on another person by which, it is assumed, he learns something that he doesn't already know. Traditionally, educational discipline is the painful communication of the past for the purpose of supporting present authority. The assumption that this is teaching is usually verified by its failure to work in any of us. You know that, don't you?

Yet the transmission of its past is of prime importance to the future of any community. It is the creation of a social memory by means of which one generation establishes and maintains its dynamic connection with another generation in a peaceful, you might say, in an evolutionary manner, and not by way of conflict and rebellion. Indeed, we might define education as the techniques of maintaining social memory. But if this were all, nobody would need to bother about a future which is different from the past. The generations would repeat each other. Yet what most of us are concerned with is not to repeat the past, but to vary from it. We are by nature concerned far more with creating a new future than we are with perpetuating an old past. Hence there is a conflict in education everywhere. Certain vested interests of body and of spirit undertake merely to perpetuate the past. They combat the lovers of growth and freedom who undertake to create a new future. Their differences do not lie in their care for the past. To both it is of supreme importance. But they differ in *how* the past is important. Too many educators think that it is important in itself and for itself, and that to conserve it and repeat it is enough for a good life. But true education uses the past as a food or as a soil or as an instrument, by which to nourish, or grow, or create something different that the past is not. The vital function of education goes far beyond merely transmitting the past. The vital function of education is to liberate the powers of the next generation. It is to set them free from the past by making them masters of it; not by abolishing but by consuming, by digesting the past so as to grow a better and richer future upon it.

Now, when you are told by gentlemen of the cloth that the world is assaulted by something unspiritual and material called secularism in education, those gentlemen are concerned primarily with the conservation of a past that will keep them presently comfortable. They are speaking on behalf of a professionally-vested interest. They do not also tell you that the reason why so-called secularism arose at all, was not that secularists scorn or quarrel with the past; it is that the *soi-disant* non-secularists killed the past. When they had a monopoly of transmitting it they made of it a dead past. They failed to do the job on which their own survival depends in such a way as to win and hold the allegiance of a growing mind to the past whose conservators they presumably are. If their teaching had been successful, no need would have arisen of alternatives to it. They can still save their bacon by doing the necessary job of education better than the dedicated men and women whom they call secularists. Let them engage the field in fair competition, without fear or favor, without demanding monopoly or privilege. Let them prove by their achievements their competency and worth. Let them not, in our free society, seek to shut out from the work of education either the Jews or the Gentiles whose concern is the growth of the generations in liberty, whose care for the past turns on its role in creating a true, a new future, one richer and freer and more intelligent. Let them be American and democratic in education. Let them consult with the secularists. Let them seek a meeting of minds based on the objective and scientific examination of the facts regarding education; the facts regarding methods; the facts regarding the relation of past content to new development; the facts regarding how the past can be absorbed in and digested by the growing future. Lacking this knowledge, you do not liberate the energies of men's minds, and education which does not set minds free is not education. Such education is only the creation of conditioned reflexes; it is animal training; it is not the evocation and nurture in men and women of the power to choose, to appreciate and to understand.

You know, of course, that the clerical assault on so-called secularism, which was intruded into our deliberations last night isn't confined to the Jewish communities of our country. It is part and parcel of a wide-spread attack on those improvements in education, which have been brought about by the existence of our American public school system, from kindergarten through university. We of the Jewish communities are simply getting our share of a conflict that pervades the nation's entire educational establishment. Protestant clergy and the Catholic hierarchy are both attacking our free tax-supported public schools for what they call secularism, and what experts in educational processes know to be the science and art by which the powers of growing youth are liberated, strengthened and brought to their appropriate excellences and some Judaistic clerics are making capital of that example.

MEANINGS OF "JEWISH"

Let us now turn to the meanings of "Jewish." How is "Jewish" related to the liberation of the powers of growing youth? What is "Jewish?" Is there one exclusive answer? If there is, you can't get it from the different denominations of Judaism. Each proffers a different answer. Nor could they be different sects, if each did not have a different answer. If there is one only answer, you can't get it from the multitude of "secular" groups, including the so-called defense groups. Each has a different personnel, program of organization and plan of action and all emphasize their differences, not their agreements. Yet, the force which makes them all Jews together, from the point of view of the non-Jew, is not their differences. That force unites them all in one community and gives the word "Jew" one meaning. Yet neither this unity nor this meaning rests on the power of Jews to establish. Both are affirmations of Christian power and are established in and by the position assigned the Jews in the Christian scheme of salvation.

Thus, there are two ways of thinking "Jew." One is the way employed by non-Jews, especially by Christians. It denotes what is known as anti-Semitism, implies a system of thought and life that is common to all anti-Semitisms and underlies those which are not theological, but economic or political. The other way of thinking "Jew" is the whole complex of variation and change, which in spite of every attempt to prevent them, makes up the history of the Jewish people everywhere in the world. Suppose you classify Jews by their religion alone. You can make a scale with the Free Synagogue at one end and the Lubavitcher's *klos* at the other. The first is a Jewish religious society, without dogmas, without ritual, without any sacerdotal impedimenta but with a certain attitude toward the values of the Jewish inheritance and a certain way of living and acting together. The second is all dogma, magic and miracle, combining the *Shulchan Arukh* with as much that is not in the *Shulchan Arukh* or in the Talmud. Between those poles you can arrange a multiplying variety of sects, ranging from Orthodox, through Mizrachist, conservative, soft reform, and hard reform until you reach the American Council for Judaism, Inc.

But obviously classification by religion only would leave out great bodies of Jews, and notable individuals proud to call themselves Jews, and active in a great variety of non-religious enterprises regarded as Jewish. It would leave out Yiddish and secular Hebrew. It would leave out the occupational and cultural economies of the Jewish community. It would leave out their social and cultural history. It would leave out the role of the English language in the transformation of the American Jewish community. It would leave out all the non-religious components of the Jewish culture-complex. That is, it would leave out the greater part of the community-being.

Now, what do the Jews identified by Judaism have in common with Jews not thus identified? Is it not that they remember and share a common past in a common way? Is it not the transmission of the past we call education? Is it not education that presents to the growing child the materials which give "Jew" content and meaning and to the Jewish child its Jewish identity, first unconsciously, then as conscious acceptance or rejection? How the school presents this material, what attitudes it stimulates, provides both the field of choice and the motives for choosing, for allegiance or aversion.

Suppose we call the field of choice Jewish culture. Obviously, its Hebraic component is not the whole of it. Hebrew is the language of the Bible which was written when Hebrew was the language of the people. But the Bible was compiled when Hebrew had ceased to be the language of the people; when the language of the people had become Aramaic. Later the language of none of the world's Jews was Hebrew, and that of the great majority had become Greek. The Jews had developed a notable Judaeo-Greek civilization of which the center was Alexandria in Egypt. Most of the Jewish community of that city had forgotten Hebrew; they couldn't read Hebrew and had to have the Bible translated into Greek. That translation survives as the Septuagint, and as a part of a new Jewish culture which rested on the Jewish tradition. But it survives altered into something different and new, a new way of thinking and living, which came to its highest expression, philosophically at least, in the writings of Philo of Alexandria. It survives in a still more radical variation from the original in the New Testament written in the Judaeo-Greek language. New Testament Greek, you will remember, is first and last the language of Greek-speaking Jews. Now our schools have dropped all that part of the cultural inheritance of our people. It has been purposely ignored if not forgotten. And the cause is intrinsic to the New Testament. Anti-Semitism as we know it has its spring and roots in the New Testament. Yet the Judaeo-Hellenic component is a rich part of the Jewish cultural inheritance. It needs to be renewed. We have need to know that part of our past even more fully and completely than we know the parts we approve of and live by precisely because we do not approve it and do not live by it.

In the course of time, Greek disappeared as a vital form of communication and expression among Jews. Other languages of life, as against literature, appeared. There was Arabic. There was the Ladino of the Spanish-speaking Jews. There was Yiddish. And Yiddish, which is now recessive among us Americans and dead in Europe, developed an enormous cultural impulsion, with a beautifully varied literature, going with an economy of life that all of you either have heard about from your parents or lived through yourselves.

When Bernard Semel tells us his inimitable stories and makes his inimitable fables in Yiddish, the effect is very much more beautiful to me and greater than when he does it in his admirable English because the genius of those tales is a Yiddish genius. This genius is a precious part of the Jewish inheritance in danger of being lost, now that the great majority of the Jews of the world are an English-speaking community the language of whose life and labors never was Hebrew, is ceasing to be Yiddish and is becoming entirely English. Indeed it is already English to the degree that the Jewish Publication Society of America found it necessary (even as the Alexandrians had found it necessary to translate the Bible into Greek) to project and publish a translation of the Bible into English. You know there is a Jewish Publication Society version of the Old Testament. There ought to be one also of the New, to provide a Jewish alternative to the various Protestant and Catholic versions.

The American Idea and the American Scene

How, now, is a Jewish school to deal with the variety of matters I have just mentioned? It might continue as in the past, to ignore all but the specific denominational interest of a sect, religious or secular. It might choose to keep the growing mind ignorant of all context and alternatives and their challenge to the chosen doxy. Or it might bring to the pupils a realistic and just awareness of all that, and arouse their curiosity about the action of cultural forces on one another, and the conditions of the survival and growth of any under the influence of free communication with all. If it did the latter, it would be adopting the methods of scientific inquiry and intellectual and moral responsibility. It would pay due attention to all the values, that in their conflicts and concords together, compose the Jewish being — the cultural heritage and the life and labor of the Jewries of today.

Those, please remember, belong not to Jews only. Because of the historic accidents from which developed what is called Judaeo-Christian civilization, they belong to the entire Western World. Whose version of the Bible then, is the authentic version? Whose alone must a free society of free men accept? Isn't the democratic answer that there cannot be such a *must?* That the different violates the principle of equality in right if it imposes itself on others different from itself? Education especially must recognize that people, if they are to live as free men in a free society, must agree that all have an equal right to differ from each other in every respect, and that they make up a free society insofar as they live together with each other in such a way that each lives more freely and abundantly than he could by living alone or by trying to subdue others and to force upon them his own works, ways and values.

What I have just said is intended simply as a brief expression of the American Idea, which I keep steadily laying before friend and foe.* This is the Idea conveyed by the ever-unfinished Bible of America whose Book of Genesis is the Declaration of Independence and whose latest book at this moment is President Truman's Inaugural Address. From the Declaration of Independence to that Address, we may read repeated in new forms, under new conditions, with varying purposes, the fundamental American principles that all men are created equal, that they are endowed by their Creator with certain inalienable rights, that among those rights are life and liberty and the pursuit of happiness, and that the purpose of all government — political, religious, economic, or any other — is to secure those rights. These principles are the foundation of what I have come to call Cultural Pluralism. They mean that all of the different communities in our country and everywhere in the world develop in their different localities, ways of life that come to expression in foodways and folkways, ways of thought and expression, of work and worship and art and play, which have an individual character singular to each region and community. They mean that each is a spring of individuality from which flows a little stream of cultural difference that crosses the others, combines with them, and finally makes the great river of the nation's cultural life, as all the tributaries make the Missouri or the Columbia or the Mississippi. They effect a cultural union — a union, not a unity, an orchestration, not a unison —

* See above, "Critical Problems in Jewish Education."

in which each different region and community has its own different part to play. There exists a sort of division of cultural labor with analogies to our economic division of labor. Economically and politically, as you know, we have become relatively the most prosperous, powerful and freest country of our time, because of these divisions of labor. The same is true spiritually and culturally. Our great superiority in knowledge and know-how, in religious freedom and cultural activity, is due to the free orchestration of the different in which as a political fact, the Unitedness of our United States of America consists.

I have already suggested what, thus, we must mean when we say, "American scene." Our country is continental. It is at least as diversified as the entire continent of Europe. Nature is bountiful. We have all the climates, practically all the animal, vegetable and mineral resources we could need. Ethnically, we are the miscellany of the world. All the peoples of the globe have sent out their shoots to this continent. Of course there are and there will be conflicts. We are all aware of intolerable injustices and inequities. Sometimes, the disability of Negroes and Mexicans is in some of our localities as great as the disability laid upon the Jewish people on the continent of Europe. But here in America, it is always a local perversity, never a national program. And it is always contrary to the American Idea. It has always been fought by Americans loyal to the American Idea, and those who are guilty of it are ashamed of it and try to fend off condemnation in terms of the American Idea. Equal liberty is making genuine progress, however great the obstructions, however powerful the interests which oppose it.

Consider the history of freedom in our world. It records how free men have often fought against the loss of their own liberty. It records how slaves have fought often to win their liberty for themselves. But the record shows only one instance where free men fought to win liberty for slaves. The instance is that of the Americans who fought our Civil War in order to liberate the slaves. This war is a unique event in the history of this nation, and in the history of mankind. The reason — the cultural and spiritual reason — of the Civil War was the American Idea. To embody this Idea in the courses of his daily life must needs be the all-embracing objective of every American as American. To achieve it, means to fight as well as to work, to struggle as well as to preach. The report of the President's Commission on Civil Rights is but one more step in this unremitting struggle, one more reaffirmation of the American Idea. The effort to get Congress to implement the Report in law is still another. And yet another, of perhaps greater importance, is the struggle to have Congress provide through Federal aid for public education, in order that those Americans who through no fault of their own are deprived of equal educational opportunity, may receive this opportunity. To fight for the equalization of educational opportunity is to endeavor so to implement the American Idea, as to liberate the growing mind from the prejudices and shackles of a merely repeated past, to give it the chance to grow toward a freer, a more hopeful, and more courageous future through sharing knowledge, understanding, fellowship and freedom with those who are different from it. Education should bring about the union of the diverse on equal terms in the American scene.

The Role of Jewish Education

We may now ask what would be the role of Jewish education in this scene? Its obvious fundamental task is so to transmit the Jewish inheritance as to save it from ever again becoming what it so often has been — an instrument which alienates the generations from this inheritance — and to perfect it as an instrument of understanding and loyalty. This task can be accomplished only in the degree that it becomes clear to the parents of American Jewish children, and to the children themselves, that the Jewish values of their inheritance are, like all values which liberal education undertakes to transmit, essential dynamics in the liberation of their own powers of growth in freedom.

To achieve this requires a preliminary study and observation of the alternatives which Jewish education, as a part of general education, must envisage. What is it that ultimately distinguishes an educated man from an uneducated one — a gentleman, as they used to say when I was a boy, from a boor? Is it not the fact that the gentleman always acknowledges the equal right to life and to growth of what is different — different in language, different in technique, different in meaning, even inimical in meaning? That the gentleman is able to understand the different sympathetically, to interpret it, to assimilate it into his own way of life and thought? That his personality, instead of being assimilated by what is different, assimilates what is different to itself?

Assimilation, as you know, can move in either of two directions. The kind of assimilation which self-respecting Jews have always felt to be degrading is the kind that was due to the fear of being freely and openly a Jew, due to the feeling of shame that people experience when they are called "Jew." In our Judaeo-Christian culture the word "Jew" is to a non-Jew a word neither of praise nor of admiration. When it is applied to a non-Jew it is an epithet of derogation. This non-Jewish appraisal spreads quite unconsciously to Jews. It makes of them anti-Semites and marks them with fears and timidities and feelings of inferiority. It develops in them attitudes averse to and of flight from a frank, open, just facing of their Jewish reality. In so far forth, their education has failed them, both by its methods and content; it has contributed to making "assimilationists" of them. Of course, success in such assimilation does not transform them into Gentiles; it only sets them up as amateur Gentiles. The Jewish component of their being has not been liquidated, it has only been suppressed.

The other direction of assimilation I take to be synonymous with liberal education. A person whose education has been genuinely and not formally liberal is not thereby alienated from his family or community or the folkways of his town or village or the intimacies of faith and affection constituting home, and friendship due to growing up together. He "belongs" more certainly than without this education. But it has made him spiritually hospitable, able to welcome and appreciate what is different as friend, not as foe. It has given him the power to cooperate with what is different in such a way that the partners in the cooperation both benefit and each is stronger through the union of the two than either could be if the two remained together un-united. This strengthening of each by its free, friendly association with all, is the import of the word "United" in our country's name. The peculiarly American task of Jewish education in America is to nourish this union by liberating the powers of the Jew as Jew to participate fruitfully and freely in contributing the Jewish values toward the strengthening of the national union. This means that Jewish education can not be exclusively religious or sectarian. It means that the different denominations whose differences together make up all of Judaism, need themselves to meet face to face on equal terms, to learn to know, to understand and to respect each other and to recognize the equal right of each other to their respective doctrines and disciplines, and to work out a teamplay of their differences, in the spirit of sportsmanship and scientific fair play. They need to achieve union in the American sense of union. Then their schools can perhaps pass on their particular teachings to their children in the spirit of cooperative democracy, and instead of alienating so many, win them to a continuing loyalty to Jewish values in the frame of reference of the American Idea.

Of course this way of conducting education in religion breaks with the tradition which has always been dogmatic and exclusively sectarian. It has always shut out and condemned and cut off what is different whether among Judaists, Christians or Mohammedans. The Jewish people have been the most tragic victims of this aggression against the different that the Western world has known since the coming of the Christian cults to power. More than any other community, Jews need first to understand, to appreciate and freely to share in each other's diversities and then to bring their united Judaism into similar teamplay with the world's residual religions. Those diversities, let me say again, are secular as well as sectarian. They embrace a variety of languages, from Aramaic and Greek to Yiddish and English, with their diverse poetries, and dramas, and journals. They embrace an unending variety of associations that range from *landsmanschaften* and *fraternities* to nationalist and national federal organizations. These together figure as largely as, if not more largely than, synagogues and temples in the life of the American Jew as Jew and in the lives of Jews everywhere. For successful education these also must be studied, understood, respected, appraised, their diversities orchestrated, and united to the rest of the subject matter from which the psyche of the American Jew is to receive the nourishment that will keep it vitally and freely Jewish.

Jewish Education and the Future

I like to think that the American Association for Jewish Education has this for its vision, and that its ten year labors have endeavored to realize vision in works. Its resources have been few, its manpower small. Great as the need was, in 1939, when World War II was beginning, it has become immensely greater, in 1949, with World War III a cloud on the global horizon. The need is not alone that of our Jewish community. It is our country's need. It is the world's need. And educators and other men of good will have so recognized it. There is now no only UNESCO, with its principles and program. There is also the Universal Declaration of Human Rights which the Assembly of the United Nations Organization adopted on December 1, 1948 — in the fulness of time this date may be as momentous as July 4, 1776 or July 17,

1789. That Declaration affirms that education is a universal human right. I cite Clauses 1 and 2 of Article 25:

> 1) Everyone has a right to education. Education shall be free at least in the elementary and fundamental stages. Elementary education shall be compulsory. Technical and professional education shall be made generally available and higher education shall be equally accessible to all on the basis of merit. 2) Education shall be directed to the full development of the human personality and to the strengthening of respect for human rights and fundamental freedoms. It shall promote understanding, tolerance and friendship among all the nations, racial or religious groups and shall further the activities of the United Nations for the maintenance of peace.

These propositions establish what shall be the purpose, the subject matter and the methods of all education in the United Nations and the United States, and of Jewish education as the characteristic Jewish contribution to education in the United States.

The times are difficult and the way is hard. It is still a way for pioneers. Men and women of vision and courage — they are much more numerous than the foes of freedom are willing to grant — are giving their entire strength to the task. They have learned the wisdom concerning dangers which Plato calls courage. They know that this vision of education as a right for every man is going to be very difficult to transform from a vision into a fact. Having the example of the American struggle for equal educational opportunity in mind, they know that what is called for is a fighting faith in democracy in education. In the United Nations Educational, Scientific and Cultural Organization, they have prepared an international instrument of this faith. They hope this instrument will parallel on a global scale the best work of the great national systems of education, of which the American provides the outstanding example of union in diversity. The educational enterprise of the Jewish communities is, though those concerned with Jewish education may not be aware of it, necessarily a participant in this union. It has its own characteristic contribution to make through its schools, its synagogues, its community centers, its lecture halls, its fraternities, its every form of communication and expression between Jews, and between Jews and non-Jews. The role of Jewish teaching and learning in the American scene is to bring to the generations of Jews an ever-deepening awareness of the union of the diverse which is Jewishness, and a feeling of pride in and devotion to its ways and works. It is to bring to the non-Jewish neighbor a realization of the democratic import of Jewish culture and ideals, and to establish and enhance free and fruitful communication with him, so that each may come into a greater abundance of life and liberty than either could in isolation, thinking and living to himself alone.